Listen First!

Listen First!

Turning Social Media Conversations into Business Advantage

STEPHEN D. RAPPAPORT

WILEY

John Wiley & Sons, Inc.

Library of Congress Cataloging-in-Publication Data:

Rappaport, Stephen D., 1952-
    Listen First!: Turning Social Media Conversations Into Business Advantage/Stephen D. Rappaport.
        p. cm.
    Includes bibliographical references and index.
    ISBN 978-0-470-93551-4 (cloth)
    ISBN 978-1-118-03372-2 (ebk)
    ISBN 978-1-118-03373-9 (ebk)
    ISBN 978-1-118-03374-6 (ebk)
            1. Internet marketing.   2. Online social networks.   3. Social media Research.
            4. Consumers—Research.   5. Branding (Marketing) I.   Title.
    HF5415.1265.R37 2011
    658.8'72—dc22

                                                                    2011005755

Printed in the United States of America

10 9 8 7 6 5 4 3 2 1

CONTENTS

Part III
LISTENING-LED MARKETING AND MEDIA INNOVATIONS

Part IV
LISTENING'S NEW FRONTIERS

FOREWORD

Listening is hip! If you are a marketer and not doing it, you are likely to be criticized by somebody. Or do you look in the mirror and think you see someone who is out of it? So, what do marketers and agencies do? They put "listening" on their to-do list. And then they go off and do some listening. Good. It's a start.

But the problem just begins here, because there are so many easy ways to check "listening" off your list. Take a look at Google Trends, talk to some companies about sentiment and brand analytics, set up a community or two, or get IT looking into software solutions.

But is this listening? Is this consistent with the historic opportunity to hear your customers talk honestly about your brand? Or recognizing, as one pundit said recently, that "Twitter is free mind-reading!" I think not.

The Advertising Research Foundation (ARF) convened its first of four Listening Workshops in November, 2009. Listening is exploding, right? Well, it is, if you count all those projects that are started to get listening checked off the list. But the disturbing thing to me was that many speakers seemed to be preoccupied with the obstacles to effective listening—no budget, nobody in charge; where is the statistical rigor; is it projectable; tough organizational issues; hard to sell internally; ROI difficult to determine; legal has major issues . . . .

So, what's up with this? True listening is scary, that's what's up. It's a big change from our traditional way of thinking.

Consequently, the single biggest opportunity in the history of consumer marketing lies dormant. The singular opportunity to tap into the brain of today's newly empowered consumer in such a natural way—that it gives us the purest "research" ever—is buried in naysaying.

The purpose of this book is to change that, to get you so excited about the promise of listening, the essentialness of listening, the unequaled power of the insight potential of listening, that you will not go another day without taking your important first step.

That little first step? Implement a continuous listening program in your company. Tomorrow. Not project listening; that's checklist stuff. This book will tell you how to do that, well. Welcome to a new world.

—Bob Barocci, ARF President

Bob, I agree. Listening changes the game for people and brands; it brings the promise of people centricity forward. As the IT sector learned, the "tyranny of the installed base" slams the brakes on modernization and innovation, because it is not compatible with existing systems, or because it may require new ways of working and people with new skills or training, or shift power toward customers. Let's hope that our readers will not cower before the "tyranny of the installed market research base" and that they figure out how best to discover, listen to, and act on the conversational "dark matter" that is all around them, and influencing the futures for their companies, products, and services.

—**Stephen D. Rappaport, ARF Knowledge Solutions Director**

INTRODUCTION

Nearly anywhere you turn online, people are talking about your products and categories, what they like and dislike, what they want, what pleases them or ticks them off, and what they would like you to do, or stop doing. Twitter, Facebook, YouTube, millions of blogs, forums, Web sites, and review sites make most of these conversations public, accessible, and researchable to every company. You also hear individuals talk about the richness and texture of their lives and your role in them. You learn about their aspirations, families, relationships, and homes; music and movies; vacations, hobbies, and sports; finances, jobs, and careers; education and technology; what they had for lunch, what they crave; and much more. By listening in on those conversations, you position yourself to develop powerful insights into people that, coupled with strategy, drive your business forward and create an enduring advantage. *Listen First! Turning Social Media Conversations into Business Advantage* will show you how.

You might be asking yourself, "How can conversational listening help create a business advantage?" The answer lies in the difference between competitive advantage and business advantage. Competitive advantage usually derives from superiority on some dimension in marketing, execution, or customer service. However, any competitive advantage can be matched or bested, every edge dulled, and any superiority lasting only until the next competing model, price cut, ad campaign, distribution change, or customer service fiasco. Business advantage is less vulnerable and longer-lasting, because it comes from you and your company's abilities to sense, respond to, and quickly adapt your business to changing customers and conditions.

Listening is ideal for sensing and responding because it interprets meaning from signals of change that are embedded in conversations. Listening tunes into what people are saying today, gives their thoughts and comments structure, and, when astutely analyzed, leads to business-building insights.

- Listening is inherently biased toward anticipating, decision making, doing, and making progress *all the time*, not at one point in time.
- Listening is an *emerging discipline* that is plainly visible on companies radars. While many are still experimenting and dipping their toes into listening's waters, a good number are moving from the experimental stage to figuring out how to "bake" listening into their business processes. Still smaller groups are already running sophisticated listening operations. Yet

each camp has questions. Newcomers want to know the basics; the more experienced want to compare notes and, especially, plan for what's next.

Listen First! is a playbook in the true sense of the word; it combines education with strategy and actions for achieving specific marketing and advertising goals, all based on the best available research and evidence from more than 50 carefully selected case studies, which feature companies of all sizes and states of maturity. You can be confident that the plays and tactics you'll read about "have legs" and provide a supported foundation for your listening initiatives. This book gives you the knowledge necessary to deep-six the hype, misinformation, and anecdotes about listening, and exploit its full potential instead.

Listen First! answers three critical questions:

- What is listening and how is it done?
- How is listening used to help achieve business objectives?
- Where is listening headed?

The book is organized into four parts that answer them:

Part I, Steps to Effective Listening: This part explains how listening research is done, step by step. It begins by defining the initiative and moves on to reporting the results and evaluating the effort. The different types of software solutions available for listening research are given in Chapter 2. The Appendix complements Chapter 2 by furnishing summaries of more than 70 vendor companies and their solutions and services.

Part II, Listening-Led Marketing and Advertising: Applying Listening Insights to Achieve Key Business Objectives: Listening contributes to achieving the full range of marketing and advertising objectives set out by most businesses. Each chapter in this part identifies a single objective—such as understanding consumer mind-sets, developing new products, increasing sales, providing customer service, or managing reputation—and details listening's contribution to its success.

Part III, Listening-Led Marketing and Media Innovations: Listening is more than insight and input into strategy; it is a data source, too. The chapters in this part look at four emerging data-driven applications that will usher changes into traditional business practices, such as social TV ratings, listening-based targeting, achieving share of market goals, and predicting near-term sales.

Part IV, Listening's New Frontiers: In this part, leading listening practitioners and researchers contribute essays on the way forward for listening, its practice, adoption, and contribution to creating business value. We will need to pick up new signals, understand people and culture, change the research paradigm, rethink what we do, and become listening organizations.

In keeping with its description as a playbook, *Listen First!* is intended as a business tool. Here are just a few of the ways that you can use it to your business advantage:

- Bring your colleagues and clients up to speed on listening research by reading Part I.
- Match a marketing problem you're working on to those in Part II.
- Sharpen your knowledge of what's next by consulting Parts III and IV.
- Jump-start the evaluation of listening solutions by turning to the Appendix, which presents summaries of more than 70 vendors.
- Learn the lingo by consulting the Glossary.

After reading *Listen First!*, it won't be business as usual. And for many people settled into their careers, that's scary—especially when listening insights challenge the status quo: When you find that the market you think you're serving turns out to be—or is becoming—something else entirely. When you know you've got a great insight and colleagues don't take it seriously. This book presents case studies of exactly these situations, and what was done to address them. You'll also learn about the ways companies recognized and seized the opportunity to build their businesses through listening.

I'm bringing up these points because of what I learned in the year it took me to write *Listen First!* It's simply this: Understanding and doing listening is essential, but not enough to create business advantage. The most successful listening companies do great work, have the guts to act on compelling insights, let go of the past, and shape their futures. Just imagine what boldness it took for Hennessy's management to transform a centuries-old cognac associated with brandy snifters, genteel surroundings, and after-dinner pleasures into an urban, music-inflected brand, where the beverage is mixed into drinks and enjoyed at parties? Or to persuade an editor who built a career on parenting publications that the readers for a new mom-targeted magazine she has in development don't want that information? There's a related factor, as well: These companies tell convincing stories from the listening research; they connect listening to the business in ways that bring people fully to life; understanding people as they are, not necessarily as a company would like them to be, makes tough decisions easier and sets a path for growth.

Listening is not just another research technique; it furnishes a new platform for business and research, and needs to be recognized as such. This book gives reasons for that recognition. It will provide you with the know-how to listen and turn conversations into enduring business advantage. Above all, listening is about learning through time and engaging with a like-minded community. Visit the Listen First companion Web site: http://listenfirst.thearf.org, for news, updates, viewpoints, and developments and for you to comment and share your knowledge and experiences.

PART I
STEPS TO EFFECTIVE LISTENING

ARF's Definition of Listening

A conversation about listening takes place nearly every day at the Advertising Research Foundation (ARF), and like most new concepts, people talk about it differently depending on their perspective. As an industry organization, we aim to be rigorous and inclusive on matters that affect our advertiser, media, research, agency association, and academic members. Since good investigators begin by standardizing definitions, that's where we will start. The ARF defines listening as:

> The study of naturally occurring conversations, behaviors, and signals that may or may not be guided, that brings the voice of people's lives into the brand.

Let's dissect this definition and explain our reasoning.

"The study of naturally occurring conversations, behavior, and signals . . ."
- *The study of*: People's authentic, unfiltered thoughts, feelings, and emotions
- *naturally occurring conversations*: Those that take place among people and through interactions with brands or companies in an open, noncoercive manner
- *behavior*: Observing what people do, such as shopping or using brands
- *and signals*: That people emit silently, such as through gesturing or biometric measures

"That may, or may not, be guided . . ."
- *That may/be guided*: Directed by other people, brands, or organizations in ways that focus naturally occurring conversations on agreed-upon topics
- *Or may not/be guided*: Conversations take their own direction

1

"To bring the voice of people's lives into the brand."

>   *To bring the voice of people's lives*: Through deep insights and con-
>   vincing stories
>
>   *Into the brand*: To evolve the relationship and take actions for mutual
>   benefit

Our definition aims to convey several key ideas. First, listening is concerned with what people say, how they act, and how they react on the "inside." In other words, it's not just focused on online conversations. Second, listening brands have responsibilities to people; they must be extraordinarily perceptive and respectful, and become their advocate. Last, brands and customers are in a learning relationship over time; both improve when each listens and responds to the other. The relationship is not reactive, but anticipatory and evolutionary.

You'll notice that our definition does not restrict conversations to online sources; rather, it acknowledges that they take place everywhere. Neither does it reference research methodology, tools, or techniques. Decisions about where and how to listen should be determined by the project, brand, customers, and expertise of those involved.

Listen First! Focuses on Social Media Conversations

This book is concerned with listening to social media conversations, because that's where the listening action is today. But since listening is also about anticipating, we sprinkle in a few instances of listening to behavior and signals. See Dr. Carl Marci's essay in Chapter 19 for a glimpse into the biometric future of listening.

Research Tasks: Social Media Listening Performs

Part II: Listening-Led Marketing and Advertising: Applying Social Media Listening Insights to Achieve Key Objectives shows how strategies based on listening research enable companies to accomplish a wide variety of marketing objectives. Social media listening provides different ways to perform many of the customary research tasks that are central to developing winning marketing and advertising strategies. In fact, listening's range of research applications often surprises people—"I didn't know it could be used for that!"—because listening is stereotypically thought of in fairly narrow terms, as a substitute for focus groups or other qualitative research, or as a way to monitor conversations for mentions of brands, people, or words or phrases of interest. Look at this range of uses, all taken from case studies in this book.

Understand mind-sets: Explore people's culture, views, values, and life-styles that influence their interests, thoughts, feelings, and behavior. Companies seek to learn how consumers cope with changing economic circumstances, or take on new roles—such as caregiving (both in Chapter 4)—or act within a product category, such as credit cards (see Chapter 9).

Profile customers and prospects: Develop insights into people for marketing and advertising products and services, as was done for spirits, motor-cycles, and e-tailer marketers (see Chapter 5). Go further by developing engaging loyalty programs (see Chapter 15).

Sense early market shifts: Anticipate changes that challenge existing business and present opportunities for new business, such as being able to recognize that customers are changing in unexpected ways—as a maker of electronic games detected (see Chapter 5).

Detect problems: Uncover the issues that impede sales and/or customer satisfaction, such as product or service issues, poor executions and experiences, or faulty retail strategy. Reveal unmet needs that companies can address, or remedies that can convert into new business opportunities or greater customer satisfaction (Chapters 8 and 14).

Analyze competitors: Compare rivals along various dimensions to develop strategies or tactics capable of creating advantage. For example, when new competitors enter the marketplace, learn and assess how customers position competing products on benefits, or size up strengths and weaknesses (see Chapter 13 for examples).

Target and segment: Categorize people based on their interests or actions as reflected in their conversations and the cultural contexts within which those conversations take place. Movie marketers, for instance, target and segment their audience according to facets such as interest in actors, type of movie, or special effects, whereas car companies target by reaching people who talk about them organically. Interest in multi-cultural listening is growing, as many realize how it can help marketers become more inclusive and expand their customer base (Chapters 5 and 14).

Uncover sales drivers and predict sales: Identify customer factors—such as the volume of social media activity, advocacy, and reviews—and the specifics within them that can be modeled to predict sales, as has been done in categories like books, consumer electronics, and entertainment (see Chapter 18).

Complement "asking" research: Bring multiple sources of data to bear on a marketing or advertising issue in order to enrich understanding. For example, one razor manufacturer surveyed and listened to lapsed users, or people who had stopped buying. The surveys documented the percentages of lapsed usage, and the listening research explained the reasons why people stopped buying (Chapter 12).

Innovation, R&D, co-creation: Develop new products, services, or enhancements by listening and, in some cases, involving customers and prospects in the process, as food companies, technology firms, and auto manufacturers have done (see Chapters 11 and 13).

Test concepts: Learn if new product ideas resonate with customers and prospects; acquire feedback on new services or features, as was done by a new food product (Chapter 11) and a venerable magazine (see Chapter 16).

Discover/evaluate brand attributes: Uncover the features most important to customers and prospects, as a car company (Chapter 14) or researchers did for a consumer electronics product (Chapter 18).

Develop and evaluate messages: Create messages that resonate with customer or prospect mind-sets, or modify them so they do. Chapter 12 shows how one personal care product learned its value proposition was off, and then repaired it accordingly. Cutting-edge techniques that gauge emotional responses to communication pave new pathways to insight and understanding effectiveness (see Chapter 19).

Identify threats to reputation: Understand and respond to the issues and events that can undermine and weaken a company, product reputation, or its future prospects (Chapter 17).

Though this list, generated solely from the cases discussed in this book, is extensive, it doesn't exhaust the research applications being explored, tested, and, probably, being kept under wraps for competitive reasons. For example, companies are developing brand trackers that incorporate listening data in two ways: as sources for attribute lists, so that the trackers are more in tune with people's conversations and interests; and as supplements to surveys, brand metrics, and regularly reported business measures like sales. Social media-based "numbers" essential to functions like media planning and buying are emerging that add insight into the quality of audiences and their marketing "fit" for specific companies, products, and services. Expect to see innovations like these and others appearing soon.

TWO TYPES OF RESEARCH USING SOCIAL MEDIA LISTENING

Social media listening divides into two categories: social media monitoring and social research. Tom O'Brien and David Rabjohns (2010) supply working definitions of these terms:

Both types of effort deliver value; the trick is matching the right type of listening to the goals of your business. Monitoring applications tends to be

Social Media Monitoring: Tracking online brand mentions on a daily basis for PR, brand protection, operations and customer service, outreach, and engagement.

Social Research: Analyzing naturally occurring online conversation categories to better understand why people do what they do; the role of brands in their lives; and the product, branding, and communications implications for brand owners.

more tactical, such as noticing comments, issues, or problems, and dealing with them expeditiously. Adept monitoring helps guide the response when someone calls out a particular product or company—whether it's negative, as it was for Hasbro (Chapter 17), or positive, as it was for Gatorade (Chapter 12). Poorly executed monitoring and response may lead to reputation problems that can range from trivial to severe. However, it's always best if these are handled properly and quickly, such as the Motrin Moms who ignited a firestorm of protest over an ad strategy, and pressured Motrin to pull the ad (Matson 2008). Chapters 12 and 14 provide many examples that rely on social media monitoring.

Social research is more strategic: It delves into underlying human concerns, attitudes, motivations, emotions, preferences, and the needs people have that shape their mind-sets and, ultimately, their actions, whether it is shopping, buying, or merely watching a TV program. Done well, social research uncovers pivotal insights that guide not only marketing and advertising, but also innovation, product development, customer service, and just about all business functions that touch customers, prospects, the trade, and other relevant stakeholders. Several of the case studies in Part II, where we show the contribution of listening research to achieving marketing objectives, provide examplary cases that all companies can learn from. Several particularly valuable ones to consider are the Hennessy Cognac and Suzuki Hayabusa cases in Chapter 10, the CPG manufacturer of home storage solutions in Chapter 12, and the example regarding X *Factor* in Chapter 15.

BENEFITS OF LISTENING RESEARCH

We interviewed a variety of researchers experienced with listening at advertisers, media companies, advertising and media agencies, and research companies to share with us their hard-won learnings about the benefits and advantages of listening, compared with traditional surveys and focus groups. In their words, listening offers the ability to detect early signals, make timely adjustments, and understand people in their own terms. They value listening for its abilities to provide:

- *Speed and timeliness*: Guidance can be acquired in days or weeks, not months.
- *Flexibility and course correction*: Changes can be made quickly if the research isn't being productive or if new avenues should be explored.
- The ability to frame research in consumer terms, not researcher language.
- Opportunities for listening to and analyzing unfiltered conversations.
- Answers to questions researchers did not think to ask.
- Large sample sizes.
- Cost advantages—although these need to be evaluated not only on dollars alone but also on efficiencies or results that are gained.

To this list we will add the ability to use "historical" data, or "backcast," for research initiatives. Unlike traditional methods, which have to start from day zero in most cases, listening research begins with an available datastream. That means that you can begin developing insights the day projects start, complete with trends, the ability to compare periods of time, and, perhaps most important, the freedom to ask new and different questions as the research proceeds, without requiring more money or extra time to collect and analyze new data. Because all data is automatically put into context, analytic and interpretive richness arises, and greater confidence in the insights results.

Listening research innovations are coming fast and furious. On the social side, researchers are gaining more experience daily by using listening data to do the nuts-and-bolts research that marketers and advertisers need, and by adapting research traditions to take advantage of social media data. An example of this is *netnography*, a digital form of ethnography (Kozinets 2010, Pettit 2010, Verhaege et al. 2009). There are more than 150 software applications and services available, and new ones appear daily that claim to address a new need or solve some problem. All this activity and innovation does not mean that we have to approach research differently; it simply requires that we do some new things and use different tools. The principles of doing good research endure.

MANAGING LISTENING RESEARCH

Planning, running, and evaluating social media listening programs require the same discipline as managing a research project or continuous research program. The differences—and they are crucial—reside in the operational specifics—the skills needed, tools, methods, data, and analysis—but not in the aims and ends to which the research insights are applied. For many readers, the differences will likely be challenging to what we know about market research

("How can we answer questions we didn't think of asking?"), but the chapters in Part I intend to explain the unfamiliar and guide the way forward to understanding listening and doing it effectively.

Principles for Effective Listening Research

The first three chapters explain the "how" of social media listening; it is intended to be a very practical, approachable guide for most readers. We do not get into very fine technical matters; rather, we highlight the issues or controversies that are generally important.

Listening initiatives follow a sequence of steps, and that is how the chapters are organized and progress:

Chapter 1: Organize for Listening and Define Objectives, Key Measures, and Conversations
- Organize for listening.
- Set objectives in relation to business goals.
- Define key performance indicators (KPIs).
- Determine the "research subjects": the voices and conversation sources best suited for the listening program.

Chapter 2: Evaluate and Select Listening Solutions
- Listening tools: overview and key features in five categories: Search, Monitoring, Text Analytics, Communities, and Full-service Vendors

Chapter 3: Field, Analyze, Report, and Evaluate
- "Field" the research: Run the listening program; establish methods and tools for "data processing"—the harvesting, cleaning, and processing of conversations.
- Analyze and report the data: Communicate the insights.
- Evaluate, appreciate, and commit to next steps.

Earlier, we distinguished social media monitoring from social media research. While both types of listening efforts share these steps, the types of work and levels of commitment are different. Those primarily monitoring conversations and alerting when something important comes up have different needs from those conducting research using heavy text analytics, working with full-service vendors, or running communities. As we move through the principles for effective listening research, we'll call attention to places where considerations for monitoring and social research differ.

SUMMARY

Social media listening research is used for many of the same purposes as traditional market research. Listening research is divided into two spheres, social media monitoring and social research, which are tactical and strategic, respectively. Listening research is innovating rapidly, and there are many solutions available to companies. Although the tools and some of the methods are different from familiar research methods like survey research and focus groups, the principles guiding research are unchanging.

CHAPTER 1

ORGANIZE FOR LISTENING AND DEFINE OBJECTIVES, KEY MEASURES, AND CONVERSATIONS

This chapter outlines the first steps for doing listening research that were outlined in the Introduction:

- Organize for listening.
- Set objectives in relation to business goals.
- Define key performance indicators (KPIs).
- Determine the research subjects: the voices and conversation sources best suited to the listening program.

We will now discuss each of these in detail.

ORGANIZE FOR LISTENING

Because listening can be done by companies of all sizes, from small businesses to globe-circling enterprises, the ways that they organize to undertake the effort will vary depending on their goals, resources, and staffing. Organizational consultant Beth Kanter (2009) proposes three concepts for listening organizations that provide a helpful framework:

Centralized listener: A person responsible for overseeing listening and, possibly, a firm's social media strategy. The J&D Bacon Salt (Chapter 6) case illustrates this model and shows that it can be very valuable for concept testing and product development, even on a shoestring, as it was for this startup.

9

Listening team: A group of people dedicated to listening, made up of individuals in the company from either a single department or cross-functional. The Vitamin Water case (Chapter 7) demonstrates the value of multidisciplinary teams in creating a new product and bringing it to market.

Listening organization: This model is meant for companies where listening data is a resource utilized by multiple departments and functions, such as marketing, sales, public relations, product development, or customer support. The Fiat MIO case study is a good example of how communications, marketing, and product development organized to co-create a car (Chapter 7).

Whatever your company size or the organizational form you eventually adopt, Chris Bourdreaux, Converseon's organizational lead, tells us there are five principles to keep in mind for success (see Chapter 23 for details):

- Establish an internal champion.
- Begin with business objectives.
- Create a social media center of excellence.
- Focus investments on business processes.
- Manage culture and communications (listening changes companies and operations).

Is there a preferred model? Not yet. Companies are figuring out what is best for them using a combination of the organizational types and principles. As for staffing, some companies dedicate people to listening, others make it a shared responsibility. However, given the importance of social communication and listening to every company's future, firms will derive more enterprise value from figuring out how to bake listening into the business and its operations instead of merely treating it as a bolt-on or "cover the bases" requirement.

SET OBJECTIVES IN RELATION TO BUSINESS GOALS

According to Coca-Cola marketing expert Stan Sthanunathan, listening research needs to be anticipatory, innovative, action-oriented, and focused on making real business impact in order to make a valued contribution (for more on this, read Sthanunathan's essay in Chapter 21). He's talking about creating marketing advantage, not researching to explain. To achieve that outcome, we need to focus first on asking the right questions, questions that make a difference instead of just confirming what we know or validating past beliefs and/or experiences.

These questions can be either broad or narrow; each has its place and purpose. Some examples from cases that we reviewed are:

Broad Questions

Broad questions are wide-scope, often concerned with areas of general interest and driving trends.

- A global food company asked: "We're considering repositioning the company on the concept of 'awesomeness,' to stay relevant with younger consumers. What does this term mean to people? And if we use one or more of those meanings, will it risk alienating our current customer base?" (Chapter 13).
- A large CPG company asked: "How do people think about the economy now? What changes will they make to their behavior? Will any of those changes last, even after the economy recovers?" (Chapter 5).

Narrow Questions

Narrow questions usually deal with specific topics, categories, or brands.

- A financial services company asked: "What are the financial issues with which people are grappling nowadays, and how is this affecting their credit and credit card use?" (Chapter 8).
- A small business providing Internet services asked: "Why are customers dissatisfied with our services, and what would they like to see us doing instead?" (Chapter 13).

This quartet of questions reveals an important point: They are asked in different contexts and for different business purposes, which, from top to bottom, are:

- Rebranding
- Understanding mind-sets
- Developing message strategy
- Managing reputation

Don't fool yourself into thinking that questions like these are mostly for big companies to ask. The small services company out to understand how to restore its reputation faces problems that are nearly identical to Dell's during its "Dell Hell" period; the only difference between the two scenarios is company size. Take the time to phrase your questions properly, and if possible, collaborate with colleagues to bring in different perspectives. In my experience of leading hands-on listening workshops, participants are often surprised by how challenging it can be to make a question researchable. Hearing "We used 15 of the 20 minutes just trying to phrase the question!" is not uncommon. The better the research question, the better the research.

DEFINE KEY PERFORMANCE INDICATORS (KPIS)

KPIs define and measure the progress of a business' initiatives and goals (performance). Just to take social media marketing as an example, an exact search on Google for "social media KPIs" turns up about 29,000 results, with the top title being "35 Social Media KPIs to Help Measure Engagement (October 29, 2010)." The results list a variety of interactions such as downloads, reviews, sharing, and so on. Making the search more specific by including "listening" in the request ("social media listening KPIs") rendered Google helpless, it couldn't find an exact match. Instead, it searched on the individual words which failed to garner very helpful results.

The crux of the matter is that listening insights in and of themselves are not revealed in standalone measures. Rather, they are often inputs to some other business process like customer service, R&D, marketing, sales, or public relations. For that reason, KPIs need to take the contribution listening makes to another process or function: their impact.

Companies that listen to social media conversations can compute metrics such as relating to *business process improvements,* which include quickening resolution time, increasing customer satisfaction levels, *cost-efficiency gains*, or *profitability enhancement*, see the JetBlue and Comcast cases (Chapter 14). Organizations also assess *contributions to strategy* by asking questions like these: How did listening insights frame our externally focused marketing, sales, or product strategies, for example, and influence the results they achieve? (See the Hennessy and Suzuki Hayabusa examples in Chapter 5.) They may also be concerned with *response and cycle times*: Did listening insights help us speed up time-to-market by improving our understanding of customers and prospects, and contribute to better coordination and teamwork? This isn't a complete list; it's merely meant to be suggestive. The KPI question can only be answered one company at a time, and needs to be asked at the front end, not the back: How will listening contribute to the work our company performs, how will we attribute its value, and what will success look like? Companies that are not able to answer those questions will never know or appreciate listening's effect on the business.

DETERMINE THE "RESEARCH SUBJECTS": THE CONVERSATIONS, SOURCES, AND VOICES BEST SUITED FOR THE LISTENING PROGRAM

Once you have defined your scope, the next step is to locate the conversations and the places they occur, so that you can collect and, later, prepare for data processing and analysis. Where you listen, as well as the appropriateness of conversations collected, directly affect the quality of the research and, eventually, the insights you're able to derive. That said, accessing the "right" conversations requires a number of steps:

1. Choose *where* to listen.
2. Determine the *footprint* of sources where your topic is talked about.
3. *Vet* the sources.
4. *Select* sources to use for listening.

Choose *Where* to Listen: The Consumer and Brand Backyards

We know people converse both online and offline. Online sources command most of listening's attention for two major reasons: one, their variety—there are sites for every conceivable interest, taste, and enthusiasm; and two, for the relative ease with which they can be located and harvested. Specialized programs called bots, agents, or spiders are set up to collect conversations that truly occur *everywhere*. We place online sources into one of two groups: *brand backyard* and *consumer backyard*.

Brand backyard sources, sometimes called "owned media," include company blogs, customer and private communities, discussion forums, e-mail, customer service logs, corporate Twitter accounts, and official presences on social networking sites like Facebook.

Consumer backyard sources include publicly available online blogs, forums, ratings and review sites, Twitter and status update features, social networks like Facebook, or media-sharing sites like YouTube and Flickr, and offline word of mouth. It is vital to capture offline word of mouth whenever possible, since it accounts for about 90 percent of brand-related conversations, and adds context or contrast for online conversations (Keller Fay 2008).

Depending on the project's aims, listening researchers use the backyards independently or mix the two in some fashion. For example, marketers of computer hardware, software, and services, like CDW (Chapter 10), concentrate on its brand backyard and professional forums, whereas a food manufacturer, like Kraft, explores consumer-oriented food and recipe sites, as well as its own sites (Chapter 11). In most listening initiatives, specialized software accesses the backyards and captures the conversations (see Chapter 2 for detailed explanations of the different types of software solutions).

A crucial point to remember: Wherever and whenever you listen, do it ethically, and harvest only publicly available or permission-based conversations. Respect the privacy policies of all the sources captured for the listening initiative.

Determine the Conversation Footprint

After deciding on the project's goals, it's time to locate the specific blogs, forums, social networks, and other sites where conversations of interest take place. You may just deal with a handful of selected sources if you are monitoring, as is often the case with customer service applications (see Chapter 14); however, if you're doing social research, it is essential to fish where the fish are. Defining the footprint is the fish finder.

This is a true research task. It's best to begin with known sources, like brand backyard ones, and then conduct searches to locate the places that are conversation-rich for your research goals. Keep in mind that you do not always need to include entire sites; only certain sections may be relevant. This is especially true for large Web sites, forums, and discussion boards, which have a variety of topics and attract different types of users or visitors. Set those that interest you aside, and get ready to take the next step: vetting the sources.

Vet and Select the Sources

The next thing you'll want to do is investigate the sources and choose which ones make the cut. Seth Grimes (2009), an authority on text mining, recommends four criteria for evaluating sources:

- *Topicality*: The source contains the information of interest, and enough of it, to justify including it.
- *Focus*: The source contains a high proportion of relevant information, and not a lot of extraneous information; said differently, the source has a high signal-to-noise ratio.
- *Currency*: The information is timely.
- *Authority*: The information is trustworthy.

The message here: Don't just use sources because they're popular ("We have to use Twitter") or easily available, or included in the set of default sources provided by vendors. Employ them because they will contribute high-quality conversations for analysis.

Select the Right Voices

The two backyards contain an array of voices, and every site will contain its unique set. Quality research depends on your ability to discover and listen to voices that are especially relevant to your company, product, or service. Practically speaking, new projects should focus on ensuring that the main voices are captured, such as moms (Chapter 3), lapsed users (Chapter 7), or caregivers (Chapter 4) for example. Unless experience counsels otherwise, avoid being overly specific at the outset. Just as in traditional research, it's difficult to know in advance what all the segments of interest in products are; let them emerge through analysis.

Listening is bringing about changes in research thinking the marketing community is working its way through, which is worth mentioning. Conventionally trained researchers often challenge the representativeness of listening research, inquiring: Do the people holding the conversations (the voices) match the demographic profile of a product's users; were they randomly selected; and are they projectable to the target market? One reason they ask is because so much of the information on public sites is not personally identifying. Failing to ascertain the characteristics that are part of almost every traditional survey makes some researchers uncomfortable because the people conversing cannot be classified with certainty, which runs counter to historical market research practice.

Listening-oriented researchers counter that representative samples are less of an issue because "the traditional model of quantitative market research based on questions asked to random probability samples is fading away . . . and providing the opportunity for the first time in probably 70 years to really revisit the methodological foundations of market research" (Poynter 2010, also see R. Scott Evan's essay in Chapter 21 for related points). Nowadays, one of the most important goals is to ensure that the research reflects the people on a site or in a community who are interested in a topic, company, or product by "sharply defining the population you are going to study, and to get as much of that population as humanly possible . . ." (Webster 2010). Manila Austin and Julie Wittes Schlack (2010) expand on that idea:

> If relevancy of insight is an important quality factor (which we believe it is), then researchers have more to gain by listening to the "right" group of people than they do by trying to generalize findings to a generic population. If you want to deepen customer loyalty, who better to engage than members of your brand's loyalty program? If your goal is to broaden your brand's appeal, then hearing from fans of your competitors' brands may be the most useful approach.

Every company needs to answer the question of voices for itself and for each initiative, as different projects may have different goals. The tensions between tradition and innovation will be resolved and lead to wider adoption of a new listening-centered research paradigm.

SUMMARY

Defining and setting up a listening initiative draw upon solid project management discipline: organizing, setting objectives, and establishing key performance indicators. Defining and vetting the conversation sources and selecting the voices to capture and analyze are vital to successful projects. Listening research represents new approaches to understanding consumers that are contributing to a new paradigm for market research.

CHAPTER 2

EVALUATE AND SELECT LISTENING SOLUTIONS

Conversational listening methods are rooted in the tradition of media-content analysis, a process that enables researchers to learn what people are saying, writing, or commenting on. Used during and since World War II, content analysis has provided insights for military, academic, and business purposes. For many years, the process relied on trained individuals ("coders") to manually extract terms, brand names, people, organizations, issues, actions, relationships, and sentiments from all types of published materials: magazines, newspapers, journals, transcripts, images, and proprietary comments from open-ended questionnaire items. The ability to process the coded information for statistical analysis has advanced from manual methods to mainframes to smaller, more powerful computers and, more recently, Web-based services.

Free or low-cost blogging tools from such service providers as Blogger, Twitter, and WordPress, along with the creation and deployment of customer feedback and ratings systems for products (Bazaarvoice), video and photo sharing (YouTube, Flickr), social bookmarks (Digg), and social networks like Facebook, Orkut, and CyWorld have broadened content analysis from the study of mass media sources to everyday conversations, especially those held online. With a few mouse clicks or touchpad taps, anyone can become a writer, replier, publisher, producer, commentator, reviewer, pundit, advocate, or even jerk, on a new and unprecedented scale.

People's thoughts, feelings and conversations, previously hard to get to, are now shared, visible, directly accessible, collectible, and analyzable. No longer are people's expressions restricted to "letters to the editor" that may or not be published, correspondence with the "complaint department" that may or may not be acted upon, or practically irretrievable remarks in customer relationship management (CRM) notes.

The result: Marketers can *listen* to great numbers of the people who are interested in their categories, who may buy or currently own their products; *learn* from them and develop insights; *engage* in conversations with these consumers if they choose; and *act* on what they hear.

16

These remarkable developments have stimulated today's widespread interest in listening, and contributed to the rapid growth of listening-related services and products, including search-term analysis, text-analysis software, full-service platform vendors, community operators, and offline word-of-mouth researchers. Innovations coming forward are providing the technology, services, and expertise that help brands listen to people and develop insights capable of creating business advantage.

The variety and growing number of solutions available to brands and their partners is mind-boggling. A Google search for "social media monitoring" garners results with titles like: "A Wiki of Social Media Monitoring Solutions," listing 149 of them, or "12 Social Media Monitoring Tools Reviewed." Go to LinkedIn and you'll see a thread in the Social Media Marketing group of 294 responses to the question: "Can anyone recommend a good social media monitoring tool?" (LinkedIn 2010). The first answer was: "My boss just showed me these two. They look pretty good." I'll spare you more examples; the point is that while many people create lists or comment, meaningful guidance is hard to come by. This chapter aims to correct that trend and provide you with the ability to navigate confidently through an active, yet often confounding, marketplace to the solutions suitable to your listening needs.

FIVE TYPES OF LISTENING SOLUTIONS

Today's solutions market leverages 30 years of product experience and addresses the most up-to-the-minute customer demands. Countless companies are backed by venture capital and private equity firms that see the enormous potential of listening. As it is in any dynamic market, it can be a challenge to sort out which solutions—or combination thereof—meet brand listening requirements and budgets. We developed a classification system based on the various properties that software solution classes share in common. Five groups that we discuss here comprise our scheme:

- Search engines
- Media monitoring
- Text analytics
- Private communities
- Full-service listening platform vendors

The following pages describe the key features and analytic capabilities of each class, and considerations for their use. Leading vendors in these categories are compiled and summarized in the Appendix, "Listening Vendor Profiles: A Resource Guide."

Search Engines

This group includes two types of solutions: general search engines and real-time search engines. Search engines are typically used to get quick reads on topics of interest in pop culture, and also for competitive analysis (see the Tassimo case in Chapter 13), or to gauge consumer interest in an issue, such as iPhone4 antenna-gate. Without being hyperbolic, the range and variety of topics that can be explored through search is virtually unlimited. The key to using them well resides in the ability to search on keywords that capture the topic of interest.

General Search Engines   Search engines index a range of online sources to make them searchable and the results accessible. Google, Yahoo!, Bing, Ask, and AOL are the top 5 engines, with Google the most popular.

Google and Yahoo!, in particular, offer useful analytic capabilities for listening. Google's robust research tools permit studying search term trends, related or contrasting concepts, and competitors (Google Trends, Google Insights for Search), whereas Yahoo! is especially strong in the areas of popular culture and buzz, providing a snapshot of a searcher's current and recent interests (Y!buzz and Yahoo Buzz Index).

For tracking, Google provides an alert system and the capability to download results from Insights for Search and import them into spreadsheets or databases for further analysis. The major engines innovate and occasionally add features that are inspired by Twitter and real-time search.

Real-Time Search Engines   This newer class of search engines specializes in social media, and chose not to duplicate the big engines' coverage. Real-time search vendors concentrate on harvesting social media sources where people are actively commenting, writing, Tweeting, uploading, or updating. Sources include blogs (e.g., Technorati), Twitter, social bookmark services (Digg, Delicious), photo-sharing sites (Flickr), video-sharing sites (YouTube), and full-on social networks like Facebook. Real-time search engines monitor and report activities as close as possible to the time they happen.

Real-time search engines often provide information about items' "sociability" by detailing the popularity of posts or tweets, identifying trending topics, assigning sentiment, linking to authors and recipients, and listing influencers. Some even provide tools for people to act on the information by e-mailing, commenting, or re-tweeting. For companies who listen, real-time search can be a no-cost, bare-bones monitoring option and entry level engagement tool for customer service and sales, for example. But keep in mind that while they are helpful, they do not offer much in the way of administration and reporting capabilities.

Search Engine Considerations

Match engines to listening requirements: It's crucial to keep in mind when using search engines or real-time search for listening that they differ from one another in various areas, including popularity, the sources they cover, their ranking routines, the audiences they attract, and their value propositions. Google sets out to "organize the world's information," whereas competitor Bing specializes in helping searchers use the information (especially in travel, shopping, and finance). Since the engines differ from one another, the results do so as well. The implication for listening is clear: Every listening initiative needs to vet the engines in light of research requirements to make sure that those selected match their needs. Additionally, real-time search engines can present spam in their results. Ensure quality in data by applying filters to remove as much noise as possible before the conversations are processed.

Social Media Monitoring

Social media monitoring provides a major step up from real-time searching. Tools and capabilities allow end users to observe, measure, analyze, and report on social media activity. Monitoring tools help organizations track mentions of their brands, products, competitors, and industry; topics and issues; words or phrases of interest; key executives; as well as marketing messages, the sentiment around them, and key influencers (which can be people, blogs, or sites). As we mentioned in Chapter 1, the primary goals of monitoring are public relations, including reputation management; company and brand protection; and customer service, outreach, and engagement. Chapter 12 on managing reputation and Chapter 14 on customer care and satisfaction present a variety of cases that use monitoring.

Most solutions offer dashboard displays that report and visualize the monitoring data as stats or trends over time, and as word clouds that reflect the popularity of keywords. Filters to narrow down results by keyword, source, or geography, for example—coupled with drill-down capabilities—enable users to access and read the individual posts, tweets, or comments underlying the numbers that help to explain the "whys." (See the M.D. Anderson case study in Chapter 13, which used social media monitoring to uncover and meet men's health needs.) Several companies offer social CRM; workflow and collaboration features that integrate monitoring with managing accounts on services like Twitter or Facebook; and alerting, escalation, routing, response, and resolution services that help with outreach, engagement, and customer care.

Most vendors provide their solutions as a service that is accessible through an Internet connection and Web browser. Though pricing and licensing schemes vary, charges may include a flat rate per user per month and/or tiered fees based on quantities or usage, such as the number of keywords tracked or the number of results returned.

Social Media Monitoring Considerations

The primary role of social media monitoring solutions is to equip companies with tactical tools and capabilities, often for customer service, such as JetBlue or Comcast show (Chapter 14) or reputation management, as seen in the Hasbro example (Chapter 12). Since these are essentially self-serve solutions, it's important to ensure that they are configured for each company's listening needs, and that companies understand the strengths and limitations of their solution. Several considerations influence the business value derived from monitoring:

Retrieving brand mentions: Organizations that conduct brand-name tracking must make certain that they're able to retrieve brand names in meaningful quantities. That is not always easy to do because—except for ratings and reviews and brand backyard sources—brand names may appear only occasionally in consumer backyard conversations. For example, only 5 percent and 40 percent of conversations in food and automobiles, respectively, specify brand names. Retrieving these mentions that are about the brand and not something else is another point to consider. O'Brien and Rabjohns (2010) found that during the Beijing Olympics it took 250 search arguments to separate out the brand Visa from the travel document. They add that car rental companies with generic names, such as Enterprise, Dollar, and Thrifty, face this problem. Research for which you are unable to separate out generic terms from the brand terms does not yield good results.

Understanding context: Because the people talking are not always mentioning brands, analysts need to search for and retrieve conversations relating to brand discussions in order to understand the different contexts in which they occur. For example, conversations about hot dogs hardly mention brand names; but they take place in the context of family gatherings, sporting events, and feeding children. Unearthing those discussions requires subject expertise and artful querying of the social media sources.

Reporting: Companies need to make sure that dashboards present data that is appropriate and relevant to their listening requirements. They must require that reporting is flexible so that they can generate reports that support their needs and apply to their decisions.

Text Analytics

Text analytics software companies are another rung up the ladder from social media monitoring. These vendors supply software that provides tools and capabilities for collecting both brand and consumer backyard conversations; processing, analyzing, and reporting them; providing workflow and collaboration tools for groups or teams; and integrating data with CRM solutions, third-party, and in-house systems to provide a comprehensive view. Although they perform the brand monitoring functions just described in the social media monitoring section, their strength resides in their advanced analytic capabilities, which include uncovering and evaluating the importance of topics and themes; discovering relationships and facts; and revealing emotions and motivations.

Several of the case examples that we cover in Part II utilize text analytics, and illustrate its powers quite well. Three that are worth looking into are: developing a new women's food product (Chapter 11); understanding the different meanings of terms and contexts for "broadband," to create messaging and inform media planning (Chapter 25); and detecting the competitive positioning of two brands, Tylenol and Advil, in the public's mind (Chapter 18). One quick example: Gaylord Hotels text-analyzed post-stay comments and discovered that although noisy rooms were not a frequently experienced problem, they were one of the most serious because they were highly correlated with "wouldn't return" or "wouldn't recommend" responses (Stodder 2010). Text analysis is also used just like quantitative data: as inputs into models that predict business outcomes. Examples in Chapter 18 show how text-analyzed listening data was used in models that predict product sales.

Text analysis solutions aim to assist in all aspects of listening initiatives. They are available as enterprise solutions installed on your company's hardware and as Web-based self-service tools made accessible as a service.

Text analysis has a long history; it's over 45 years old, and is a very technical field that has emerged from computer science and computational linguistics. Describing it technically is beyond our scope. If you are interested in an excellent and accessible primer, read Seth Grimes's two-part series on text analytics basics (Grimes 2008).

Text Analytics Considerations

Complexity: Text analytics is a complex undertaking that requires specialized expertise. Many listening initiatives that use it do so through vendor and consultant services that offer the right mix of people, process, and technology. Companies that purchase this kind of assistance should carefully evaluate suppliers for their knowledge, practical experience, and capacity. Text analytic services are not commodities; the related people, skills sets, and domain expertise vary from one company to another, as does their capacity. In fact, one large company buyer we interviewed declared that while some companies did great work, many of them couldn't handle several projects simultaneously, which left them with the option of waiting or selecting a less-preferred supplier.

Project focus: As with any major initiative, establishing and sticking to clear goals up front improve one's chances of getting a completed—and, hopefully, fruitful—research outcome. Clear leadership, excellent project management, and communication are vital, as is the willpower to resist the temptation to expand the initiative's scope as it unfolds, and thereby risk losing focus. It is occasionally necessary to change scope; if this is the case, then operate in a change-and-control fashion, whereby you first approve changes and then establish their impacts on project budget and timeline.

Staff resources and new skills: Every solution discussed requires hiring people who are trained in the use of the various tools and have an aptitude for listening. Initiatives that incorporate text analytics require employing staff with a higher level of skills in working with unstructured data, such as content analyzing, coding, classifying, clustering, and taxonomy building. These individuals must also understand the business, industry, and customers. Software, of course, is not perfect. For example, though it will suggest topics, categories, and themes, it usually takes a human being or team of them to make sure that these parameters are relevant and meaningful to the research objectives; and if not, to tweak and modify them so they are, and iterate until they're right. Companies that purchase text analytic services need at least one knowledgeable staffer who can interact with and guide the vendors, and serve as the bridge between the company and the research team.

Private Communities

Private online communities invite qualified customers and prospects to engage with brands in prearranged ways through projects, assignments, and conversations, and with other community members in free, natural, unstructured methods by using social media. In these respects, communities are best regarded as "brand-backyard" sources. By referring again to Part II, you can see how NASCAR listened to its community and took their suggestions to change racing to make it more exciting (Chapter 13), or how publisher Meredith used its community to reposition *Ladies' Home Journal* (Chapter 16), or the way CDW listened to its community and developed an effective sales strategy (Chapter 14).

Companies that run communities manage sizable "living labs" for marketing research. By having members participate for varying periods—from at least one month to several months or longer—these communities make it possible for brands to run multiple projects simultaneously or progressively, and to listen to the evolution of their core customers' and prospects' discussions. Communities aid marketers in developing customer insights, brand strategy, new products, and innovation strategies. Community vendors typically provide benefits such as member recruitment, qualification, and activation; member accounts and social networking; market research capabilities; deployment; analysis and reporting; and professional services for community operation and ongoing engagement.

Community Considerations

Be open to community guidance: Use communities for more than just "quick answers" to marketer-initiated questions and routine evaluations. Connect with members to explore concepts—like wellness—or behaviors—such as stocking up on products—more deeply and develop richer insights. Companies that run communities, like Communispace, strongly advise marketers to remain open and receptive to the guidance the community gives. That requires humility and the capacity for marketers or advertisers to see themselves in their customers' lives, rather than as consumers of their products.

Full-Service Listening Platform Vendors

Listening platform vendors provide technology, services, and consulting that offer end-to-end solutions for analyzing both offline and online word of mouth.

Full-service vendors furnish many research capabilities, including those of the text analysis vendors, but surround them with value-added services. Consulting and service offerings focus on listening project management; analysis; reporting; and evaluation; and, sometimes, creation, implementation, and evaluation of marketing, media, advertising, and public relations programs.

Considerations

Match vendor strengths to listening requirements: Although vendors may have the right mix of offerings and business strategy, they differ from one another on various dimensions, like the availability of consulting, the strength of their services and analytic capabilities, the robustness of their technology, data source coverage, or ease of use (Forrester 2010). Additionally, strong project management and clear communication are essential for initiatives to keep momentum, stay on track, and meet milestones. Taking on a solution is always more than the technical capabilities of software; it's an engagement and relationship in which both parties should contribute and benefit.

SUMMARY

Listening solutions—the software and methods for doing social media listening research—fit into five groups: search, media monitoring, text analytics, private communities, and full-service listening platform vendors. Each category has its own capabilities and value, ranging from tracking search terms to counting and trending mentions to slicing and dicing to predictive modeling of business outcomes. Solutions can be used alone or in combination, depending on how they fit with goals for the listening initiative.

CHAPTER 3

FIELD, ANALYZE AND REPORT, AND EVALUATE LISTENING RESEARCH

Now that we know how to set up listening initiatives (Chapter 1) and choose from among the many and various solution options (Chapter 2), it's time to run the listening initiative, learn, share, and evaluate the results.

FIELD THE RESEARCH

Before putting the research into "production," employ pretest procedures to make sure that the data is top quality and that essential procedures are working properly. The following four tactics will help verify quality of data to derive the highest-value results and insights:

Ensure Data Quality: Four Tactics

- *Test connections to listening sources you want to harvest to make certain they are working*: Sometimes sources will change URLs, site organization, access schemes, or even cease operations altogether. Any of these can prevent you from making successful connections. Check periodically if you're running your listening effort over a period of time.
- *Test that content is being harvested correctly*: Test the queries that locate and retrieve content from sites to ensure that they return what you want; and keep iterating and testing until the results meet your needs. Writing queries is an art, one that requires knowledge of the business, insights into customers, and some technical skill in search logic. If you are listening in a regulated industry like pharma or financial services, consult with legal and compliance colleagues to ascertain that your listening harvesting conforms to requirements.

- *Filter spam out and deal with vernacular*: Spam is a common nuisance on social media sites, and much of it is auto-generated. This extraneous material hurts quality and gives leading vendors a black eye. Large companies that purchased listening services expressed disappointment in the levels of spam (and irrelevant information) in the datasets their vendors provided (Forrester 2010).

    Texting and instant messaging have brought about all sorts of language innovation; you've undoubtedly seen "4" used for the word "for" or "cul8r" for "see you later." Solutions for handling these types of substitutions should be used, such as dictionaries for slang, new words, text abbreviations, or common misspellings.
- *Determine that basic processing routines perform properly and accurately*: When software reads posts, tweets, or reviews, it breaks them down into elements and assigns them to content categories. These categories can be such things as brand names, people names, or geographies; product types like "hair care"; topics such as customer service; or attributes like color. Categorization errors lower quality because the data inside the categories is not the same. When software classifies both "Earl Grey tea" and "Charlie Brown" as colors instead of the correct classes of "beverage" and "name," respectively, computations will be thrown off and the insight will be invalid (Pettit 2010). Test and modify categorization until the content is classified satisfactorily; and don't assume that errors will cancel themselves out. If you are using workflow and collaboration functions, test these, too.

Go Live

Once you've addressed pretests and quality concerns, it's time to throw the switch and take an active stance toward listening. Ensure quality by spot-checking harvesting and processing, and then make necessary adjustments. The social world is dynamic, so it's critical to keep in step to obtain the highest-quality results. Keep in mind that going live can also mean "backcasting," or conducting historical analysis on a content collection.

ANALYZE AND REPORT

It's best to have a plan when it comes to analyzing, and reporting should be close to an event in its impact. In this section, we recommend an analytic strategy and raise two related concerns: the importance of using multiple data sources to both confirm findings and improve confidence in sentiment. Following those discussions, we take on the topic of reporting.

Analytic Strategy

It's not uncommon for people to get a little anxious shortly after a listening initiative starts generating data: "There's so much data: What does it mean?

And what do I do with it?" That feeling can apply whether you're getting machine-processed streams of Web data or dealing with reams of qualitative verbatim statements from communities.

Developing and following a plan to guide the analysis not only alleviates the anxiety; more importantly, it sets the path to developing insights. The pragmatic approach to analyzing listening data is to consider the nature of the data and connect it to the business goals the listening effort supports. Because listening data comes from conversations, a question-based analytic approach makes sense; then the data can provide answers. Questions provide a context that directs data interpretation. From a reporting standpoint, the results are presented in another important context, that of the decisions your organization needs to make to drive business forward.

The standard "4Ps" marketing framework—product, price, promotion, and place—will serve to illustrate. For each, we note the type of research solution used to show some of the ways they are applied.

- *What improvements would people like to see in our product?* NASCAR drew upon its private community to learn what would make its racing events more exciting to fans. Through its listening, the organization made two improvements, including racing rules (Chapter 13).
  Research technique: private community
- *How do people feel about the price?* Gillette looked into this question through traditional survey and listening research among lapsed users for its Fusion razor (Chapter 12). The survey findings showed that a "too high" price drove shavers to drop the Fusion, and the listening research put that into context and explained why: The price was too high for the expected quality of the shave. The shave was better, but not enough to justify the price premium. That more nuanced interpretation led Gillette to better align price with shave quality and then communicate that to shavers.
  Research technique: text analytics
- *How should we position our product in advertising?* Listening research reveals the "people's positioning" that can be used to evaluate current positioning strategy or suggest changes that will make it resonate more with customers and prospects. Although Tylenol and Advil are popular analgesics, results showed that people positioned each product differently in their minds. Tylenol was seen as safer for children, while Advil was seen as an effective pain reliever (see Chapter 18).
  Research technique: text analytics (content analysis)
- *Where should our product be available to help increase sales?* Looking to boost sales for its Tassimo pod coffee maker, Kraft sought to find where a competitive advantage would lie. After sizing up Tassimo in comparison with category leader Keurig, Kraft discovered that people considered the two brands to be parity products: They didn't see differences in features or likes or dislikes. Still looking for an edge, Kraft turned to search, which

provided the "aha" moment: Tassimo interest concentrated on the East Coast, with hot spots in the Middle Atlantic and New England states. Kraft had its insight and used it to recommend improvements to distribution and retail strategy.

Research technique: social media monitoring and search analysis

As you see, questions about listening data can be asked across the marketing spectrum and, by extension, within any framework that you choose. For example, you might have a framework for comparing competitor strategy, or one for innovation; either one will work. The trick is to have one and repurpose it to frame research questions for listening.

Bring as many different voices to bear as appropriate when analyzing. Conversations are always open to interpretation, and a variety of perspectives can strengthen both insight and its eventual contribution.

Triangulate to Increase Confidence *Triangulation* means to use multiple and different sources to confirm a finding or insight. In effect, it is a way of "building the case." This method is vital for proper listening, for several reasons. First, the process of listening is still unfamiliar; since many people don't fully trust it yet, it helps to be able to show supporting evidence. Second, no single data source contains the answer, and any single data source is limited in its perspective (Grimes 2008a).

Let's take a case of a quick-service restaurant to see triangulation in action. Looking to reach a younger audience, a popular quick-service restaurant chain decided to enlarge its menu and develop new advertising; it offered new items and launched a humorous campaign. Franchisees wanted to know: Would the campaign raise awareness of the new products and increase same-store sales? The brand needed to know: Should we continue to invest in this effort?

The brand engaged full-service social media listening vendor J.D. Power and Associates Web Intelligence, which monitored the blogosphere for discussions about the brand and the new items for the first three months of the new advertising run.

People's online conversations are influenced by offline conversations and advertising. J.D. Power's analysis looked at the relationships between the ad spend, the media plan and commercial schedule, and the buzz. It determined that the new ad campaign "had an immediate and long-lasting impact on total blog postings about the brand, as well as dramatically increasing the brand's percentage of positive versus negative postings. Analyzing verbatims, bloggers proactively played back the storyline of the various commercials, accurately identifying the new menu items and responding positively to the humor used in the campaign." Same-store sales increased shortly after the ads hit. The chain reported that the franchisees were satisfied with the campaign and performance of new items; based on these results, the brand invested more money in the national media to sustain the momentum (J.D. Power and Associates 2009).

Increasing Confidence in Sentiment   Sentiment is a computation about people's feelings—positive, negative, or neutral—toward people, products, companies, and topics discussed in social media conversations. The accepted wisdom is that positive sentiment has positive effects and negative sentiment has negative impacts. While that's an oversimplification—there are times when negative sentiment can have positive impacts (Berger et al. 2009)—we are concerned with gaining confidence that the scoring is accurate: that positive is positive and negative is negative. We face a conundrum, however: Sentiment scoring is important yet imperfect. As a practical matter, machines need to score sentiment because the volume of content is so great. Listening efforts do not deal with 500 posts; they deal with thousands, tens or hundreds of thousands. It is, therefore, out of the question to have humans analyze the complete data collection.

Here are five tactics for improving confidence in sentiment scoring:

- Clean the data to a reasonable extent to make sure that categorization is accurate.
- Use machine-scored sentiment to identify trends in a data collection.
- Use human analysis of sentiment when context and pinpoint accuracy for individual posts are required.
- If the listening solution used allows for its sentiment engine to be trained, use a hybrid approach: take two passes. First use the machine, and then manually code a sample of the machine-scored text for confirmation, augmentation, and correction. As accuracy improves, the human pass will fade (Grimes 2008b).
- Consider using additional information about sentiment, such as star ratings or like/dislike ratios.

More than knowing, but also having confidence in sentiment can provide marketers and advertisers with better guidance for engaging in conversation with customers and prospects; recalibrating the brand to consumer mood; or taking marketing or public relations actions that aim to maximize brand advantages and minimize risk or harm. That said, the guidance is only as good as the quality of the sentiment scoring.

Reporting

There are two types of reports: real-time dashboards and reporting results and insights to colleagues in presentations or using conventional documents with text and graphics. Real-time dashboards are better suited to listening efforts where monitoring and responding are central to the effort. Gatorade offers a stellar example (see Chapter 12), and such dashboards also provide statistical reports on activity.

Though some organizations report listening findings and insights using conventional formats, they are usually boring. The reason is because the reports don't capture or reflect the tenor or excitement of the conversations from which the data emerges. A number of companies recognize this and see it as necessary for listening research to make an impact on the company as a whole, not just on the insights department. As Coke's Stan Sthanunathan writes in Chapter 21, research must be "inspiring"; if it isn't, it's failing.

Companies are training staff in the art of storytelling to help make this trend more prevalent. Stories provide context, connection among ideas through narrative, and—most importantly—an emotional connection with the audience. The best stories meet the needs and interests of the people listening. You must first and foremost understand what's important to your audience when you tell stories. If you're talking to product development or the CFO, craft your tale to leave them with the most relevant information for their purposes. Avoid the trap of making up a standard story about the research that you tell to everybody else; instead, truly cater the information to the person to whom you're presenting it.

EVALUATE THE LISTENING INITIATIVE

Evaluate listening initiatives according to their capability to meet the key performance indicators (KPIs) cited in Chapter 2. The point we stressed earlier is that listening's contribution comes from the application of findings and insights to other business processes, and that listening should be judged on the value of its contribution to them. That is what giants like Comcast, JetBlue, AT&T, and smaller ones like True Citrus do (see Chapters 14 and 8). Don't just grab metrics from popular lists circulating on the Web; develop ones that have meaning in your business and for your business.

SUMMARY

The contribution listening makes to business advantage comes from doing solid research. This chapter builds on Chapters 1 and 2, stressing the importance of data quality, ongoing checking of data and procedures, and instilling confidence in the analysis. More engaging reporting—that which conveys the dynamics of conversations and makes emotional connections with colleagues—increases the value and contribution of listening efforts. Last, listening needs to be evaluated in the terms of its contribution to the business processes it supports.

PART II

LISTENING-LED MARKETING AND ADVERTISING

Applying Listening Insights to Achieve Key Business Objectives

It's one thing to be excited about social media listening. After all, you've probably heard countless people claim that, "It's the world's largest focus group," "It's practically free mind-reading!", or something similarly grandiose and unhelpful. It's quite another to *apply* social media listening in ways that impact marketing and advertising performance. Chances are that if you're reading this book, the role social media listening played—and continues to play—in frequently cited successes for brands like Starbucks, JetBlue, and Dell is familiar, or at least rings a bell, and interests you. Those companies faced critical business challenges that had the potential to erase years of stellar reputation, impede their growth, and lower their level of competitiveness. Instead, this trio of companies adopted effective listening techniques and eventually engaged with prospects and customers.

- Dell counteracted "My Dell Hell" with IdeaStorm.
- Starbucks reinvigorated itself with "My Starbucks Idea."
- JetBlue put customer service on Twitter.

At this point you might be saying, "But those are special cases; they're big companies facing big problems." You might also be wondering, "How exactly did they use social media listening to help build and improve their businesses? And how do *I* gauge the value of listening for my company?"

The best way to answer those questions for an emerging field like social media listening is by looking at case studies. These scenarios enable you to learn from what others have done; they show you methods to take onto the field, practice, and maybe put in your company's playbook. To that end, we researched and selected cases that used social media listening to:

- Generate consumer insights,
- Leverage those insights, and
- Report marketplace results or specific actions these brands took.

In other words, it wasn't enough that companies listened; they had to act on what they heard and experience a positive or negative outcome. Each case we present in the following pages passed these screening criteria. We can look to all of them to highlight how companies use social media listening to create business advantage.

Cases with the most successful results:

- Started with clear objectives and strategy.
- Combined online and traditional media in their programs, with social media an important component in the mix.
- Included a defined role for social media listening—not a "bolt-on" or afterthought.
- Conducted research that drew upon the principles for effective listening research (see Part I for a detailed discussion).
- Partnered social media listening research with other marketing study sources and data—such as secondary research, surveys, and directed activities.
- Boldly acted on the research insights, even when they contradicted their conventional wisdom.

Reviewing the points in these cases led us to several conclusions about social media listening research and demonstrated that it is:

- Appropriate for companies of all sizes, from startups to established brands
- Applicable for both B2B and B2C products and services
- Complementary to traditional "asking" research and understanding marketing effectiveness, and can stand alone
- Capable of providing business guidance that runs the gamut from free and low-cost tools to the most sophisticated implementations (to varying degrees of depth and richness)
- Far-ranging, spanning the spectrum of communications objectives from discovering new customers to customer loyalty, service, and reputation management
- Suitable for setting strategic direction, tactical plans, and in-market actions
- Valuable for solving or handling tough, complex, challenging problems and public issues

However, even companies that actively listen to social media occasionally find that they are working against themselves and may not fully reap the benefits of these initiatives. The case analysis we did revealed a number of challenges that less successful social media listening efforts faced, specifically when:

- Company policies sometimes get in the way.
- Violating research principles, such as listening to the right sources and voices, can miss important conversations and lead to faulty insights.
- Core customer groups were not involved, yielding a distorted picture.
- Response to issues often used outdated strategies and tactics that may have worked a decade ago but need to be overhauled for the social media era.
- Companies failed to listen continuously after addressing needs and concerns to learn whether solutions were working.
- Social media listening did not maintain a civil tone and/or avoid public arguments.

We organized the cases into a progression of brand objectives. You'll see through these examples how social media listening is not limited to simply generating insights from "the world's largest focus group" or to customer service; it truly contributes to *all* of the tasks that marketers and advertisers typically perform. Our aim is to provide a reference for you and your colleagues to consult when planning a social media listening project for your brand to achieve a specific goal. The chapters in this part will provide guidance on how to achieve the following aims:

- Understand the consumer's mind-set—"get in their heads."
- Discover new customers.
- Drive new product development and innovation.
- Create messages that resonate.
- Improve products and services.
- Increase sales.
- Look forward to drive business forward.
- Rebrand and reposition products and services.
- Manage reputation.
- Compete strategically.
- Customer care and customer satisfaction.

Each case describes the business objective, role for social media listening, insights leveraged, program implemented, and marketplace results or decisions that the findings helped produce. Where the cases allow, steps in their research processes are outlined. You'll notice they conform to the principles summarized in the introduction to Part I and discussed in detail in Chapters 1–3. When reading the cases, flip back to them from time-to-time for a refresher and for more detailed discussion. Doing so will raise appreciation for the valuable role that listening research plays in achieving marketing objectives and creating business advantage.

The cases reviewed differ in the sophistication of their social media listening; for that reason we indicated each one's level:

- *Fundamental*: Companies just getting started in this area and relying on free or low-cost tools
- *Intermediate*: Companies with some experience under their belt that may have a listening toolkit that includes traditional research
- *Advanced*: Companies with a commitment to social media listening, investment in tools and people, and additional resources

Additionally, to help you understand the type of listening research conducted in each case—search-based, social media monitoring, or social research—it is included in parentheses following the level.

Though social media listening is becoming more widely known and utilized, it is still an emerging practice for a lot of organizations. Most companies are at the fundamental level; very few are advanced. But whatever your company's level of sophistication, all can learn from one another, in terms of both accomplishments and setbacks. While fundamental-level companies may not have the same capabilities, they may see approaches that they can approximate and borrow to improve their own efforts, or aspire to.

CHAPTER 4

UNDERSTAND THE CONSUMER'S MIND-SET

START WITH THE BIG PICTURE

When you or your team meets to plan strategy, one of the first questions asked is: What's going on out there in our industry, and how is it affecting people? The textbook response is to undertake a business environment review, identify trends, extend them, and consider their impacts. Of course, while that type of work is necessary, important, and valuable, it's essentially descriptive and backward-looking—even when the deck gets spiced-up with short-term projections. As when driving a car, business should be steered forward by looking straight ahead, while continually adapting to the traffic, twists and turns, and weather.

Some years ago, I conducted a mammoth study for a global CPG company that tracked trends driving the food business in Europe and Asia. The results included demographics and appliance details like the varying sizes of freezers, microwave penetration, and food categories. Taken together, this data did a very good job relating market conditions and the ability to freeze or zap food. It also led to an important conclusion: The infrastructure for microwaveable food was emerging, providing several of the CPG firm's frozen-food brands with new global potential.

The ability to convert potential results into insightful guidance requires consumer-centered strategies and programs that are grounded in perceptive, timely consumer research. The consumer research available to draw upon for this food trends project was survey or focus group based. The research was not notable for what it told us, but for what it could *not*: customers' concerns about the economy and budgeting; feelings on prices, taste, health, freshness, nutrition, or package size; indulgence, convenience, or mealtimes; what they plan to buy, how they will stock their freezers and use their microwaves; what trade-offs will be made; or if they will skip the hassle altogether and go out (but where, when, and why?). In other words, we lacked insights about their mind-sets that influenced their behavior (see Wind and Crook 2004, or Moskowitz and Goffman 2007, for authoritative treatments on this topic).

The strategy team could only make assumptions, an exercise of limited value, because they were often constrained by past experience, legacy thinking, and corporate mind-sets. None of these were up to the task of understanding, marketing, and advertising to a rapidly changing consumer. Revealing consumer mind-sets through social media listening does, as the winning plays and cases will show.

WINNING PLAYS THAT REVEAL CONSUMER MIND-SETS

Our case analysis revealed the following five winning approaches to discover consumer mind-sets.

- *Choose a specific area to explore that is relevant to your products and services; listen to the right people, and draw from appropriate sources.* While some of these areas might be broad-based, with an aim to figure out a general direction—"How do people feel about the economy, and what are they doing about it?"—some are category-specific concerns, such as "What is the mind-set of the credit card holder in this challenging economy?" It goes on to understanding attitudes in terms of roles people perform, such as giving care or parenting, among many others. See Chapter 1 for a fuller discussion of this listening research principle.
- *At a minimum, research consumer mind-sets by trending words and phrases.* Start by using free or low-cost tools with effective features like Google Insights for Search (see Chapter 2 and the Appendix), or investigate terms of interest. If you're equipped with robust listening tools that allow you to "roll up" phrases into clusters or topics, you can perform more detailed analysis. Choose words or phrases that reflect consumer language and are central to the area you're researching. Avoid using marketing-speak and jargon when considering words or labels; it's essential to capture the language and reality of your potential and current *customers*, not those of marketers and advertisers.
- *Track and analyze conversations over time to reveal how consumer mind-sets are evolving.* Pay attention to which elements are staying the same, which have come and gone, and which appear to cycle in and out. In the credit card category, several themes—like debt reduction—remained constant, while others—such as the concern over amount of credit card debt—appeared, exited, and then returned, reflecting consumers' shifting emphasis (see "Mind-set of Credit Card Holders," later in this chapter). Marketers and advertisers that track the ebb and flow of consumer mind-sets anticipate and respond quickly to change, and work to minimize their

impacts by quickly adapting their strategy, tactics, and messaging. Companies further up the listening curve—like credit card issuers—should leverage their social media listening data to optimize products, features, and communications by combining with other types of research and analysis, such as trade-offs.

- *Recognize that some consumer markets today are mosaics, composed of people facing shared situations, needs, and desired benefits that cross traditional definitions such as age, gender, geography, or income.* The "sandwich situation" research, discussed elsewhere in this chapter, on the tensions of simultaneously caring for older parents and children shows that consumer insights and market opportunities were caregiver-oriented, not specific to a given generation. This highlights how we can use social media listening to find the commonalities among people, which can lead to nontraditional insights into customers' and prospects' minds across a wide range of product and service categories (see "Explore Widely to Understand Consumers and Their Life's Context," later in this chapter, and the essays in Chapter 20).

- *Encourage all relevant departments or functions to draw upon social media listening research.* Kraft's research, for its sales organization reviewed below, had actionable impacts across various units, including marketing, distribution, product development, Web and magazine content development, and in-store merchandising. Sharing results, demonstrating their value, and connecting them widely throughout an organization promote awareness and adoption of listening as a valuable enterprise capability. This shows that some companies are becoming true listening organizations centered around people.

Regarding tactics, our cases revealed three that companies use, which we will detail:

- Search, to discover consumers' mind-sets.
- Home in, to understand category mind-sets.
- Explore widely, to understand consumers and the context of their lives.

SEARCH: GATEWAY TO DISCOVERING CONSUMERS' MIND-SETS

Tapping into consumers' minds can be as easy as studying trends in search terms, analyzing the words and phrases people punch into search boxes. In the United States alone, July 2010 saw *more than 16 billion* searches performed across the five core properties measured by audience research company comScore: Google sites, Yahoo! sites, Microsoft sites, Ask Network, and AOL LLC Network (comScore 2010).

Every word and phrase that *anyone* searches online is captured, put into a database, and can be made available for analysis and reporting. These are the unfiltered, everyday terms that motivate people to find any type of information, products, and services in just about every category. They are not the forced choices typical of conventional research designs, which often require people to describe their likes, agreements, hopes, fears, motives, and desires using language or numbers that are not their own.

Search queries are like verbatims from traditional research, except that they are ripe for analysis and potentially much richer. Although this is changing a bit as text analytics are applied to survey responses, open-ended questions in surveys have traditionally been underanalyzed, primarily because people, time, and expense are required to code them. Typically, a single person or small group would read these, draw some inferences, and add them to the report as "color." Search engine listening, on the other hand, allows any person or company to analyze not merely a few hundred or thousand verbatim statements, but thousands upon thousands. This is possible with the aid of a Web browser and readily available tools, such as Google Trends and Google Insight for Search, both of which are free and have very capable features for basic tasks (see Chapter 2 for details).

During 2008–2009, when the dislocating forces of the great recession hit, every company wanted to know how consumers were reacting, setting them off on a mad dash to vacuum up whatever information was available. Inquiries into the Advertising Research Foundation's Knowledge Center skyrocketed. The available studies on "advertising and recession" explored changes in sales and market shares, companies that decreased or increased advertising, store brand impacts, and other business factors. But one important component was missing from all that: the consumer mind-set. What does a consumer think about and do during a recession?

We can begin to find the answer to this question by searching for the terms consumers use. We selected recession-relevant terms like "coupons," "unemployment benefits," "bankruptcy," and "foreclosure," and plugged them into Google Trends. Figure 4.1 compares indices of search volumes and news volumes for the terms in the top and bottom parts of the graph, respectively. Looking at them, it's clear to see that consumers and the media have different priorities. Though causal factors like foreclosure and bankruptcy of major companies drew relatively little consumer interest, we're all aware that they dominated media coverage. In stark contrast, consumers were concerned with ways to cope with the eroding economy and their worries about employment. The shock of the recession caused coupon and unemployment searches to rise sharply in mid to late 2008, and search activity has continued to remain higher.

Search tells us that during times like these, the typical consumer mind-set comprises enduring concerns with economic uncertainty: fear of job losses,

Figure 4.1

Trends in "unemployment," "coupons," "foreclosure," and "chapter 11" search volumes and news volumes reveal that people are concerned with their jobs and family budget, while the media is focused on unemployment and foreclosure to a lesser degree.

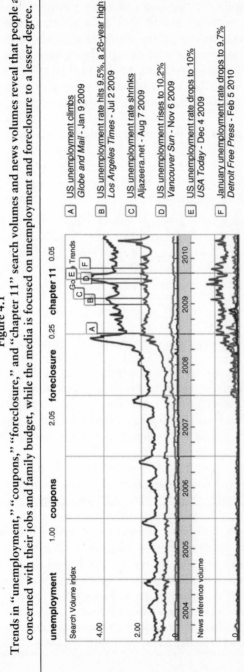

A   US unemployment climbs
    Globe and Mail - Jan 9 2009

B   US unemployment rate hits 9.5%, a 26-year high
    Los Angeles Times - Jul 2 2009

C   US unemployment rate shrinks
    Aljazeera.net - Aug 7 2009

D   US unemployment rises to 10.2%
    Vancouver Sun - Nov 6 2009

E   US unemployment rate drops to 10%
    USA Today - Dec 4 2009

F   January unemployment rate drops to 9.7%
    Detroit Free Press - Feb 5 2010

Source: ARF, Google Trends, August 28, 2010. Used with permission.

along with a strong desire to cope, save money, and continue to be able to afford the products and services they want and need.

The graph in Figure 4.1 required just a few moments of thought to create and was available without cost. Listening to search conversations allows marketers and advertisers to garner clues quickly about consumers, which they can further explore. They're able to learn how their customers and prospects feel about money-saving tools, like coupons, to gain a richer understanding of likes, dislikes, and emotions—factors they can then consider when designing couponing strategies and programs.

Listening Level and Type: Fundamental (Search listening)

HOME IN TO UNDERSTAND CATEGORY MIND-SETS

Consumers hold many mind-sets, they can be specific to broad swaths of life—like parenting or health—or be more specific to a product category, like automobiles or electronics. Two cases, one concerning financial services, the other regarding food, reveal the ways social media listening aids in understanding these consumer mind-sets and the implications they have for marketing, advertising, and sales.

Mind-set of Credit Card Holders

Imagine running a financial institution today. You would want to know how to market to investors, depositors, credit card account holders, and policy holders. You would also need to know how to do this *profitably* in a climate of rock-bottom institutional confidence, people shaken by loss of, or who fear losing, their homes through foreclosure, and postponed retirement due to plummeting 401(k) values.

Despite the dreary economic climate, people and financial institutions still need one another, perhaps now more than ever, to work out the problems, market more effectively, and get back onto solid footing. Social media listening can help play a vital role in this process, as we will see in the following example.

One leading credit card issuer wanted to understand the significant topics people were talking about in order to respond with timely and relevant card features and new offerings to improve its brand's health and competitiveness. The company's three-pronged research program comprised conventional qualitative research, such as focus groups and ideation sessions, and quantitative work such as attitude and usage studies and trade-off (conjoint) analysis, and social media listening. In combination with the traditional research methods, it could explore the social media listening insights systematically to develop the optimal program.

The company's social media listening research partner, Collective Intellect, worked with the issuer to first define who it should listen to, and where. This crucial step focused on collecting conversations from relevant participants via blogs, online forums, and message boards. The vendor's text mining and analysis research revealed credit card consumers' sentiment around the category, credit cards, and their providers—especially the issuer's own brand and customers. More than 650,000 posts were analyzed to identify conversation drivers, along with positive and negative themes. It's important to note that the analysis ran over a one-year period, enabling the card company to see how conversations and themes evolved over time. The issuer found that some stayed constant (such as rewards), and several cycled in or out (like credit card debt) in response to circumstances. Collective Intellect CEO Don Springer summarized the results (2009):

> Even in times when consumers are concerned about their balances and changes in credit card terms, they still see benefits in using credit. Specifically, we learned that consumers spend more time sharing and talking about responsible spending, debt reduction, and incentives and rewards than they do "bashing" providers of credit.

The credit card issuer discovered that despite its distress regarding the economy and its own situation, people were generally engaged in sensible, practical discussion about what to do next. According to Springer, these insights

> armed the client with the ability to emphasize traditional features that matter, like rewards, cash back, and travel, to build new product and feature offerings that gave consumers more control over their debt, including debt management options and services, and to tailor messaging to mitigate any negative sentiment and reinforce brand affinity around those benefits most relevant to their consumers.

Listening Level and Type: Advanced (Social research)

The next case we examine shows how a similar research approach was used to understand a different group: food shoppers.

Mind-set of the Food Shopper

With economic recovery coming slowly, megabrand Kraft Foods knew that shoppers' attitudes and behaviors were changing to meet current conditions, and sought to understand their new attitudes. The company's aim was "to inform the sales organization of the rapidly changing consumer mind-set in order for them to be agile in designing relevant merchandising and sales strategies with retailers." But as we'll see shortly, it turned out to do much more.

The most important point here is the stance that Kraft took toward change. It wanted to be proactive, identify the emerging mind-set, and respond in ways that matched consumer outlooks and kept it ahead of, and differentiated from, the competition.

Kraft's social media listening research method resembled the approach described earlier: social media listening coupled with quantitative research that, when analyzed together, resulted in rich insights derived from conversations and their importance to their market. Kraft worked with vendor TNS Cymfony for social media listening, and Synovate for the survey research.

As the world's second-largest food company, Kraft products line the pantries and cupboards of over 99 percent of American households (Engelbart and Mats 2010). In contrast to the credit card case, Kraft focused its research across all product types; it was not restricted to a specific category or customer. The company's social media study required a very broad definition of what to listen for, whom to listen to, and where to listen. The resulting research uncovered four key insights into the Kraft consumer's mind-set. It found that:

- Shoppers who change their behavior do not just drop new behaviors for old. Rather, they are on an "emotional journey," traveling from denial to shock/guilt, to confidence, and, finally, to empowerment. It is a transforming experience through which they embrace the lessons they've learned along the way.
- Shoppers discussed meal planning most often. The research uncovered a number of concerns and coping behaviors such as: making lists and sticking to them; using a few basic ingredients across a number of meals; stockpiling, planning, and budgeting; cutting back on meat; and cooking in bulk and using leftovers for later meals.
- Shoppers experienced a resurgent interest in home gardens and seasonal eating as a way to save money and derive gratification from growing and eating their harvest, eat more healthfully, reduce their carbon footprint, and support local farmers' markets.
- Shoppers view coupons as more complex than just "buying for less." Though many realized that economizing is important, and even has an emotional component, it is accompanied by a concern that coupons are for products that don't contribute to eating healthfully and work against their goals. Coupons also served the purpose of enabling people to donate to food pantries.

Though this likely wasn't a thought one expected to hear at the outset, the link between coupon savings and charitable giving was very illuminating. One shopper described it as follows:

> Well, it's a sort of a money-saving way of donating food to food pantries in our areas that are in more need now with our poor economy.

> Whenever I stock up on buy one/get one canned or boxed items at the grocery store, the "free" one gets put aside to take to the local center.

These statements clearly exhibit consumers' very textured and nuanced ways of looking at the world. The coupon insight shows that people weigh associated benefits and potential costs all together. It is not easy to glean that kind of richness from surveys, which usually consider and score attributes separately. Notice as well that these comments tie back to larger cultural trends, such as healthy eating, sustainability, and generosity. This reminds us that social media listening should not occur in a vacuum, but rather should be put into context in order to be meaningfully interpreted, or to challenge the conventional view about the trends.

Kraft was able to draw a number of crucial business implications from these mind-set insights. The study's authors, Larissa Mats (Kraft) and Christina Engelbart (Cymfony), discovered one important best practice: Tie implications to specific insights. Without that, insights are merely observations without business impact. To that end, Mats and Engelbart listed several implications for each insight. For our purposes, we will just take one example from each that reveals a range of recommendations across the "4Ps"—product, price, promotion, and place—that ultimately enabled Kraft to connect its sales strategies with their consumers' frame of mind.

After completing the study, Kraft initiated the following programs:

- *Shopper's Emotional Journey*: "Communications should focus on positive emotions—'the light at the end of the tunnel.'"
- *Meal Planning*: Help consumers who are new to meal planning with the basics: design, shopping lists, and ideas for incorporating variety.
- *Gardening and Seasonal Shopping*: Partner with retailers to create merchandising displays that borrow themes from farmers' markets and create community-supported agriculturelike boxes of complementary items in stores.
- *Coupon Revival*: As consumers continue to strive for healthy eating, suggest ways to create balanced meals with family favorites that are promoted.

The power of these insights and their applications was strengthened by placing them in a business framework nearly everyone understands and communicating them in a relevant way, for this reason. Kraft was able to utilize the social media listening work more widely throughout the organization, for a broader variety of purposes. The research was also used by distribution, marketing, and advertising units, and for Web site and magazine content, recipe development, and product innovation. Because they expanded beyond the original audience—the sales organization—Kraft researchers raised both awareness and adoption of social media listening research. In so doing, they demonstrated a fundamental property of listening: It is relevant and valuable throughout an organization, not just a single department or function.

Listening Level and Type: Intermediate (Social research)

EXPLORE WIDELY TO UNDERSTAND CONSUMERS AND THE CONTEXT OF THEIR LIVES

Societal shifts, like juxtaposing an aging population with the maturing of the millennial generation, inevitably cause stresses and strains. They also generate new needs, while creating opportunities and raising challenges for marketers and advertisers. The result is certainly not a new, easily defined and segmented market; it's nowhere as neat and tidy as the current market (e.g., women 25–54 or men 18–34). Instead, some markets are taking on the less conventionally defined characteristics of mind-sets: unique outlooks that are drawn from shared life circumstances, priorities, and values.

It has become essential for marketers and advertisers looking for new growth from new markets and customers to understand these "mind-set markets." Because the markets are defined primarily by commonalities among apparently dissimilar individuals, social media listening research can identify them by uncovering the conversational themes and topics uniting them. (If this idea interests you, John Zogby and Joe Plummer's piece on neo-tribes in Chapter 20 offers a related but slightly different take.)

Case in point: the "sandwich generation," the group of middle-age people caring for both their elderly parents and for teens and children. This "generation" rose to prominence about a decade ago. Is it really a generation, as boomers or Gen X-ers are, or should these caregivers be understood differently and more fully in ways that represent new opportunities?

Insight community company Communispace decided to take a more penetrating look at these caregivers to understand their "lives, needs, and choices." Its study of roughly 75 people employed a variety of research techniques. Participants engaged in activities like image galleries and collage projects designed to elicit perceptions, emotions, and inner feelings; they were also involved in various topical discussions and brainstorming sessions. Additionally, Communispace surveyed nearly 500 members across four of its private communities—financial services, health care, pharma, and travel—to identify advertising and marketing implications in these categories (Communispace 2009). Its key findings included:

- The sandwich generation is more of a "situation" than a quantifiable age group since members range from millennial 20-somethings through 60-something boomers, facing challenges that span all income groups and geographies. Among the millennials, 83 percent are already thinking about how they'll cope with their challenges.

- While participants admitted that it was often stressful, they also saw caregiving as being "central to one's moral identity." They claimed that it satisfies many needs, including a personal source of pride, feeling thanked and appreciated in ways that children can't provide, and peace of mind in the knowledge that their parents are getting the best care possible.
- Sandwiched caregivers are "overwhelmingly" more likely to make sacrifices for their parents than for their children. These sacrifices might be giving them a spare room, moving closer to them even if it means their children will have to change schools, or buying a larger car to accommodate new needs like walkers or wheelchairs.
- These individuals want authentic messaging; realistic, reassuring, and empowering information that balances tradition and innovation. They found overly optimistic, sugar-coated messages and those engendering fear or anxiety to be "absolutely repellant."
- New product and service needs were identified in categories like insurance (which enabled caregivers to put the entire family—children and their parents—on one policy), air travel, medical reminder services, and security.
- Last, study participants talked about product categories and brands not usually associated with eldercare. Some of these included personal care, speed scratch foods, mass merchandisers, beverages, household cleaning products, and even small indulgences like chocolate. These categories fulfill caregivers' concerns about helping their charges become more comfortable and healthy in their homes, while making their own lives more pleasurable and satisfying.

This "sandwich situation" research not only takes us into the heads of caregivers; it goes on to highlight the applications of caregiver insights, like providing clear direction for commercial copy. By coupling insights with survey data, researchers were able to start the important task of establishing demand for both expected and nontraditional products and services meant to fulfill needs and deliver benefits for these "sandwiched" individuals.

Listening Level and Type: Advanced (Social research)

SUMMARY

Social media listening is helpful in detecting consumer mind-sets from conversations. They reflect the ways people look at the world, how and what they choose, and also influence their behavior. Of course, people hold a variety of mind-sets about countless topics. Companies that understand mind-sets relevant to their business are truly at an advantage. They put themselves in a better position to calibrate and adjust their marketing and advertising to their customers more quickly, and improve their chances of marketplace success. Companies should promote their listening results and implications, and leverage them throughout their organizations. Doing so builds awareness of listening, promotes adoption, and ultimately puts the customer at the center of the business.

CHAPTER 5

DISCOVER NEW CUSTOMERS

A failure to generate new customers can hurt an organization dramatically. It limits the company's ability to expand its base of owners and prospects, increase revenue, and generate profits necessary to grow the business and reward investors. While lead-generation tools can be helpful, their strength is in locating prospects based on profiles of the customers you currently *have*. Social media listening, on the other hand, helps companies discover people who are interested in their products or services but currently invisible to them.

Why do potentially valuable customers and growth prospects remain "hidden in plain sight"? One reason is that advertisers and marketers collectively remain trapped by conventional mind-sets. Social media listening techniques enable marketers and advertisers to "pan for customer gold" by helping us to reframe and rethink conventional wisdom, encourage us to link disparate data, and open our minds to what that data tells us. Our case studies uncovered a variety of faint signals that [after being amplified through analysis] located new customers who exhibited real business potential.

WINNING PLAYS FOR DISCOVERING NEW CUSTOMERS

Case study analysis led us to identify the following winning plays for discovering new customers.

- *Challenge "conventional wisdom" and the widely held beliefs you currently have about customers.* Break free of your current customer definitions, and look outside them. The Hennessy and Suzuki cases, below, show how the companies transformed their marketing strategies from clubby and performance-oriented, respectively, to urban, after learning of exceptionally passionate customers flying well beneath their radar.

47

- *Use social media listening to learn about customers and prospects in ways that provide richer insight than surveys alone can do.* Profile and understand nonconventional users. Though in-house research may identify lapsed users, it does not convey what these people are doing now, what they may be looking for, or what untapped opportunities exist. The same goes for light or infrequent users.

- *Listen to multicultural consumers.* Make sure that your social media listening is inclusive and free of bias. Today's world is a mosaic of peoples, cultures, languages, and values, all of which represent new market opportunities, when understood in the correct terms. Two cases we present— one for French Cognac, the other for a Japanese motorcycle—reveal how companies can open themselves up to new, lucrative markets by listening to multicultural consumers. Glean additional knowledge from understanding which ethnicities and cultures use certain popular online services. For example, Twitter overindexes on African-Americans: Nearly 25 percent of tweets—twice their population percentage—relate to African-American themes, culture, and topics that may be valuable for marketing and advertising.

- *Analyze related data.* Find new clues by following trails of customer activities expressed through Web site linking patterns, site visitation, and other related log file analyses. These are useful not only for meeting objectives like improving customer experience or optimizing search engine effectiveness; they can also reveal the kind of information that will help grow your business. Hennessy's case vividly demonstrates how companies can stumble on a pattern of Web links and, by being open-minded, uncover a market they did not know existed that can become their central focus.

- *Listen for changes in speakers' voices.* Monitor conversations to detect shifts in who's talking, which you can do easily by reading posts or engaging in sophisticated processes such as text analytics. One computer game maker tuned into a major trend, the rise of female gamers, by tracking variations in the ratio of male to female posters on forums. This gave it valuable lead time for creating a new marketing strategy (see "Track Voices in the Conversations," later in the chapter).

- *Be bold; have the courage to act on social media listening findings.* Companies uncovering new customers through social media listening may sometimes find themselves challenged by the insights because the prospects were not just "off the radar"; they were not in line with ingrained assumptions. The Hennessy and Suzuki cases revealed a fairly unexpected group of core urban customers, not the clubby and strict horsepower junkies, respectively, whereas the game company saw that its customers were changing from male to female. These new discoveries prompted those companies to confront traditionally accepted models, which posed tough choices between staying the course or adapting in order to grow. Changing takes guts; after all, how many of us would completely alter the image and marketing approach of an iconic brand like Hennessy? However, the company reduced risk by triangulating and cross-checking its listening with a variety of sources. The result was that management confidence increased to the level necessary to support game-changing decisions and create compelling social media strategies.

The companies whose stories we explore in this chapter used social media listening in ways that uncovered potential among multicultural markets and light users. As you read through them, take note that the approaches and methods used are not limited to their particular organization or industry; rather, they are applicable to discovering any new market and exploring any customer group.

From case review, we identified four tactics:

- Listen to the story in people's behavior.
- Track voices in conversations.
- Look at customer data with fresh eyes.
- Listen to light purchasers.

LISTEN TO THE STORY IN PEOPLE'S BEHAVIOR

Back in 2005, world-leading cognac brand Hennessy conducted an analysis of links coming into its Web site and spotted a trend: The number of links between its company Web site and BlackPlanet.com—the largest social network for African-Americans—was unexpected and substantial. This kind of link analysis is one of the studies conducted by companies looking to improve their search engine optimization and search results ranking. By discerning which sites are linking to their own, this analysis provides some (albeit, weak) signals about audiences and site content appeal. Hennessy stumbled on a passionate market, one they were completely unaware of.

By digging deeper, Hennessy learned that some BlackPlanet members simply linked personal pages to Hennessy's site. However, some went further by decorating their pages with borrowed images of Hennessy brands. In an attempt to learn more about these potential consumers, Hennessy then studied a random sample of BlackPlanet member Web pages to understand their themes and use of brand imagery. They also commissioned an online survey with research partner CRM Metrix to profile these users' attitudes, usage, and influence.

According to the study's results, Hennessy discovered that visions of their brand expressed in the member pages "were not necessarily ours, but this does not make them any less valid." Research showed that "the brand belongs as much to its consumers as to its managers . . . . We must listen without prejudice." Stated another way, this is a shining illustration of customer "co-creation" and extraordinary brand engagement. The survey data described these individuals attractively, in that 8 out of 10 were "high-value" consumers, and they had a strong influence on the alcohol choices of people around them. About half the respondents were opinion leaders, a higher than usual percentage than that found generally, which is about 10 percent–20 percent in many categories.

Recognizing the inherent and potential long-term value in BlackPlanet members, Hennessy next sought to learn what would improve its site and make it more interesting and enjoyable for them. But Hennessy went further than just tweaking the site; it also asked for and listened to suggestions about "what would make the *experience* of drinking Hennessy cognacs more enjoyable?"

Equipped with insights, Hennessy's improvements pivoted on providing service. The first thing the company did was to beef up the site's download sections with wallpapers and shareable images for page decoration and brand identification. Realizing that BlackPlanet members enjoyed drinking socially and mixing Hennessy's product into drinks, the company added recipes highlighting cognac as an ingredient, and offered Hennessy-branded e-invitations for parties.

Five years after the initial round of responses, the Hennessy site showed the brand's ongoing commitment to social media listening and evolving

Figure 5.1
**After applying social media listening to consumers, Hennessy revamped
its marketing approach to center around music, art, and mixing.**

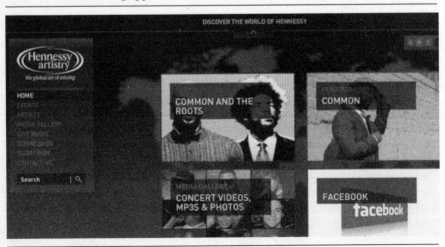

the relationship and experience. In 2009, Hennessy's "Artistry" initiative sponsored musicians, music tours, and streamed music, showcasing artists. Building on the ingredient insight, the brand's tagline became "the global art of mixing." Hennessy also added a social networking component by creating a presence on Facebook and YouTube to give people the chance to take their mixing online.

Listening Level and Type: Intermediate (Social research)

TRACK VOICES IN THE CONVERSATIONS

Tracking topics and themes about products, services, or entire categories sheds light on consumer concerns and, over time, can be used to identify trends within markets. When coupled with analytics that reveal who is speaking, these shifts in voices send early signals of market changes. These are not just blips or fads; rather, they're long-term and structural differences that suggest new market opportunity.

As part of its customer listening program, one digital game publisher routinely monitored relevant sites for issues, problems, likes, dislikes, and so on. One aspect of its social media listening research identified the gender of people posting. To the company's surprise, it spotted an interesting and unexpected statistic in 2004: Women wrote about 40 percent of the posts. This discovery contradicted the company's and the industry's widely held impression that gamers were predominately young men. Just five years later, male gamers had become the minority. M16 and ePoll research found that "women are now gaming more often than men, a first in the gaming industry" (J.D. Power and Associates 2005, Knight 2009). By taking a previously "accepted" user trait into account, this company caught a market shift early, created new games for the female market, and benefitted from the lead-time advance warning social media listening provides.

Listening Level and Type: Fundamental (Social research)

LOOK AT CUSTOMER DATA WITH FRESH EYES

Like Hennessy, Suzuki hit upon a new market, not through link listening, but by being open-minded to and pivoting on survey data. One month after launching its second-generation high-end bike Hayabusa, the fastest production bike in the world, Suzuki with its marketing and research agency Questus looked at the customer data they had on hand. They zoomed in on one impressive stat: Forty percent of buyers were "minority"—a "huge hidden audience," in the words of Questus CEO Jeff Rosenblum.

Suzuki's Hayabusa team then started looking more deeply at this particular group by using a combination of social media listening, observational and ethnographics studies, surveys, and secondary analysis of statistics and trends. This work led Suzuki to realize that not all of its Hayabusa buyers were the strict racing and performance enthusiasts they targeted historically; instead, a substantial number were people participating in a heart-pumping, thriving global bike culture in the streets and online. Social media listening exposed the deep passions that owners and fans expressed on discussion boards and Web sites. They covered every topic imaginable—design, sounds, upgrading components, repairs, products, where to ride—and showed off photos and videos of their bikes. Hayabusa.org, one of the largest and most active forums, is independent of Suzuki; Busa fanatics built and maintain it. Manufacturers and retailers sponsor their own forum areas to attract and serve customers and prospects.

Historically, Suzuki advertising had been highly corporate in nature, and covered the different lines of their bikes together. But given the strength of the listening insights, Suzuki green-lighted its first marketing and advertising program for a single model centered on the urban/street customer revealed through its research. That effort culminated in creating the BusaBeats campaign, initiated in 2008, and still running today. Suzuki makes extensive use of social media to create exceptional levels of Busa fan interaction and engagement, with both the brand and each other.

The program's introductory year stylishly integrated music, art, video, and a variety of digital media with a soft-sell, street-level approach that highlighted entertainment more than the company's typical corporate advertising agenda. Suzuki then intensified the campaign's level of consumer involvement by sponsoring "MC Battle," a contest for rappers and hip-hop artists to produce tracks about the Hayabusa, based on beats created by leading MCs and celebrity producers directly on the BusaBeats.com Web site. Site visitors voted on tracks and ultimately picked the winner, who was awarded the top prize of a customized Hayabusa.

Social media metrics, especially plays and votes, emphasize the program's success. The top five music tracks racked up more than 67,000 plays and received more than 37,000 votes. There were more than 179,000 plays and nearly 100,000 votes across all submissions. In fact, the number of plays may have been even higher, since users were able to forward their tracks and challenge friends to battle outside the formal competition. Average visitor time spent, one measure of engagement, was an "impressive" 21.4 minutes. Questus's Rosenblum added that Hayabusa's share of social media voice exceeded its share of media spending, a fact that pointed toward a very efficient and successful investment inspired by social media listening (Ultimatemotorcycling. com 2010; Rosenblum 2010).

Listening Level and Type: Intermediate (Social research)

LISTEN TO LIGHT PURCHASERS

Converting sporadic users to more frequent purchasers is one way that companies can gain additional business. An essential step in creating or improving the product mix, marketing, and advertising strategy is to understand what makes them intermittent (versus regular) purchasers in the first place.

Case in point: One particular direct-mail order retailer was frequently disappointed by its unremarkable sales from African-Americans. It wasn't for lack of effort; the company communicated frequently. However, its messages, positioning, and product mix simply did not resonate. The retailer sought to remedy the situation by better understanding this market; to do so, it turned to social media listening.

Like much of the population today, African-Americans are well represented online. They often belong to social networks, like the previously mentioned BlackPlanet.com, to engage around shared interests, culture, and needs. This retailer worked with its listening vendor, Networked Insights, to identify the best online resources for listening to African-Americans—relevant blogs, forums, and communities with substantial traffic and visitor interaction. They used text analysis to break down the discussions on topics related to the mail order company's product lines, from which they identified key themes and consumer sentiment. They followed the steps for effective listening research outlined in Part I.

Discussions mentioning the company were minimal—an important point to keep in mind. When people talk about topics online, they do not always mention brands. In fact, brand mentions are a minority in many instances. One large food company with which we spoke and that has numerous brands in global distribution told us that 95 percent of the conversations in its categories were unbranded. Instead, discourse often relates to a category, usage occasions, or performance and emotional benefits. Companies that look only at mentions of their brands via social media monitoring may not make important observations that can lead to sharp insights.

Realizing that they were working with fundamentally category-level conversations, this retailer and Networked Insights expanded keywords and topics, a move that led them to identify hair-related issues as those that stood out as a major concern. People didn't talk about brands or competitors, but they did talk about topics like natural long hair, shampoo, wefts, virgin hair, corn rows, weaves, relaxed hair, wigs, and protein treatments. These conversations also included dialogue about culture, music, values, and emotions.

This analysis prompted the retailer to attempt to develop a strong emotional connection with African-Americans to help them reconnect with their heritage and raise their confidence, themes that surfaced through the research. The retailer chose to focus on three product areas tied to culture: wigs, weaves, and wefts. It capitalized on the interest in music by creating its own branded label, featuring affordable gospel, smooth jazz, and soul CDs. Online advertising co-branded the music label with the wigs and ran on their branded media properties, as banners on relevant sites coupons, and in opt-in e-newsletters.

Results showed that their strategy was a success. According to CEO Dan Neely of Networked Insights, "Thirty-six percent of product page views were linked back to the record offers through search and link referrals. Sales for the wigs surpassed first-year marketing goals by 18 percent. The CD business, designed as a loss leader, turned a modest profit just a few months after launch. But its real value is not in the profit, but in the emotional connection it created and reinforced for the retailer" (Networked Insights 2010; Neely 2010).

Listening Level and Type: Advanced (Social research)

SUMMARY

Social media listening enables companies to identify potentially valuable new markets from faint signals that emanate from related information, such as patterns of Web site links, data in routine reports, and conversations about categories, not specific brands. Signals need to be amplified and cross-checked with additional data sources; these enable marketers and advertisers to home in on the signals in order to define the market and develop strategies for maximizing emergent opportunities.

CHAPTER 6

DRIVE NEW PRODUCT DEVELOPMENT AND INNOVATION

Most companies rely on new product development and innovation to generate revenue growth. Yet it's a constant challenge to develop successful offerings. Failure is an all too likely option for companies of all sizes; in fact, over half of new products that are brought to market fail or underperform. The number-one reason? Marketers neglect to understand the customer (Janowski 2008).

Companies that have turned to social media listening for innovation and new product work find that it has opened their eyes in important ways. It allows them to gauge market interest; hear suggestions for potential product features; and fine-tune concepts, products, marketing, and advertising.

WINNING PLAYS FOR INNOVATION AND NEW PRODUCT DEVELOPMENT

The cases we review in this chapter span efforts in industries ranging from automobile design to foods to Web site editorial content. From these, we've distilled six winning plays:

- *Gauge potential market interest in new product concepts by searching publicly available social media profiles.* These can be exceptionally rich sources for basic market reconnaissance. They take little time and can provide valuable early guidance. Successful new product Bacon Salt got its start when two entrepreneurs tested a hunch by searching for, and contacting, people who wrote "I love bacon" in their social media site profiles (see "Search Social Media Profiles," later in the chapter). Profile analysis is suitable for companies of any size, and it readily identifies potential markets.

- *Listen-engage-listen-engage. Repeat as necessary.* Iterate through cycles of listening and engaging during product development and innovation. Companies that receive ideas, reflect upon them, return them to the community, then "rinse and repeat" are more likely to provide a truly customer-centric product or service. Update your community on the status of ideas while the cycle is underway; transparency and timeliness are key. For example, MyStarbucksIdea.com and the Fiat MIO (described below) put tallies of the status of these ideas smack on the home page, which promoted a sense of connection and co-ownership. Establish criteria that measure the value of ideas submitted. Use voting or community rating systems to evaluate their merits and promote competition among ideas; and make sure that you have an objective system that conveys integrity in the process.

- *Carve out an explicit role for listening in your new product identification or development process.* Companies that utilize social media listening successfully articulate and follow a series of steps for collecting and using related data. One example of this is vitaminwater's "flavor creator" project, which asked the product's Facebook fans to co-create a new drink. Their effort started with defining the flavor, then determining the functional benefits of the drink. It concluded with naming and label design. Similarly, Fiat MIO first collected features and design suggestions, then branding and marketing ideas, and last, solicited feedback on the prototype. Frameworks like these help the company and its customers establish expectations and stay in sync throughout the product development or innovation process. Both cases are discussed in the "Co-Create New Products" section later in the chapter.

  Companies that use frameworks have a leg up, because frameworks provide a context for collecting, interpreting, and acting on insights. Companies without a formal or systematic process often struggle to handle and make sense of a hodgepodge of insights, which are hard, if not impossible, to act upon confidently and to gain and select business advantage.

  Although a primary reason for social media listening is to identify attributes or features for product development, discoveries may apply to other areas, such as targeting. Fiat MIO, for example, discovered that its most passionate advocates are located in cities, not in the rural areas as originally thought.

- *Co-create products and services that your customers and prospects desire by utilizing social media listening to support the process.* Recognize that many great ideas for new products or innovations reside outside the company. A number of organizations, such as MyStarbucksIdea.com, Fiat MIO, and vitaminwater, have undertaken co-creation projects. Keep these collaborative projects on track by adhering to an explicit process and being transparent, as just discussed.

- *Fine-tune new product features before you release them by listening to your brand's most committed customers.* Use panels or communities to test concepts that you are strongly considering bringing to market, as well as to garner suggestions and implementation ideas. Take advantage of conversation listening along with surveys and moderated discussions. Prior to launching its recipe-sharing site MixingBowl.com, publishing powerhouse Meredith turned to its private Real Women Talking community for feedback on content and design, and feelings about advertising sponsorship. Thanks to their help, Meredith launched MixingBowl.com and secured the revenue it needed (more on this in the "Fine-Tune New Products, Services, or Features" section later in the chapter).

- *Apply insights from new product development to in-market products and services.* Look across your product lines to see if you can transfer learning from new product development. Fiat MIO had a better idea of consumers' interests through the features, marketing, branding, and prototype reactions it elicited. The company planned to leverage those for marketing and advertising its current lineup. Repurpose findings and insights from one social media initiative and apply them to others; doing so will increase the return on investment and create further value for the enterprise.

The cases we review in this chapter used social media listening tactically to:

- Search social media profiles to identify consumer interest in a new product.
- Uncover mind-sets and locate unmet or undermet needs.
- Co-create, design, build, and market new products.
- Fine-tune new products, services, or features.

New product tactics that use social media are nearly identical to those used traditionally; the key difference is in the data. Let's turn to our first case: a product called Bacon Salt whose origin shows how searching social media profiles can quickly and easily suggest market opportunity for a newcomer.

SEARCH SOCIAL MEDIA PROFILES TO GAUGE MARKET INTEREST

Two bacon-loving friends, Justin Esch and Dave Lefkow, joked one day about how awesome it would be if there were a bacon-flavored seasoning. From this conversation, they hatched a brilliant business idea.

Most of us have taken part in similar conversations. We've concocted all sorts of services, solutions, foods, or infomercial fantasies around the dinner table or barbecue. But there's a big gap between thinking that your idea is a slam dunk and hearing from the market that it is—or, more likely, it isn't. Everyone involved in new product generation needs to test their ideas to see if they resonate beyond their inner circles to potential markets. Because research requires a substantial amount of time and money, it is infrequently or incompletely conducted by small and midsized businesses.

Social networks, however, enable both garage-based entrepreneurs and large companies alike to conduct quick exploratory research that can yield some early guidance for testing ideas and concepts. Publicly available social network member profiles reveal information including the tastes, interests, ages, geographies, favorite brands, and favorite bands of millions upon millions of people—without even needing to ask. These are only a fraction of the attributes available to marketers and advertisers through searching, or "crawling," social networks.

So Esch and Lefkow opted to take a research step. They searched social networks for fellow bacon aficionados and found more than 35,000 people mentioning "I love bacon" on MySpace alone (Qualman 2009). By capitalizing on social network tools, the two budding entrepreneurs reached out to these folks in order to gauge their interest in bacon-flavored salt. Their conversations ignited interest and created buzz, so much so that people placed advance orders even before they created the product and made it available.

The company succeeded right out of the gate, in 2007, selling out of supplies during its first week in business. In 2008, profits reached $1 million, and sales today exceed 650,000 orders of this widely distributed product.

Figure 6.1
Bacon Salt started by listening to social media,
and retains its commitment to the process.

The company is not a one-hit wonder, either; social media listening led it to release sandwich spread Baconnaise, as well as many new line extensions and new products, such as bacon popcorn, bacon ranch dressing, and even bacon-flavored envelopes. The two entrepreneurs' commitments to social media listening and a social network presence remain strong, as evidenced on MySpace, Facebook, Twitter, and YouTube, and consider the many comments submitted that endorse the current lineup, share opinions on new products, or suggest new products, such as bacon-flavored yogurt. They understand the power of listening and engaging continuously through social media—the forum that helped bring their dream product to life.

Listening Level: Fundamental (Social media monitoring)

DEVELOP NEW PRODUCT IDEAS FROM MIND-SETS

Social media listening for understanding consumer mind-sets—how people put the world together and act in accordance with it—is valuable not just for giving insights into people's minds. It can also be an effective opportunity for generating new product ideas (see Chapter 4 for details on mind-sets).

One major food manufacturer capitalized on this very approach. It sought to develop new product ideas for women's food products by using social media listening research. Taking a rigorous approach to social media listening, it undertook the following progression of research steps, which are very similar to those outlined in Chapters 1 through 3:

1. *Define the scope.* The food manufacturer chose to explore the "emotional landscape of women and food," in order to understand women's mind-sets, identify unmet or poorly met needs, and propose new product ideas.
2. *Define who to listen to, what to listen for, and where to listen.* The answer here was social media devoted to women's lives and food—especially blogs, forums, and message boards.
3. *Segment conversations into topics.* The research uncovered four major subject areas: "Me Time," "Weight Management," "Balance and Wellness," and "Beauty from Within." Both text and human analysis were used to identify the topics.
4. *Analyze conversations by issue and need state.* Researchers put conversations in context by creating a matrix of four "states of need" through which women progress each day—focus, energize, connect, and relax—along with the four topics. This allowed them to understand each topic individually and in terms of how it evolved throughout the morning, afternoon, and evening. Conversations were further analyzed within each group to discern which goals women wanted to reach, the actions

they were taking to achieve them, the positive and negative emotions they experienced, and the foods they consumed. From this analysis, the company was able to achieve a holistic and nuanced understanding of women's mind-sets, something that's considerably more valuable than counts of words or phrases—which can be "observations without wings" (Banas 2010).

5. *Draw new product ideas from mind-sets.* By distilling and synthesizing findings, the food manufacturer developed a set of strategic insights for each topic and need state. With those insights providing guidance, the company was able to score and filter potential solutions that the blogosphere had suggested.

Let's make this concrete by looking at one example: the "Me Time" topic within the energize need state. This mind-set focuses on restoring and renewing one's energy. The company developed a key strategic insight from its analysis: Women's energy isn't inexhaustible. It can go in a flash ("then it hit me"). Women's unmet need: Find foods that will give them a needed lift while they are aiming to refuel mentally and physically.

Listening for inspiring new product ideas from blogs was important to the research as the company was looking to bring about worthwhile consumer-led ideas. Two promising opportunities emerged: One, a pick-me-up that lasts, especially in the form of healthy, convenient snacks that will help women feel "invincible" and pass on the less nutritious food they aimed to avoid.

Figure 6.2
Strategic insights following from the need state analysis are linked to blogger-inspired innovations that become candidates for new product development.

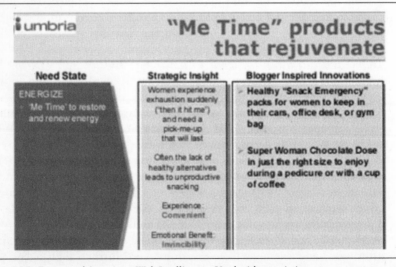

Source: J.D. Power and Associates Web Intelligence. Used with permission.

The other, a "just right"-sized chocolate dose that could be enjoyed with a cup of coffee or tea, or during a small indulgence like a manicure or pedicure.

Listening Level: Intermediate (Social research)

CO-CREATE NEW PRODUCTS: DESIGN TO CONSUMER-GENERATED REQUIREMENTS

A longtime staple of consumer-friendly businesses, "suggestion boxes" brought the customer's voice inside companies, but often faintly. Some organizations, like grocery chain Stew Leonard's, still prominently feature an old-school one—a pen, paper, and slot—at exits. Today, advances in social media have transformed that simple solution into fully blown idea and innovation factories. MyStarbucksIdea.com—one of the earliest, most popular, and highly regarded of these initiatives—allows enthusiasts to share, discuss, and vote on ideas. Transparency is key here; site visitors are able to see popular ideas under consideration and those that have already been put into action right on the home page. By late 2010, the MyStarbucksIdea.com Web site had received nearly 100,000 ideas regarding products, the Starbucks experience, and the company's involvement in local communities and its social responsibility.

Because companies now recognize that ideas, suggestions, and solutions exist in great numbers outside their office walls, their interest in co-creating products and services has vastly increased. The following two case studies— that of the Fiat MIO Concept Car and a recently launched vitaminwater flavor called Connect—highlight these organizations' willingness to "think outside the (suggestion) box." Take note of the rigor each company applied to its co-creation effort. The efforts are very tightly managed, pass through a set of progressive stages, and cycle repeatedly between listening and engaging in order to gauge consumer input and refine product development.

Fiat MIO

Car companies routinely develop "want lists" from their customers. Often cultivated through surveys, focus groups, or customer panels, such lists result in some product improvement and new ideas—for example, cup holders, in-car entertainment systems, and configurable seating. However, it's fairly unusual for automobile companies to collaborate with an open community of people to co-design a major advance, such as a concept car, that will be displayed and whose ideas may eventually go into production. Yet this is exactly what Fiat did with the MIO.

This project (which concluded in October 2010 with the unveiling of the co-created MIO prototype) focused on discovering ideas that made a car *personal*. Whether or not the car makes it into production, Fiat has learned and developed expertise in leveraging social media tools and research techniques.

These advantages will help it create, market, and advertise products grounded in the deep understanding of the elements that its customers and prospects desire and request.

The MIO project is Fiat's third initiative to attempt to include customers in its thinking and direction as a company. This passage from the MIO Web site reflects that commitment (AgenciaClick 2010):

> We must think of the future in a collective and participative form. Fiat therefore assumes the commitment to continue the Fiat MIO project, converting your ideas into reality. They may be simple or complex; it doesn't matter. Everyone has an idea of how the future should be, or what to do to make it better. It is therefore essential that you participate in this more than democratic forum. Let's combine your ideas with our capacity to produce them. We wish to create a new project with you, a new car, a new form of transport for the next generations.

Fiat runs the program out of the Brazilian agency AgenciaClick, which created a Web site (with translation tools) and presence on Twitter and other social networks (see Figure 6.3). Why Brazil? For one thing, it's a digitally savvy country. For another, Fiat is the country's largest carmaker, with roughly 25 percent of the market, and its fifth-largest advertiser. Last, Fiat planned to unveil the prototype car at the International Automobile Fair in Sao Paolo in 2010.

Figure 6.3
The Fiat MIO Web site invites people to create "a car to call your own." Translation tools make the site multilingual and invite contributions from all over the globe.

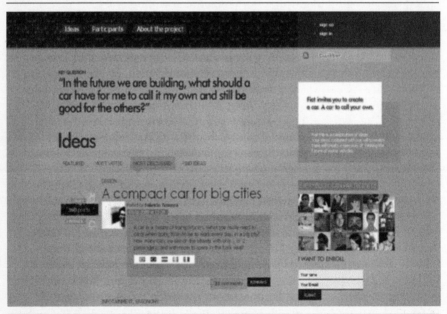

Although the use of social media alone does not guarantee that companies will reach large, interested audiences, stories about this innovative project, in both traditional and digital media, amplified project news, created awareness, spawned word of mouth, and spurred participation. *Advertising Age* magazine reported that ". . . in the two weeks starting August 3, 2009, the Fiat Mio site had 67,000 unique visitors who submitted 1,700 ideas, and more than 40,000 comments were posted on Twitter" (Wentz 2009). Four months later, the site had about 10,000 registered users in more than 40 countries who submitted more than 7,000 ideas, comments, and suggestions in seven categories: general, safety, design, propulsion, ergonomics, materials, and infotainment (Agencia-Click 2010). Contributors wrote or shared pictures and videos, and voting by site visitors allowed MIO to gauge the popularity and appeal of the different suggestions. One important component was that the ideas didn't have to be new. Some people uploaded information from competing brands about the various features they desired. But whatever their source of inspiration, people clearly wanted to be a part of the process and have Fiat listen to their voices.

Along with encouraging conversation and comments, MIO conducted its social media listening program in a progressively staged manner that moved from:

Stage 1: Features and design
Stage 2: Branding and marketing ideas
Stage 3: Feedback on the prototype, with more specific recommendations for the final assembly of the car

These three stages provided a coherent framework for the co-creation effort, which allowed Fiat and its community to understand expectations and proceed in sync with the concept car's development needs. What makes Fiat's method especially notable is its virtuous cycling of listening and engagement into a feedback loop over time, as well as the depth of the company's commitment. It was not a casual checklist type of effort.

Apart from learning about the attributes of the car that the community desired—which included comfort, safety, and "green-ness" and being connected for communication, navigation, and media access—Fiat also uncovered insights into potential customers' mind-sets and motivations. It learned that people who lived in big cities craved the car the most because they were looking for a meaningful solution to the pollution, noise, and traffic jams that they frequently encountered.

This co-creation effort allowed Fiat to gain valuable insight into the kind of car its customers desired. It gave the company an important sense of direction that it could apply to marketing and advertising its current lineup. Fiat marketers will know which available features are most attractive, which they can then emphasize broadly or narrowly. For a global company like Fiat, understanding the geography of interest in features, for example, can help localize and tailor cars to each market, while messaging and creative can be tuned to match the motivations, aspirations, and benefits expressed by a customer community.

By tightening the match between offering and customer, Fiat increases its chances for success.

Listening Level: Advanced (Social research)

Vitaminwater Connect

Nutriceutical beverage line vitaminwater (now owned by Coca-Cola) wanted to connect more deeply with its younger consumers. Putting "the consumer in control," quite literally, vitaminwater turned to its Facebook fans to create a new flavor, select its benefits, and design its label, a move the company hoped would ultimately instill a sense of brand ownership. Its objective was summarized in the words of Jason Harty, the vitaminwater manager in charge at the time: "Vitaminwater was our idea. The next one will be yours" (Harty 2010a, Kincaid 2010).

The company developed a "flavor creator" tool that simulated its lab environment, and carefully structured its program by combining solicited choices from fans with social media listening. Here are the steps it followed:

1. *Determine the flavor.* Flavor candidates were harvested through conversation mining, using feeds from Facebook, Flickr, foodgawker, Twitter, and Google News. Fans could suggest their own flavors or a two-flavor combo. The community voted on the top 10 flavors, and the top vote-getter won—black cherry-lime.
2. *Choose the functional benefits.* Vitaminwater did this cleverly through a game that was made up of different contests. After completing the game, a score tied to specific benefits was computed. The winner was "super energy," a cocktail of caffeine and eight key nutrients.
3. *Design the label.* Vitaminwater sponsored a cash prize contest for the best design and name submitted by an individual or group of three. Bottle designs were "hung" in a gallery, and creators were encouraged to campaign for their bottles. Eventually, all bottle designs were voted on, with Connect taking first place.

It is important to note that vitaminwater's flavor creator Web site provided a variety of social networking features, such as discussion areas, sharing, and fanning. By doing so, the brand helped ensure that the contest truly engaged the fan community, and was not a gimmick like a simple sweepstakes contest.

Connect launched in March 2010. Coke's Stan Sthanunathan (2010) explained the benefits: "A process that normally takes two years and millions of dollars of investment in formal market research and trials was turned on its head and conducted in three months for a few thousand dollars by harnessing the power of the crowd to co-create a new product."

Listening Level: Intermediate (Social media monitoring)

Adoption of Social Media Listening

Vitaminwater Connect is not only an excellent case for accelerating innovation. Jason Harty told us how critical it was to turn the company into a true listening organization (Harty 2010b). Although the company had internal experts, "listening" was just another word with little specific meaning. Few of the experts themselves appreciated the value that social media listening could bring to consumer research—and to the myriad daily decisions that must be made in a fast-growing company and competitive category.

Harty related that the social media listening the company did to identify flavors became the Trojan horse that brought the practice of listening across the corporate drawbridge. Its proven ability to collect data on consumer preferences on flavor—a topic squarely at the center of the business—opened people's eyes easily, naturally, and unobtrusively. From there, colleagues started asking how consumers felt about campaigns in the market, their sentiment and their effectiveness. After a short while, social media listening research didn't just become expected; it was closely scrutinized. When senior management began asking for reports, adoption was de facto.

Harty believes that listening's adoption begins with a success tied to vital company goals or issues. Adoption occurs in stages, as listening insights are effectively shared and prove themselves with meaningful outcomes—as opposed to shallow and glib findings that are tangential or of the "look what we did, isn't that cool" variety. Though companies vary in how they adopt and utilize listening, as in any paradigm shift, hard-nosed results and socialization of the findings eventually bring it about (Kuhn 1996, and see Austin & Ware's essay in Chapter 21).

FINE-TUNE NEW PRODUCTS, SERVICES, OR FEATURES

The cases discussed so far concern developing new product concepts (Bacon Salt) or co-creating prototypes and actual products (Fiat MIO, vitaminwater). We'll now look into how social media listening is used to help companies fine-tune ideas they already have under consideration or that are in early stages of development.

Diversified media powerhouse Meredith Corporation publishes magazines and owns broadcast outlets and a number of digital properties. The company's goals are to ensure that its properties are relevant, that its audiences are high-quality, and that the combination is attractive to advertisers.

Meredith publication *Better Homes & Gardens* (BHG) decided to augment its print presence with a social network it called the MixingBowl.com (see Figure 6.4). Its team had some fairly well-established ideas about content and design, but wanted to test them out in real digital time.

Figure 6.4
Meredith's MixingBowl.com social networking site features, design, and
editorial/advertising approach were guided by the company's private online
community Real Women Talking.

Meredith Research Solutions runs a private Communispace community
called Real Women Talking to engage with and partake in social media
listening with its target female audience. Communispace prepared a concept test and then asked for reactions on overall feel, uniqueness, and participants' likelihood of using the new site. Community members endorsed
the approach. While that was good news, the BHG/Communispace team
had to be confident; very important decisions were on the line. They absolutely needed to know: "Will social media listening guide us, or is it just
confirmatory?"

Editorially, Meredith heard that members wanted fresh material. So the
team developed a plan to update content weekly, just the kind of decision that
might have been made using traditional methods.

The real value for Meredith came when the team analyzed conversations
and activities regarding content direction and advertising. Women wanted to
see food within the context of occasions—entertaining, family meals, or shopping—not in isolation from their daily lives. Additionally, they wanted to do
more than just read recipes. They said they wanted to trade and exchange ideas
with other members of the community so that they could benefit from each
other's input, and by so doing, add to their lives.

Meredith discovered through social media listening that it already had the
features and services for an appealing site. To generate revenue, however, it
needed to sell sponsorships, and that required another set of deliberations: What
was the right mix of editorial and sponsorship? Would too much advertising
be a turnoff? Again using social media listening, Meredith learned that women
would be receptive to editorial supplied by well-known and well-liked brands.

With that insight, the MixingBowl.com team created a "back-of-the-box" recipe section—what it called "an engaging resource that simultaneously enhanced consumers' experiences of client's brands."

With community comments in hand, Meredith's ad sales team was primed and able to demonstrate MixingBowl.com's value to potential advertisers. The company's ability to tap into this real-time market knowledge "has been a key point of difference that builds relationships with advertisers, and drives innovation" (Ware and Austin, 2008). Meredith, in fact, also has used Real Women Talking in conjunction with advertisers, to generate insights for special opportunities and programs.

Powered by Ripple6, a social business platform, MixingBowl.com also began offering a full set of social networking features—including groups, profiles, forums, sharing, and updates—that provided Meredith with additional social media listening posts, which it now mines for insights and ideas for content and features.

Listening Level: Advanced (Social research)

Summary

Social media listening is a data source for developing new products, supporting ideas, testing concepts, co-creating, and refining new products prior to launch. The most important step is to define a process and clear role for social media listening, one that includes ongoing engagement with a community. Put voting or rating systems in place to provide objective measures of popularity, and assign priority for development. Always remain transparent, in order to instill a sense of participation, co-ownership, and trust between customers and companies.

CHAPTER 7

CREATE MESSAGES
THAT RESONATE

Communications in recent years have been transitioning, from rational features and benefits that marketers promoted to include more context, emotional content, and imagery that customers and prospects desire. This evolution is an important reason why social media listening has begun playing a larger role in message creation: to generate insights for communications that resonate with, and within, customers and prospects at a deep level. Harvesting and analyzing conversations around product categories, specific products and services, and issues of all sorts can unmask the motives, drivers, emotions, and images that move people today. Resonant messages help marketers and advertisers move away from old-school "tell and sell" toward connecting, engaging, and building their businesses—as we'll see shortly.

WINNING PLAYS THAT CREATE RESONANT MESSAGES

Four winning plays emerged from our analysis of cases:

- *Listen to the people you are interested in, and locate the conversation hubs where they talk about your product, service, or category.* These are the places you'll get the strongest and clearest signals. Be specific about whom you listen to, and organize comments, topics, or themes according to groups that are most pertinent to your business (see Chapters 1 and 3 for discussion of these listening research principles). For Harrah's Casino, this meant people considering trips to Las Vegas—particularly their hotel, entertainment, and restaurant properties—as you'll read in the "Search Social Media for Resonant Topics" section.

  The company settled on TripAdvisor.com, a popular travel Web site that focuses on consumer discussion and reviews. For one specific consumer packaged goods (CPG) company, it was millennial moms dealing with storage issues in families with young children (see the section "Discover and Use Customer Language in Messaging"). A home storage manufacturer zoomed-in on "mommy blogger" sites and specialized areas on forums and Web sites like iVillage.com. Gillette's Fusion razor focused on lapsed users from sites where men discussed shaving. Resist the temptation to be broad, unless you have solid marketing or research-based reasons.

- *Resonant messages often combine ideas, so look for those that "hang together," and create messages grounded in the combination.* People generally hold impressions of products or services that are shaped by evaluating performance, price, emotional benefits, and their experiences. Address these factors in an integrated way to construct resonant communications. For example, by studying lapsed users, Gillette Fusion found that men quit the brand not because of performance or price as separate issues, but because the price was too high for the level of performance the razor delivered. To that end, the company created messages to win back lapsed users that treated performance and price together, thereby addressing perception head-on. (For additional background on marketing to lapsed users, Rishad Tobaccowala, head of strategy and insights for VivaKi, explains the merits in his Chapter 21 viewpoint.)

  Similarly, Harrah's learned that potential guests were interested in both views and amenities, which prompted the company to blend and communicate these two components together (see below). As the Gillette and Harrah's examples show, the ability to combine several elements is a different approach from old-school advertising, which likely would have treated each point separately in different ads.

- *Consider message length and benefits.* Depending on the goal and consumer, short, simple messages can work just as well as longer, more complex ones. Gatorade discovered this to be quite effective when it tweeted or posted news about the sudden availability of a music track that became available for download, thereby creating resonant messages in near-real time. Test message length and benefits when feasible and develop guidelines for different situations and applications.

- *Monitor buzz following advertising exposure to discover and fix communications problems or amplify wins so that ads resonate.* Television advertising often has an afterlife online, as people turn to social networks, blogs, Web sites, and forums to discuss them. Listening to those conversations will allow you to discover how customers are receiving, understanding, and acting upon your advertising. Then use those analyses to pick up on early signals that pinpoint problems and successes. This will let you adjust messaging in near-real time to get advertising back on track or exploit opportunity. For example, one international mobile phone company realized that its customers and prospects misunderstood some points of its service, which was turning them off to the company entirely. Correcting the problem shortly after discovery enabled the company to make its advertising much more effective. On the other side, following a new campaign launch, Gatorade picked up on a groundswell of positive buzz and used it to take near-real time actions, such as messaging and engaging with followers and fans, and even adjusting their brand experience.

Let's turn now to the tactics and cases that led us to diagram the plays. There are four:

- Search social media for resonant topics.
- Discover and use customer language in messaging.
- Combine ideas to address consumer perception.
- Monitor buzz after ad exposure to adjust messaging.

SEARCH SOCIAL MEDIA FOR RESONANT TOPICS

Renowned spa and hotel chain Harrah's sought to increase bookings by sharpening its messaging to increase its relevance and resonance with potential guests. Working with ad agency Ogilvy, Harrah's undertook a social media listening effort to identify the most important conversation topics and themes. It wanted to answer questions like: "What do people look forward to?" "What will make their stay special?"

Those who are familiar with Ogilvy know that the firm employs exceptionally sophisticated techniques and technologies of social media listening (Doublethink 2009). Yet despite the fact that it could have used state-of-the-art text analytics, Ogilvy instead took a straightforward, practical and manual approach by:

1. Scraping the top 50 posts from leading travel Web site TripAdvisor.com, which is chockablock with consumer reviews and comments.
2. Breaking them down into key topics and putting them in order of importance.
3. Drawing insights from them to recommend changes to communications and the Harrah's Web site.

Harrah's learned that travelers frequently discussed the "iconic views" from, and the hotel amenities at, its Paris Las Vegas hotel. It acted on these insights by changing its home page to show the view and nearby attractions, and started communicating details about the stay experience and features such as room sizes, menus, and spa services.

Harrah's marketing VP Monica Sullivan allowed that Web ad changes "boosted online bookings by a double-digit percentage" (quoted in Steel 2009).

Additionally, the hotel chain leveraged the social media listening findings into a broader media strategy, eventually introducing a series of TV, print, radio, and Web ads. There's power and profit in small changes.

This case reinforces an important point about social media listening research: Any size company, from startups to globe-circling behemoths, can do basic work quickly and affordably. Simple and straightforward methods—that require little more than a Web browser, search box, cut-and-paste skills and following listening research principles (see Part I)—can yield productive insights. Although this example focused on travel, studies like these can tackle any topic. Keep in mind, however, that they are best suited to small, easily managed projects with a narrow scope.

Listening Level and Type: Fundamental (Social research)

DISCOVER AND USE CUSTOMER LANGUAGE IN MESSAGING

A large CPG manufacturer of home storage solutions had transformed its business from a franchise model to one that sold its products through a large home center chain. Almost immediately, it had to completely revamp its marketing. The company's messaging, which had been mass-media-oriented but now included direct mail and promotions, such as e-mails, catalogs, and coupons, was no longer working. The issue was resonance. Though the target audience—millennial, time-stressed mothers—understood the company's offerings functionally, they did not see how the products fit into their families' lives: the CPG manufacturer had to overcome a mind-set mismatch. (See Chapter 4 for details and cases on mind-sets.)

Language influences what we think about and how we behave (Wikipedia 2010). Closing this gap meant that the CPG company would have to identify the language and themes that millennial moms used and which with they identified. The company would later have to draw upon these results for its messaging. So the manufacturer turned to social media listening to discover and analyze conversations that would provide these very insights.

The company's marketers knew that moms congregate, discuss, and share their experiences online. Many flock to sections of popular Web sites, post in forums, or follow "mommy bloggers" for advice, to get questions answered, even to commiserate. Because of this, the manufacturer's social media listening research:

- Identified the most relevant mom communities that overindexed on millennial moms. The company used custom studies with third-party audience data to discover them.
- Narrowed down the communities to those that had high levels of discussion regarding family issues and household organization.

- Harvested and analyzed discussion threads that uncovered the language, issues, and concerns, and sentiment around them, that reflected the daily lives of millennial moms.
- Provided a lexicon of terms to use in messaging. For example, "soccer mom" was viewed negatively, whereas SAHM ("stay at home mom") was used positively.
- Created personas around this language that helped visualize consumers and guide messaging to look and sound like them—a move that significantly increased resonance.

Their research approach should seem familiar; they follow those outlined in Part I. Operationally, new messaging created based on the social media findings brought about a variety of results, both among consumers and for the bottom line (Neely 2010):

- The manufacturer reduced creative development costs. Tapping into relevant consumer language enabled the company to test just one or two versions, instead of iterating and testing multiple alternatives with unknown language.
- Brand metrics registered gains across the board, from awareness to purchase intent. Initially, the company was concerned that these would drop as its business model and messaging changed, but they did not.
- Profitability exceeded goals by a "significant" amount.

Listening Level and Type: Intermediate (Social research)

COMBINE IDEAS TO ADDRESS CONSUMER PERCEPTION

Procter & Gamble's (P&G) Gillette division faced the following situation after the introduction of the Fusion, a five-blade razor promising an exceptionally close shave: "brisk" year-one sales, followed by a softening of refill cartridges sales the following year. In an attempt to diagnose the problem, Gillette conducted both a survey and a social media listening project among lapsed users. This was particularly wise, since, as Rishad Tobaccowala notes in his piece in Chapter 21, it is equally valuable to learn why people have *stopped* buying as to concentrate on understanding heavy users. Recapturing and winning back lapsed users can be a powerful driver of brand growth.

Survey results found two potential reasons for this: 80 percent of Fusion users concluded that other razors were just as good, and 54 percent that the Fusion was pricey. However, the social media listening analysis revealed a more nuanced take on the problem: the value/price relationship. Former users felt that although the shave they got was a bit better than alternatives, the price they had to pay for a little extra quality wasn't worth it (Figure 7.1).

Figure 7.1
Comparison of survey and social media listening results show that social media
listening links the issues of price and performance in a way that a survey could not.

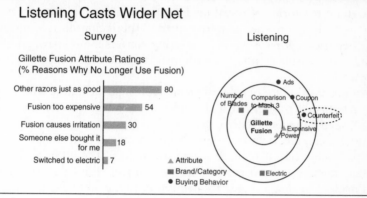

Source: Wiesenfeld et al. 2009. Used with permission.

The survey told Gillette which attributes were most important, and ranked them one by one. The listening analysis showed that lapsed users weighed and balanced their experience, price, and value into a brand perception, which led them to stop buying in this case.

Had Gillette acted only on the survey findings, it might have just lowered the price and conveyed that change to customers without addressing the parity perception. However, based on listening, it set a different course for its product messaging: to remind consumers that Fusion provides a superior shave, and align its pricing with that level of superiority (Wiesenfeld et al. 2009). Or, as stated more directly by P&G CFO Jon Mueller: "We want to make sure consumers know that Gillette Fusion can provide the best shave available for as little as a buck a week." He went on to add that, "[M]essages like these, and messages that drive trial and new innovations, will continue to be a prime focus in our communications with consumers" (quoted in WARC 2009).

Listening Level and Type: Intermediate (Social research)

MONITOR BUZZ AFTER AD EXPOSURE TO ADJUST MESSAGING

This vital postlaunch or postcampaign step provides fast feedback on effectiveness and suggests ways to either repair the damage or exploit sensational reaction. In the following examples, we see how two organizations, a global cellular phone outfit and beverage giant Gatorade, benefit from acting quickly on the results from their social media listening.

Listen to Correct Problems

Television advertising plays a key role in driving search queries, directing traffic online to company Web sites, and provoking visits to social networks, blogs, and other forms of social media. Once there, people discuss ads, their reactions to them, or other matters related to specific products and services or their categories. Monitoring and analyzing conversations spawned by television ads can provide companies with insight on how well their advertising is working.

Such was the case for one international mobile phone brand, which launched a four-month advertising campaign with heavy primetime television advertising in the United Kingdom. Rather than wait weeks for sales data, the company measured social media buzz at launch time to assess how things were going. After just one week, it realized it had a problem: The ad caused confusion among customers and prospects. Once the company learned the specifics from social media listening, it made a small tweak to the ad to fix the troublesome points—an adjustment that paid off considerably: "The remainder of the campaign was a great success, but had they not intervened so rapidly (a matter of hours after evidence of the confusion first appeared), this would most likely not have been the case" (Onalytica 2009).

Listening Level and Type: Intermediate (Social media monitoring)

Listen to Exploit Communications Opportunity

Sports drink Gatorade monitors social media activity from its Mission Control Center, a dedicated command post for listening, engaging with customers, and adjusting the brand experience to consumer interest in real time. The center occupies a prominent location: It's not in a back room or surplus space, but smack in the middle of the company's Chicago headquarters' marketing department. Five analysts track brand mentions and sentiment examination around key topics, while chattering about the industry, sports nutrition, and Gatorade's sports spokespersons across a wide range of social media.

After launching its "Gatorade has evolved" campaign, which featured an ad with a song written and produced by renowned rapper David Banner, the Mission Control Center observed a high level of approval about the track across its social media universe. Gatorade took action by releasing a full-length version of the song and engaging with Facebook fans and Twitter followers. Their posts and tweets drove traffic to the Gatorade Web site for a free download, enabling the brand to quickly capitalize on buzz early, when consumer interest was at its initial peak.

Seeking to become the "largest participatory brand in the world," Gatorade is placing a premium on engagement, connecting consumers to sports nutritionists, company scientists, and even athletes through Facebook and video services. If this approach succeeds with consumers, Gatorade's parent company

PepsiCo is likely to apply the Mission Control method to other brands within the business (Ostrow 2010).

Gatorade's case points us in the direction of social media listening's future: companywide, $24 \times 7 \times 365$ monitoring and engaging in order to create lasting enterprise value.

Listening Level and Type: Advanced (Social media monitoring)

SUMMARY

Social media listening helps companies create or adjust messaging that resonates with customers and prospects. While some resonant messages often combine multiple ideas that address consumer perceptions, others may be simple and short, depending on communications goals. Continuous listening that creates meaningful messages in near-real time points to a future of always-on listening that strengthens the relationships between companies and their customers.

CHAPTER 8

IMPROVE PRODUCTS
AND SERVICES

As soon as a product or service becomes available and people begin to use it, marketers and advertisers face the task of improving it in ways that keep it relevant and resonant. Consumers often want the product or service to better fit their needs and preferences. Some of these are needs and preferences that they didn't even know they had before, but that have come about from experience or new social/economic circumstances, such as recession or recovery or changed family situations. Products that have been with us for a century or more (Kraft Foods alone has more than 40 of them; Kraft 2010) have succeeded for so long because the companies that own them paid close attention and adapted to evolving consumer tastes. Improved products and services that resonate add to consumer happiness, have extensive life spans, and make long-term financial contributions to their companies.

Social media listening enables companies to uncover areas that are ripe for improvement and that can harmonize the relationships between products, services, and customers. The examples we cover in this chapter clearly demonstrate the ways that signals from even the most basic listening posts can help companies make timely adjustments to their changing consumers.

WINNING PLAYS THAT HELP IMPROVE PRODUCTS AND SERVICES

We developed three winning plays from the case studies we reviewed:

- *Align content to conversations and discussions.* The content that your product or service provides to customers and prospects is an important aspect of their experience. Improve this content by implementing an editorial plan based on how topics and themes are trending for your product, service, or category, and how site visitors are sharing content. Deemphasize those subjects that are losing popularity, exploit those that are gaining recognition, and continue to support evergreen topics. For example, Procter & Gamble's (P&G) BeingGirl.com Web site creates content by closely listening to product-related discussions that are concerned with the girls' experiences (discussed in the section "Keep Site Content Fresh and Relevant"). Similarly, the MD Anderson Cancer Center follows discussions about the disease and uses the findings to offer awareness and education programs that are more closely tied to these popular conversation topics than to objective measures like the disease incidence. While the latter serves to rate and rank medical importance, it may not represent what is on people's minds and claiming their attention (see the section "Tune Marketing to Meet Consumer Needs and Interests," in this chapter).

- *Capture ideas that improve the fit between products, services, and consumers.* Listen to social media to uncover issues, concerns, and improvements as they're happening and being voiced, rather than waiting for customer satisfaction research or reports from call centers to point them out. Make timely course corrections to keep consumers in sync with your products or services. Companies of all sizes can do this. Startup flavor company True Citrus, for example, drew upon its Facebook fan comments, Twitter tweets, and customer service records to learn about interest in new flavors, frustrations that not all retailers carried the full product line, and needs for larger serving sizes to accommodate families. Even Twitter, a medium used by many for social monitoring, itself listens to conversations about desired features and third-party enhancements (see below).

- *Respond to listening-led insights with decisive, superbly executed marketing actions.* True Citrus responded to their customers' needs by creating line extensions, offering bigger package sizes, and launching an e-store—all of which contributed to revenue and profit growth. Twitter added and improved upon user-created features that have broad appeal. The site can significantly improve. Why would customers show any interest in your offering if it is inferior to what is currently available? The moves described here are not radical, but incremental adaptations that arise from taking part in the conversation, listening, and engaging when appropriate. Companies that act upon listening insights are committed to implementing them, often in bold ways. For instance, NASCAR made changes to its races and TV schedule based on guidance from fans, not from a competition committee or other experts. Show your customers and prospects that you listened and acted on their advice in order to improve their experience.

Firms that enhanced their products or services used one of the following three tactics that we uncovered through our case study research:

- Keep site content fresh and relevant.
- Add user-desired features into the core product.
- Tune marketing to meet changing consumer interests.

We'll discuss each one in detail next.

KEEP SITE CONTENT FRESH AND RELEVANT

Along with pulling customers and prospects into sites, content keeps them there and encourages their return. Because Web sites have morphed from page-based brochureware that offered a one-dimensional experience—"Here's what you need to know to buy our product"—to interactive, social sites that allow people to engage with content and each other, the role of traditional advertising has often become secondary. People are returning to Web sites because of the experiences they have, the emotional connections they make, and the knowledge they acquire. For this reason, many organizations are committing to developing and offering branded content, engagement, and networking services that are relevant to their customers. This promotes an environment that supports overall marketing of products or services and their growth, as BeingGirl.com illustrates.

Launched in 2005, P&G's BeingGirl.com site is a branded community exclusively for young women. Visitors go there to discuss concerns related to being a girl, request and comment on existing or developing products, or just to entertain themselves. Sponsored by feminine care brands Tampax and Always, the site teems with information about personal health matters and the issues many young females face; at the same time, it offers fun features like quizzes, games, horoscopes, and beauty and social tips. By 2007, BeingGirl.com showcased its global appeal: It was available in 18 languages and had nearly 2 million registered users (see Figure 8.1).

By mining girls' conversations, comments, and product reviews, and tracking some behaviors, like content sharing and product requests in this brand backyard source, P&G developed insights into the motivations, likes and dislikes, and the "whys" underlying the views of younger females. Moreover, as with the earlier Fiat MIO example in Chapter 6, P&G efficiently and rapidly gained a global grasp of its customers across many cultures and regions, while hastening its ability to respond to market shifts and innovate with confidence.

P&G uses these insights to periodically restructure its content, based on issues that the girls raise, and to keep an eye on trending topics. Tampax and Always marketers pay close attention to discussions around their test and in-market brands, as well as any refinements and improvements they made that solved problems or enhanced the products or the girls' experiences with them.

In addition to the adjustments P&G made after interpreting social media listening program signals, BeingGirl helped with branding and the bottom line. Forrester research analyst Josh Bernoff reports that BeingGirl is a wise investment, claiming that the community "is four times as effective as a similarly priced marketing program in traditional media" (quoted in Morrissey 2008). Branding research shows that the effort appears to influence purchase consideration of Tampax and Always.

Listening Level: Advanced (Social research and social media monitoring)

Figure 8.1
Branded community BeingGirl.com, sponsored by P&G's Always and Tampax brands,
serves as a social media listening post for generating insights from girls worldwide. This
screenshot shows an Arabic version of the site.

ADD USER-DESIRED FEATURES INTO THE CORE BRAND

Building new features into products, or modifying them to more closely match user preferences and concerns, is the approach taken by our next two example companies—Twitter and NASCAR. By using social media listening, both made changes designed to strengthen the support for their products. Twitter adapted customer innovations, while NASCAR acted on customer recommendations.

Adapt Customer Innovations

Twitter's release of two product innovations, Lists and Retweets, landed the company on the front page of the *New York Times* business section (Miller 2009), in an article headlined "Twitter Serves Up Ideas from Its Followers." The piece described how this enormously popular company—one of the poster children for social media—maintains resonance through listening that involves various tactics. These include monitoring tweets, tracking how users augment their service with third-party applications, evaluating which features have broad appeal, and developing and incorporating them into the core product set.

Twitter added the Lists feature to help people more easily follow others, like celebrities or politicians, and help users organize and manage the posts

Figure 8.2
Twitter added Lists in response to community interest in the feature.

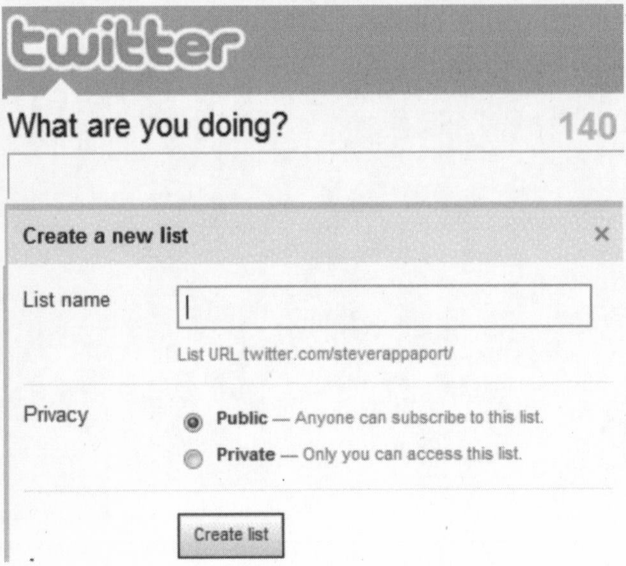

they get from the people they follow (see Figure 8.2). Retweeting, which is similar to message forwarding, became a popular element in numerous third-party Twitter applications. This method of spreading tweets is used by some social media listening companies as a factor in calculating an individual's authority or influence. Twitter's Retweet tool improves on the "field versions" by eliminating redundant posts—which simplifies their management and improves their integrity—while clarifying authorship and preventing people from changing the original post.

Twitter's ability to implement community-developed features connects to its platform and the perspectives of founders Evan Williams and Biz Stone. The site struck an interesting balance of flexibility and malleability that allowed users to invent unanticipated uses for it. As Williams said, "You get a bunch of users interacting and it's hard to predict what they're going to do. We say, 'Why are people using this, and how could we make that better?'" (quoted in Miller 2009).

Listening Level: Fundamental (Social media monitoring)

Let Fans Drive

Ever since experiencing explosive growth from 2004–2006, NASCAR has faced the issue of declining attendance and TV ratings (Sigala 2010). Though the sport is healthy—ranking third in popularity after the National Football League and Major League Baseball—the key to the association's future is holding on to core fans and rebuilding its base by making its product more fan-friendly.

NASCAR listens to its fans through the Fan Council, a private online community of 12,000 run by Vision Critical, a full-service research provider that manages brand communities. Through its social research, NASCAR made two major changes to its live competition on the ovals: It adopted the more exciting double-file race restarts after cautions, and implemented earlier and more consistent TV start times, to make watching more predictable and convenient.

In the first instance, NASCAR discovered and validated fans' suggestions. It implemented the restart rule and continued social media listening, and received positive reviews. In terms of TV start times, NASCAR quantified the sentiment around the discussions, starting with the NASCAR Sprint Cup Series, launched in 2010.

It is innovative, bold, and fairly unprecedented to let fan comments guide such major changes to a sport. In most, if not all, other professional sports, competition changes are usually the province of owners, league management, and special committees, but not fans. Apart from asking for fan input into popularity contests like All-Star games, it is nearly impossible to imagine that Major League Baseball might act on fan views regarding designated hitters, or the National Football League on whether or not fair catches should still be allowed.

The example of NASCAR demonstrates that social media listening insights can influence major business decisions throughout organizations and their brands—even at the highest levels. NASCAR's Managing Director of Market and Media Research, Brian Moyer, pointed out that, "The Fan Council has created a shift in company culture as it relates to consumer research. Nearly all departments have embraced the Fan Council for a variety of topics related to the sport. The council members, representative of our avid fan base, do an excellent job engaging us" (quoted in Vision Critical 2009). Indeed, the role of Fan Council member is such a coveted position that there's actually a waiting list to get in.

Listening Level: Advanced (Social research)

TUNE MARKETING TO MEET
CONSUMER INTERESTS

Service providers and product manufacturers attune their marketing with social media listening. Two such organizations, MD Anderson Cancer Center and flavor manufacturer True Citrus, adjusted their marketing in ways that benefitted both their customers and their companies.

Choose Programs to Market

Service providers, such as health care systems, must remain constantly in sync with the communities and populations they serve and plan to serve. An example from health care is the renowned MD Anderson Cancer Center. The center knew that people were talking about living with cancer more than ever before; so it aimed to understand those conversations in order to learn how it might align the center's services and enhance marketing. Initially relying on Google and Twitter, the center later moved to a more fully featured social media monitoring initiative that would dig deeply into cancer-themed forums, conversations about cancer that were occurring, mentions of the center, and the sentiments expressed regarding conversation topics and the center itself.

Listening helped the MD Anderson Cancer Center market its education and awareness programs, usually around specific health care topics. Focusing on men's health, the center's social media listening findings enabled the organization to reevaluate its programs. Discovering that related discussion levels were low and sentiment flat, it scrapped the prior year's Prostate Cancer Awareness Month. Instead of focusing on a single illness, the center broadened the program to include a variety of cancer-related topics under the umbrella of Men's Health Month. That effort went on to achieve higher levels of center awareness and health discussion. According to Communication Program Manager Jennifer Texada, "Over the last year, we've witnessed an increase in the number of mentions of MD Anderson . . . ; word is spreading that we're listening via Twitter, Facebook, cancer blogs, and message boards, etc., and responding to our various audiences" (quoted in Alterian 2010).

Social media listening enabled the center to adjust to its market based on audience conversations, *not* on the basis of disease-centric measures that typically guide education and awareness programs like incidence and treatability. By doing so, MD Anderson avoided another dud program. Aligning itself to community interests brought forth a successful program that resonated with its audience.

Listening Level: Intermediate (Social media monitoring)

EVOLVE PRODUCTS AND SERVICES

Few small, up-and-coming companies have leveraged social media listening to address the evolving needs of its customers better than True Citrus. The Baltimore-based company produces natural crystallized citrus powders, such as True Lemon and True Lime, that were originally created to transform water into refreshing, naturally flavored beverages.

True Citrus consumer marketing VP Heidi Carney says the company's social media listening program has directed its line extensions, packaging, advertising, and e-commerce. Its straightforward approach collects and aggregates direct consumer contacts, such as letters, e-mails, and phone call notes, which range from 1,500 to 5,000 each week. An active social media presence on both Facebook and Twitter allows fans and followers to discuss topics among themselves, make suggestions to the company, and foster engagement among True Citrus and its communities. Tracking and analyzing conversations led the company to adjust its marketing in ways that kept the brand in sync with its rapidly growing fan base: In just six months, Facebook fans quickly climbed from 1,000 to 25,000—and they are indeed demanding customers. Here's a rundown of the five ways True Citrus responded, each of which is rooted in listening insights (Carney 2010):

- *Create line extensions.* All products offered since the original True Lemon were developed based on customer feedback. After True Lemon hit the market, people asked for True Lime, then True Orange, then True Raspberry Lemonade, and continue to ask for new flavors.
- *Offer new formats and package sizes.* Initially, True Citrus flavors were packaged in individual-use tubes—one tube, one drink. The company is blessed with creative users who started using True Lemon and True Orange in unforeseen "off label" ways—for cooking, baking, or seasoning. Single-serve packets are inconvenient for those uses, which prompted customers to request a format better suited to them. Additionally, some customers, primarily young mothers with children, wanted bigger sizes to make larger quantities for their families, play groups, and entertaining needs. The company responded to both requests, introducing True Lemon and True Lime shakers, and packages for making a quart of each.
- *Test advertising.* True Citrus includes customers in the development of new taglines. For this purpose, it supplements listening with surveys and focus groups.
- *Redesign Web site features.* Listening-led changes aim to make the Web site more usable and provide a wider variety of services. The company added an expanded recipe section to the site, improved the store locator to make it easier to find outlets, and improved overall navigation.
- *Launch an online store.* True Citrus products are still gaining distribution; they are not universally available yet, and some stores carrying its products do not sell the complete line. Therefore, the company created an online store expressly to satisfy customers' desire to be able to purchase the complete range of products. The store is now one of its most profitable sales channels.

Although social media monitoring and related efforts at True Citrus comprise just 10 percent of its marketing budget, Carney says it is "worth much more." Despite the many companies that receive letters and calls from customers, and have—or think about having—some type of social media presence, not all are able to harness those consumer suggestions and voices effectively. Doing so requires management commitment, prioritization of these initiatives, and implementation of processes to aggregate, analyze, and report. When companies like True Citrus manage to do this, the entire organization feels its impact and is able to respond fully to its customers, and finely tune the fit between them.

Listening Level: Fundamental (Social media monitoring)

SUMMARY

Social media listening identifies ways that products and services can be improved and, over time, stay resonant with consumers. Marketers and advertisers acting on signals from social media listening make certain that their offerings remain in sync with their customers.

Maintain synchronicity by making changes or innovating in a number of ways, including: modifying the product, improving on the online experience, refreshing content to meet evergreen and new interests, simplifying transactions, and/or focusing on unmet or underserved needs. Do not limit listening insights to just one or two areas; look comprehensively for insights on all aspects of product improvement.

CHAPTER 9

INCREASE SALES

Growing a product's or service's top line means growing sales. However, in today's era of higher-quality items at all price points, many competing offerings are similar and, therefore, hard to distinguish. Certainly, product features, performance, and their price and advertising imagery are still important, and have to be up to snuff. But consumers are increasingly paying closer attention to emotional connection, attachment, and experience—all of which are becoming important drivers of sales.

Take the hot dog, for example. People appreciate franks nowadays for their contribution to enjoying family get-togethers, barbecues, and sporting events, and for their less obvious role in improving kids' nutrition, as parents today serve hot dogs with other foods they sneak in to broaden their children's diets. Selling hot dogs is really about selling love, nurturing, and good times.

Social media listening plays an important role in tuning companies in to their customers and prospects, and providing the knowledge that leads to the creation of compelling and effective sales strategies, programs, and tactics. This chapter looks across the range of sales situations that firms of every size face, to varying degrees and complexity. Our case examples demonstrate applications for social media listening that contributed to successful sales results. Listening assisted in: developing a meaningful sales strategy; finding, and helping to resolve, "pain points" that discourage sales; coping with fallow periods during which companies do not offer updated or new products; and influencing the influencers who hold power over a company's success or failure.

WINNING PLAYS TO INCREASE SALES

The cases we reviewed, and their tactics, led us to identify seven winning plays:

- *Transform sales from a product-centered and transactional strategy to one that is service-oriented and builds relationships.* Customers and prospects want salespeople to understand their needs and requirements and respect their purchase process. They don't want to be sold to merely because they satisfy vendor or retailer criteria for qualified prospects. This is why it is vital to use social media listening to understand customer and prospect preferences. The case of computer hardware, software, and services vendor CDW clearly demonstrates the value of listening to your best customers. In this scenario, the customers effectively determined the strategy, as described in the section "Develop and Implement a Listening-Led Sales Strategy." They advised CDW of their views on cold-calling, relationship building, and thought leadership. Matching its sales approach to customer preferences enabled CDW to succeed in a cutthroat business during a challenging economy.

Relationships are crucial here. With the exception of one-off purchases, companies often look to have trusted connections with suppliers; they add value by simplifying decisions, making business more efficient, and maintaining preference for reorders and the next major purchase. Although CDW is a large, national company, the lesson it teaches applies to just about every company: Listen to how your customers would like you to do business with them. Then make that happen.

- *Pick up on early signals of operational or product issues that affect sales; listen to consumers to make timely in-market corrections.* Listen for problems that stall sales or erect barriers to purchase, and find ways to overcome them. While rolling out Steam n' Mash, potato product maker Ore-Ida discovered that consumers were confused—and a bit frustrated—about where to find their speed-scratch mashed potato in the supermarket. Ore-Ida turned to consumers for guidance on solving this findability problem, and eventually received hundreds of suggestions to consider (see "Adjust to Real-Time Feedback for Product Rollouts," later in the chapter). WhiteWave Foods' soy beverage Silk faced a perception problem that hindered sales when the company found that people assumed healthy beverages could not taste good. To counter that, WhiteWave ran a program designed to stimulate a product trial by activating social networks of product advocates and listening to consumer reactions. Listening showed the company what consumers appreciated about the product—good-for-you nutrition and good taste—and adjusted its marketing and advertising in response (described under "Stimulate Trial for Products In-Market"). Keep sales moving by removing the hurdles that customers tell you they face.

- *Engage customers as a way to battle slow periods or seasonality.* For those times when your company faces a slow period or seasonal dropoffs, identify passion points and generate engagement around them. Auto brand MINI did just that when it encountered a year of potential sales decline, because no new model or updates were scheduled. MINI listened to identify and engage owner passions as a way to strengthen relationships, give customers reasons to stay in the fold, and keep sales moving. MINI undoubtedly enjoyed some of these great results because it had advance warning and so was able to develop and maneuver its engagement program, as described under "Engage Customers Around Their Passions," later in this chapter. This example shows that understanding, supporting, and engaging customer communities can help companies succeed during fallow or slack periods.

Furthermore, rather than listening and engaging just in response to a business event that can be planned for, continuously listen to and support customers through time to keep the connections tight year-round. Doing so helps make companies proactive, effectively increases lead time, and avoids the problems that arise from being reactive—such as slow or inadequate response that can cause dissatisfaction and may damage reputations.

- *Determine whether personal influence helps drive sales in your category.* Some product categories, such as movies, are driven in part by recommendations from family and friends. If word of mouth is important to the success of your category, product, or service, consider using social media listening to identify influencers, their opinions, and sentiments, and then engage them to minimize or maximize their impact on sales.

  It is especially important to understand the timing of conversations and their sentiment to develop an effective strategy. Ethan Titelman of market research firm Penn, Schoen & Berland studies movie buzz (see the "Track Buzz and Influence the Influencers" section). Speaking at an ARF Industry Leader Forum in 2010, Titelman told participants that what people talk about, and the sentiments they express, change before and after a movie's release date. He found that prior conversations are frequently based on expectations and cast, and sentiment is often neutral. People form opinions after the release, once they have made a financial and emotional investment. This results in a different set of topics and reactions, which can be more positive or negative and will influence sales. Companies introducing new products or services that listen only during the lead-up period before new products or services are introduced will get a different impression of their prospects than those who tune in both before and after release. Listen continuously over time to detect and adjust strategy as needed.

  Titelman makes a second important point about strategy: Not all people interested in a movie want to see it for the same reasons. Some are keen on effects, others on actors, still others on the production itself. Still others view it simply as a way to pass the time or go out on a date. Not only must companies understand their influencers; they must segment them into domains and engage with them according to their interests. (If you are interested in segmentation, it is discussed again in Chapter 16.)

- *Use social media and listening to re-create or reinvent basic sales tactics.* Every product or service needs to promote trial in order to attract new customers and build sales over time. New snack food entrant Pretzel Crisps innovated "social sampling" to deliver just-in-time sampling by: listening to social media to find people expressing the need for snacks; engaging with them; and delivering product to their door, office, or public place (see "Personalize Product Sampling"). The tweets, posts, and reviews generated substantial earned media mentions, which helped consumers get to know the company better and spark increased interest in its products. Silk Soy enlisted advocates to spur trial, and then listened carefully to what people liked and didn't like. Applying the insights it developed, Silk refined its marketing communications to resonate more clearly with customers. Consider the sales tactics your business relies on or would like to execute, and think about how you can apply social media listening to refresh or reinvent them.

- *Share insights from sales with other departments or units.* Maximize your company's social media listening investment by sharing data and helping colleagues apply this information to their business needs. Insights surfaced in both the Steam n' Mash and Silk cases that were applicable to marketing, advertising, and product development. Marketers for Steam n' Mash discovered that despite a flavor disaster with one variety, they had an opportunity for a new flavor, which they subsequently developed and launched. Silk learned that consumers cited the product's nutritional value, variety of flavors, and taste as reasons to keep buying it. Silk incorporated those ideas into its marketing and advertising.
- *Do not confine listening data in corporate silos.* Consider the many places where listening insights can deliver value in your business and work with colleagues to apply them.

The cases we uncovered and reviewed utilize the following five tactics to keep sales moving:

- Develop and implement a listening-led sales strategy.
- Adjust to real-time feedback for product rollouts.
- Stimulate trial for new and in-market products.
- Engage customers based on their passions.
- Track buzz and influence the influencers.

DEVELOP AND IMPLEMENT A LISTENING-LED SALES STRATEGY

Who knows how to sell to customers better than the customers themselves? By tapping into their priorities, preferences, and engagement styles, companies are able to create true customer-centric sales approaches. Executing such strategies promotes relationship building and a sense of confidence. This is important in any economy, but it may be especially valuable during challenging times, when competition is red-hot and closing pressure is intense.

Companies have started using social media listening to get into their customers' minds and hearts. The example we'll review here leverages a private branded community that involved customers in a program of guided activities, yet did not constrain the free flow of conversation and feedback essential for listening.

Since 2004, computer software company CDW has listened to its small, midsized, and large clients through three private communities, which were

Figure 9.1
CDW runs communities tailored to its customer groups. This example showcases the community for large companies. It provides a rundown on events, and social networking features allow members to engage with one another and with the brand.

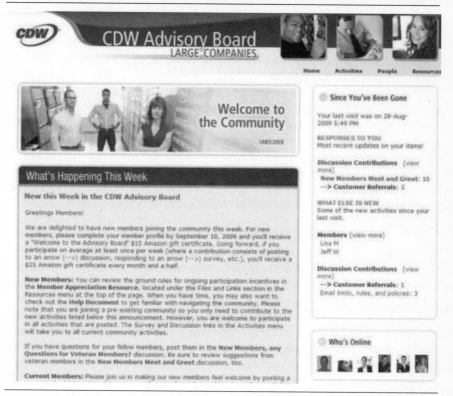

built and managed by Communispace, a leading vendor (see Figure 9.1). Community members influence or make IT decisions and interact with peers to help shape CDW's policies, products, and services.

Reseller businesses—especially IT-related enterprises—are known for being brutally competitive and having very thin margins. They thrive on acquisition, repeat business, and customer satisfaction. In the grips of an economic recession, CDW decided to task its communities with helping the company improve its approach to prospects and to building productive relationships. Based on its social media listening work with the community, CDW sought to make improvements in three areas:

- Efficacy of the cold call
- Sales practices for beginning relationships successfully
- Establishing thought leadership for the brand

Community members reported receiving more cold calls than ever. This was a pivotal finding, one that indicated that CDW had a big obstacle to overcome: to break through the noise caused by the cold-call clutter, then meaningfully differentiate itself, or risk being ignored, and potentially lose future sales. Members provided insights on what made a good first call, advising on language and key points that would help connect callers to customers effectively. The members essentially created a communication approach that reflected their understanding of their own needs and interests while eliminating vendor-centric pitches.

Best practices that the community developed revolved around three elements: the need to truly understand business requirements; service; and "sweeteners" that reduced purchase risk and left a positive feeling. One key suggestion for the sales managers taken from a cold-call idea was: "Think harder about your recommendations for a client's initial purchase." In other words, don't just sell for the sake of selling; sell to meet needs and establish a relationship. Members also gave guidance on valued offers and promotions, preparing for meetings, and personalizing both e-mail and marketing materials.

Factors including the variety of configurations available, specifications, reliability, software licensing terms, pricing, and trade-offs tend to complicate IT sales. IT buyers and influencers usually turn to independent tests and advice from third parties, whose guidance is a critical input into the process of evaluating, recommending, and deciding on purchases. CDW community members identified five sources that they deemed reliable, and in turn, CDW developed strategic partnerships with a number of those information suppliers. By doing so, the company helped its best customers make better-informed decisions, and thus paved a smoother path to purchase.

Using social media listening to communicate with its communities led CDW to formalize those insights and practices into its Sales Academy training. The change is paying off: Account managers are recruiting more high-quality customers, valued four times greater than over-the-transom buyers they acquire from the Web site or other sources. Average customer value increased 17 percent over the prior year, a testimony to the power of a social media listening-derived customer strategy (Communispace 2009).

Listening Level and Type: Advanced (Social research)

STIMULATE PRODUCT TRIAL FOR NEW AND IN-MARKET PRODUCTS

Programs promoting consumer trials traditionally offer special package sizes, financial incentives, education, or sampling and promoting in stores or at live events. Whichever tactic or combination is used, these programs effectively lower barriers for consumers and encourage them to try new products or services. Listening to and analyzing conversations and feedback from trial programs can better equip companies to understand consumers, thereby enabling them to market and advertise to them more effectively. Trial programs are not just for big companies; they work very well for midsized and entrepreneurial firms, too. Bear Naked is a smaller startup, known for granola and natural foods. It succeeded in growing sales and broadening distribution by providing samples in local specialized stores like Stew Leonard's in Norwalk, Connecticut. The company was eventually acquired by Kellogg's.

Innovative companies that leverage social media and social networks are creating and promoting trial in breakthrough ways, and using listening insights to improve their sales and marketing. The cases we review, Pretzel Crisps and Silk Soy beverage, provide a compelling guide on how to do so.

Personalize Product Sampling

Pretzel Crisps, a thin snack cracker, seeks to move from new entrant to established brand in the highly competitive snack food market. In addition to the standard promotional tactics companies use to build their brands, secure distribution, and generate sales, Pretzel Crisps had an inspired idea for its sampling effort: Listen to social media to locate people who tweeted or posted their need for a snack, find them, and deliver samples to them right away. The company's Field Marketing Director Jason Harty calls this innovation "social sampling"; he provided an example of one such conversation and how social sampling works, shown in Figure 9.2 (Harty 2010).

Social sampling uses social media not only to find the conversations but also to multiply the news in this realm by selecting people in offices, public places, and those with active social networks and followers. Fitarella and tamadear, the women tweeting in Figure 9.2, fit that bill perfectly: Both have active and popular blogs, as well as several thousand Twitter followers. They conveyed their enthusiasm and positive experiences through tweets, blog posts, and product reviews. A single "interception" reached nearly 23,000 people; in this way, social sampling revolutionized field marketing for Pretzel Crisps and contributed to building the company.

Listening Level and Type: Fundamental (Social media monitoring)

Stimulate Trial for Products In-Market

Rollouts convey a sense of excitement; the products are new, and marketing and advertising is amped up. Products that have been in the market for some time are, on the other hand, considerably less interesting. The marketing challenge for these is to increase trial, sales, and profitability, and build a customer base. Though we often think of social networks as being online, we overlook the networks that exist offline as well, those that are composed of the people we know, see, visit, and work alongside. These flesh-and-blood networks are especially important because they are formed and cultivated in the places where we deal with one another, and are also where 85 to 90 percent of all

Figure 9.2
Pretzel Crisps "social sampling" discovers conversations through social
media and then delivers samples to the conversants.

tamadear: In need of a wee **snack**. Something with nutella will fit the bill nicely.
Twitter - Aug 31, 2010 10:31:17 PM - Boston, MA, USA

Fitarella: YES! ANYTHING w Nutella ALWAYS fits the bill! RT @tamadear: In need of a
wee **snack**. Something with nutella will fit the bill nicely.
Twitter - Aug 31, 2010 10:33:16 PM - Boston, MA, USA

PretzelCrisps @fitarella @tamadear **Must try Nutella (&PB) on
Pretzel Crisps!** Amazing and light snack. http://tweetphoto.com
/42653708
8:19 AM Sep 1st via TweetPhoto from Downtown, Boston 📍

PretzelCrisps @fitarella @tamadear **DM me an addy and** I'll
deliver PC to your doorstep or office TODAY! If you request I'll even
pick up the nutella :)
8:21 AM Sep 1st via web

tamadear TWITTER BRINGS ME FOOD. Thank you, @PretzelCrisps
for stopping by with samples...and Nutella!! (As promised, a delicious
combo!)
about 21 hours ago via Seesmic Desktop

Fitarella SO FRICKIN COOL @PretzelCrisps brought crisps &
nutella to our home for us 2 try! Im at office, but daughter is SO
excited!! Thank u!
2:36 PM Sep 1st via TweetDeck

Source: Pretzel Crisps.

conversations about products or services take place (Keller 2009). This is
where face-to-face influence can happen.

Some companies are capitalizing on using influencers who leverage their
social networks to stimulate trial and collect their conversations. Silk, a leader
in soy beverages known for their health benefits, has enjoyed great success
with this approach.

Prior research conducted by Silk shows that many people assumed healthy
products simply could not taste good. Silk's parent company, WhiteWave
Foods, wanted to overcome that perception—an obvious obstacle to sales—by
getting people to try the product and talk about it. It embarked on a word-of-
mouth campaign designed to stimulate trial by working with word-of-mouth
agency BzzAgent.

BzzAgent has a network of roughly 500,000 individuals called (unsurprisingly) BzzAgents, who like to try brands and are encouraged, but not
required, to instigate conversations and spread the word about them within
their offline and online social networks. After agreeing to participate in a program, agents are matched to brands based on their interests, and report

Figure 9.3
BzzAgent's campaign for soy beverage Silk involved 3,000 agents driving
word of mouth, which was responsible for stimulating trial and sales,
and generating consumer insight that explained brand performance.

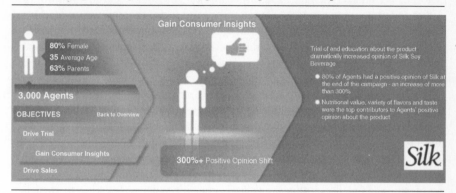

the substance of their conversations back to BzzAgent. The agency then extensively analyzes the content and categories based on such factors as agent demographics, number of people involved, geography, and actions taken—for example, the number of coupons or trial packages distributed (see Figure 9.3). The company then evaluates the data for themes and favorability.

The Silk campaign attracted 3,000 agents (see Figure 9.3). More than 90 percent tried the product, and those who did gave out about three coupons each. Of the coupons distributed, 24 percent were redeemed. At campaign's end, nearly 70 percent of the agents said they were likely to continue purchasing Silk, and 78 percent said they knew at least one person whom they had influenced.

Though the raw numbers are impressive, what's even more important is the explanation of why the program had been so successful. Insights from analysis of the word-of-mouth reports revealed that "nutritional value," "variety of flavors," and "taste" drove the agents' favorable opinions. Those findings gave Silk the opportunity to improve its ability to market and advertise more effectively. Silk's example shows the value of listening to offline sources.

Listening Level and Type: Intermediate (Social research)

ADJUST TO REAL-TIME FEEDBACK FOR PRODUCT ROLLOUTS

Sales success occasionally depends on making small, quick changes in marketing, retail, or distribution in order to make it easier for consumers to purchase products or services. This is especially true when new products or updates are first appearing across markets. Getting information about problems as early as possible enables companies to quickly respond to them, and keep products rolling.

Monitoring social media conversations is one way to capture those signals. Another is to directly engage the target market through research communities. These social networks match women, men, and kids (all community members) to products and product trials, encourage product usage, and capture feedback and discussion through conversations, comments, polls, and surveys. Participating in communities and their activities usually requires companies to register and profile in order to recruit the right people.

Potato giant Ore-Ida, a division of H.J. Heinz Co., opted to use a community approach when it began distributing its Steam n' Mash product nationally. The product was meant to help busy moms simplify mealtimes by making it easier and faster to prepare a comfort food staple—mashed potatoes—and to add variety by offering different flavors. Steam n' Mash, a frozen speed-scratch product, puts peeled, precut potatoes into a microwaveable bag and provides instructions on mashing, as well as adding milk and other ingredients. Looking to stimulate trial, build word of mouth, and garner feedback for insights, Ore-Ida turned to SheSpeaks, a by-invitation-only social network for women, which has features explicitly designed for research purposes and creating branded experiences.

SheSpeaks considers its members "everyday influencers." The 16,000 participating moms received free product and discount coupons for additional purchases—premiums that they could use themselves or share with friends—along with an information card and a free potato masher.

Participants filled out a pretest form to establish baseline information. Once underway, these "potato moms" had access to a Test Center (microcommunity) for recipe ideas, a discussion forum in which they conversed with other members and Ore-Ida, and an end-of-program evaluation survey. Since SheSpeaks is a social network, the moms could blog, comment, and engage with other community members. Additionally, moms blogged and commented on other sites, like Modern Mommyhood and Nifty Thrifty, spreading word of mouth and expanding the voices that others were listening to.

From a branding standpoint, the program rang up big numbers; it nearly doubled traditional measures, including awareness, purchase, and recommendation intent, over the baseline. Word of mouth reached 1.2 million women.

The insights gleaned from detailed analysis of nearly 1 million posts and the evaluation surveys gave Ore-Ida crucial knowledge on problems to address that affected sales. These problems were that:

- Shoppers could not find the product in stores; it either wasn't stocked, wasn't located where expected, or the package design blended in too closely with other products.
- One flavor tasted terrible and needed to be reformulated.
- Some saw the price point as too high.
- Package size was a bit skimpy; moms desired larger ones that would yield more servings to feed an entire family.

Ore-Ida used the observations to fix its rollout. It asked community members how to solve the findability problem, and users submitted more than 200 suggestions, which the company categorized and used to make changes. Additionally, Ore-Ida earned some extra mileage by deriving insights applicable for other marketing purposes, such as line extension ideas. Cut Red Potatoes, a creamier skin-on potato, eventually joined the family of varieties.

Impressed by Ore-Ida's performance, Heinz CEO William Johnson declared Steam n' Mash one of the most successful launches in company history. Presenting to a Word of Mouth Marketing Association University session, Brand Manager Kimberly Lang said that social media listening also helped secure product distribution because Ore-Ida could show the data, richness of conversations, and moms' potato passion. Lang also mentioned that social media listening would become a standard part of the Ore-Ida toolkit, and that other Heinz brands had expressed interest in the approach and results (SheSpeaks, 2009; Pietruski and Lang, 2009).

Listening Level and Type: Intermediate (Social media research)

Engage Customers Around Their Passions

Companies look for growth from improvement and new product innovations. But not all companies have "bright, new shiny objects" for the market every product cycle, so their task is to maintain or expand sales for their current product or service lineups until they do. Since competitors are rarely staying still, but are instead pressing for advantages, poised to pounce on those failing to keep up, this is not a simple exercise at all. Companies without new offerings not only need to protect their products from predation; they also need to remain in their customers' minds. And they need to do it in a way that's profitable, which usually means avoiding dealing and cost-cutting as much as possible, since both drag on bottom lines. BMW's MINI provides an excellent case in point and showcases the role of social media listening in contributing to its success through engagement.

MINI enjoyed great results following its reintroduction in 2005. But in 2006, it faced a potential problem: No new model would be introduced into a category that is driven by new product introductions. This raised the issue: How could the MINI maintain its sales momentum without a fresh model to add excitement? What could the automaker offer and tell customers? To answer these questions, MINI retained full-service social media listening vendor MotiveQuest to devise a solution focused on increasing online engagement that would keep sales moving.

MINI first listened to social media conversations around the brand and its closest rivals in order to find what made owners tick. The company identified, extracted, and compared category drivers and lined them up by brand. Results showed that drivers clustered in two segments: around the car and around the community. Table 9.1 shows that MINI sentiment around the conversations

TABLE 9.1 Conversations and sentiment around the MINI concentrate on customization and sharing, and serve to set conversations about the car apart from competing brands.

		GTI	MINI	Jetta	Scion	Solstice	
			NET SENTIMENT INDEX				
CAR	The Performance/Engine	250	124	82	93	40	Ranked by overall buzz
	Exterior Features	118	100	109	14	129	
	Driving	169	106	104	107	45	
	Cost (positive)	118	118	114	107	147	
	Overall Looks/Style	109	110	102	77	123	
	Interior	110	106	98	107	56	
	Handling	160	123	71	200	164	
	Fuel Efficiency	188	99	114	94	–	
	Customization	59	128	101	–	–	
COM-MUNITY	Sharing Pics/Dedications	77	108	97	62	19	Ranked by overall buzz
	Relationships	121	177	28	0	138	
	Event's Gaterings	117	105	78	84	–	
	Clubs/Organizations	69	136	104	49	–	
	Comfort/Space	122	73	116	128	–	
	Enthusiasts	5	198	4	–	–	

highest index   – Buzz volume is too small to calculate sentiment

Source: MotiveQuest. Used with permission.

was unique and clustered differently from competitors. MINI owners viewed the car as a blank canvas onto which they could project their personalities, through customizations and molding—something they enjoy doing and sharing virtually and with others.

Upon digging deeper, MINI learned that creativity, discovery, participation, collaboration, fun/play, and self-expression drove these findings. This quote illustrates the points well (MotiveQuest 2007):

> I have never been involved in another car culture. Friends who are tell me when they meet MINI owners that our culture is in some ways very familiar—complete obsession with the MINIS—and in some ways very different—it seems to transcend the car. We get to know each other on a much more personal level.

With these insights at hand, MINI developed an advertising strategy and tactics for messaging and community engagement. The program it created included three elements, which were launched sequentially and with time in between them: special invitation mailing; live events; and because each MINI contains a digital identification chip, digital billboards that personalized messages to drivers passing by. These led to sales.

The impacts of the mailings, events, and billboards raised MotiveQuest's proprietary Online Promoter Score, a measure of the number of people online recommending the brand to others. The Online Promoter Score is predictive: Any increases or declines foreshadow ups and downs in sales. MINI's score increased with each campaign event, which predicted an uptick in sales about one month in advance. (We will look at this measure more closely when we turn our attention to social media listening-based measures and analytics in Chapter 18.)

Listening Level and Type: Intermediate (Social media research)

TRACK BUZZ AND INFLUENCE THE INFLUENCERS

Social media shifts authority and influence from traditional mainstream voices (e.g., institutional chiefs, professionals, pundits, critics, fashion editors, and other tastemakers) to respected online voices, and eventually to people conversing and sharing their opinions with one another. The availability, transparency, and accessibility of knowledge gained online has broken, in Harold Innis's apt phrase, "the monopolies of knowledge" enjoyed and controlled by companies, institutions, governments, and elites. This transfer is not new or unique to social media; it occurs whenever new communications technologies take hold. Innis himself researched these changes in his book *Empire and Communications*, which began by exploring the impacts of moving from stone tablets to adopting papyrus in ancient Egypt and on through millenia to the printing press; each new change in media put one empire in decline and gave rise to a successor (Innis 1972). Today, that successor is the "empire of the customer," whose knowledge, values, and tastes increasingly influence one another, and influence marketing and advertising every day.

Companies know how powerful word of mouth from friends, family, and trusted associates can be. Ninety percent of consumers in over 50 countries claim that these referrals are the most "trusted form of advertising," with review-writing from "virtual strangers" coming in second at 70 percent (Nielsen 2009). Consequently, they're discovering the value of social media listening to pick up the signals about what people are saying, feeling, experiencing, and sharing about their products and services. The movie industry, which typically measures success in weeks, understands this and has been among the earliest adopters of regular social media listening for marketing.

One major studio listens to online conversations as a means of evaluating marketing efforts for all its films in distribution. It then drills down into individual movie performance to determine if it needs to take actions to increase ticket sales.

The movie studio consults customized reports, prepared by its partner, Collective Intellect, that provide granular insights and analyses that are derived from text analytic software (see Chapter 2 for a discussion). Those reports contain lists of topics, themes, and influential authors for a specific film or actor, or for movies in general. If the studio decides it should, it will dig deeper to segment people's interests and concerns and develop communications targeted to them, or it may engage with those individuals and present them with special offers and promotions, like early viewing or tailored content, to boost attendance and sales for specific releases.

The movie studio example is more nuanced than a generic PR-type "influencer" program, where companies reach out to, say, key bloggers in the hope that they will choose to write about them. Social media listening identifies people who are influential in a specific area, understands their viewpoints and sentiments around a particular product or service, and generates insights for developing programs and messaging designed for them. Applying those insights can help companies make the adjustments necessary to their marketing and advertising, and increase their chances for sales success. However, influencer programs require balancing reach and scale, which every company needs to assess for itself.

Listening Level and Type: Advanced (Social research)

SUMMARY

Emotions, connections, and relationships between companies and customers are sales drivers that are growing in importance; traditional differentiators are the price of entry. Social media listening provides companies with the signals needed to craft sales efforts that are grounded in customer understanding. Companies using social media listening have kept sales rolling by developing and implementing customer-centric sales programs; re-creating or reinventing sales tactics, such as sampling and stimulating product trials; and overcoming problems or changing perceptions that stall sales growth.

CHAPTER 10

SENSE CHANGE TO COMPETE
IN THE PRESENT

Institute for the Future forecaster Bob Johansen characterizes today's business environment as a "VUCA" world, one marked by volatility, uncertainty, chaos, and ambiguity. Few, if any, of us would argue this point. According to Johansen, the key to succeeding requires that we [sense] "the future to compete in the present," a theme that runs throughout this book and gives us part of this chapter's title. Businesses that are able to sense and compete can "turn the VUCA world around with a combination of vision, understanding, clarity, and agility" (Johansen 2007).

Listening's near-real-time conversation harvesting and analysis provides companies with exceptional sensing capabilities. Listening is about today and tomorrow, not yesterday and the past. This chapter details the ways in which companies anticipate or quickly detect change among consumers by listening and then responding in ways valued by their customers and prospects. Skillful and adroit execution enables companies to build and grow while staying tuned into a changing, challenging environment.

WINNING PLAYS TO SENSE CHANGE
AND COMPETE IN THE PRESENT

From the cases we reviewed for this chapter, we distilled four winning plays:

- *Listen for the pivotal insight that can serve as a platform for growth over time*. Develop and exploit the insights that are capable of transforming your business. Old Spice Body Wash, for example, reversed share losses and built a new path for itself by reconceptualizing its target from men to the women who buy grooming products for men, and understanding their motivations for doing so (described in the section "Build on Consumer Excitement"). Camping supplier Trek Light started reinventing itself after grasping that customers viewed it not as a one-product company selling great hammocks, but as a lifestyle company from which they wanted to buy a variety of products (read "Expand Business Line"). Similarly, Lion Brand Yarn created a community for deepening relationships and identifying emerging interests. Business-building insights are not merely observations; they are conclusions that fundamentally influence the company's forward momentum (see "Increase Loyalty").

- *Build marketing, advertising, and promotion programs on listening findings.* Let listening supply the details for your efforts. One food brand looking to drive usage by promoting its product as an ingredient listened to learn about the ways consumers used it. The brand picked up on specific types of dishes cooks prepared and leveraged that information for recipe development and sharing, creating Web site content, and blogger outreach. The result was a number of resonant and relevant recipes that cooks wanted to learn about and prepare, and the discovery of new, unexpected uses for products and services. Provo Craft, a manufacturer and global distributor of craft, hobby, and education products, used listening techniques that signaled product uses of which they were completely unaware. It responded by creating line extensions, which prompted the company to meet new needs and realize significant gains in sales (see "Create Line Extensions").

- *Choose between the two Cs: campaign tactic or continuous program.* Companies face a crucial choice: to engage in tactical listening to boost short-term performance, or to adopt strategic listening for longer-term engagement, relationships, and results. Old Spice's wildly successful listening and engagement program appears to serve a tactical purpose, whereas Kraft's "Real Women of Philadelphia," and Lion Brand Yarn—both winners in their own right—appear to be strategic efforts enabling the companies to compete through time and produce growth over time while stimulating near-term sales. Factors such as goals, budgets, resources, and company commitment to listening are a few factors that can influence listening choices.

  Short-term listening may have immediate benefits, but companies run the risk that its impact will merely support traditional campaign-oriented command-and-control marketing tactics—still the comfort zone for most businesses today. If you engage in project-oriented listening, try to achieve some of the benefits of continuous listening, as well. One method that is available to every company is to aggregate and synthesize findings and customer insights across all listening projects. This knowledge sharing and transfer, especially among departments and throughout companies, is not a substitute for an ongoing program tuned to business needs; however, this practical and workable approach can pay dividends.

- *Evaluate the importance of engagement to building your business.* Rigorously analyze the impact that this engagement has on your business. While current hype surrounding social media marketing sings the praises of participation, companies need to determine whether this kind of involvement is valuable to customers—and, in particular, *which* customers or segments. Some customers are content just to use a product, while others may want a full-on immersive experience (as seen in the ESPN example, described later in the chapter). For that reason, it's critical to listen to *all* customers, and implement an engagement strategy that is relevant and consequential to those who truly want to become involved with a specific company, product, or service.

The Old Spice Body Wash example raises a related point: the need to understand the contribution that various elements of the marketing mix make toward achieving business results. Although its social media campaign leveraged listening to generate lots of real-time online interactivity, Old Spice also advertised and promoted heavily at the same time, doubling its television advertising budget and couponing aggressively, which effectively lowered the brand's price. Marketers and advertisers need to answer the question: What is the business value of high levels of interaction with a company or its products in categories where advertising and promotional activities strongly influence sales?

The tactics these organizations use for growing business are proven and forward-looking. Our review uncovered six listening-led tactics:

- Build on consumer excitement.
- Champion new uses.
- Selectively include new product features.
- Create product line extensions.
- Expand business line.
- Create a vibrant community to increase loyalty.

BUILD ON CONSUMER EXCITEMENT

A breakthrough creative advertising and marketing strategy sparked a sensation for Procter & Gamble's Old Spice Body Wash. While the brand's target has traditionally been its male users, P&G's research revealed that women, in fact, buy the bulk of men's toiletries. Pivoting on what was truly an insight—a conclusion that makes a significant difference to the business and becomes a platform for growth—Old Spice and its agency, Wieden + Kennedy, launched a campaign geared toward women's pleasure. The resulting commercial, "The Man Your Man Could Smell Like," became an overnight classic and bona fide social media phenomenon.

P&G truly listened to the findings, in the same spirit embraced by two other cases we reviewed: the Suzuki Hayabusa and Hennessy Cognac, both in Chapter 5. P&G could have gone along with legacy category advertising and appealed to men in various ways; instead, like Suzuki and Hennessy, the company had the guts to reject convention, sense opportunity, and blaze a new path. The key principle: Go where the customers and sales are, not where you think they should be or where they were.

To drive growth of Old Spice, P&G sought to capitalize on the nearly ear-splitting buzz generated by the TV spot and ensuing consumer interest. The plan: Have the "man," former NFL wide receiver Isaiah Mustafa, answer the most interesting comments, questions, and videos from across social networks and YouTube. The agency set up a social media monitoring center to collect, sift through, and select the best candidates for video replies. It engaged with and responded to everyday bloggers and Twitter users, as well as a raft of celebrities, to help increase chatter and newsworthiness. Old Spice produced and uploaded 186 videos, with most of the responses completed within an hour after selection. That near-real time engagement fostered a sense that consumers and Old Spice were in it together, and that it was fun, immediate, and honest—not your typical corporate response.

Social media numbers were staggering: Within a week of airing the response videos, Old Spice generated 34 million views, a billion PR impressions, a multiplying of Twitter followers by 27 times, and Facebook fan interaction rates increasing by 800 percent (Neff 2010; Morrissey 2010). As of September 2010, Old Spice's total video views on YouTube stood at more than 143 million, and the Old Spice channel was second only to *The Twilight Saga* for subscribers in the sponsor's category. In terms of the top line, Old Spice Body Wash sales increased 57 percent after the first commercial, and then another 107 percent overall, in conjunction with the airing of subsequent advertising and the YouTube blitz. Old Spice's market share increased nearly 5 percent in a category that grew about 18 percent overall.

Social media listening was absolutely essential to the success of Old Spice Body Wash's social media campaign, which in turn creatively supported the brand's overall marketing program and helped generate its results. However, as pointed out above in the winning play, "Evaluate the importance of listening and engagement to building your business," make sure that the engagement is meaningful and its contribution related to achieving agreed-upon goals, otherwise it's merely entertainment.

Listening Level: Intermediate (Social media monitoring)

CHAMPION NEW USES

Companies occasionally face the situation where one of their successful, highly regarded products is falling flat or barely keeping pace with market growth. To bump sales, companies may resort to lowering price through coupons and trade deals, or increasing volume through programs such as buy-one/get-one promotions and special package sizes for limited times ("now 15% more!"). These tested and valid tactics benefit companies, and make it easier for their heavier users to buy and consume more. However, promotional activities and their benefits tend to be short term, to help companies meet quarterly or annual targets. Marketers and advertisers seeking long-term growth look instead to new or complementary uses for a particular product, and applications to increase sales and volume from core and less frequent customers over time.

Arm & Hammer may be the prototypical example of one company's ability to find new and different uses for a single product: its baking soda. It changed the image of the product from a baking ingredient measured out by the teaspoon to a multipurpose miracle product used by the box for cleaning, deodorizing, and personal care. Nowadays, Arm & Hammer baking soda is racking up sales in many different categories by itself or licensed to third-party brands for use in their products.

Food and beverage marketers, especially those that make basic items, know how valuable it is to encourage use of their products in recipes. How many people enjoy Campbell's Cream of Mushroom soup from the bowl, versus those who prepare meals with the soup as an ingredient? Recipe development and sharing are vital to the growth of many food products.

If recipes are going to serve up sales, then their content must be contemporary and pertinent to cooks' interests, preferences, tastes, and benefits. No matter how wonderful a product may be in a dish, if the dish isn't suitable (for whatever reason), the recipe won't do its marketing job. This is why some food marketers have turned to social media listening for guidance in finding and promoting recipes. We will take a close look at two that did: Kraft, which listened in their backyard, and an unnamed condiment manufacturer, which listened in the consumer backyard.

LISTENING IN A BRAND'S BACKYARD

Although Kraft's Philadelphia Cream Cheese (Philly), a roughly $700 million brand, perennially enjoyed a top sales rank, it experienced low year-over-year growth. In an attempt to put the brand on a stronger growth path, the company looked to counter the consumer mind-set that limited Philly primarily to topping bagels and making tasty cheesecakes. Kraft opted to popularize new uses and reignite interest by emphasizing Philly's versatility in cooking and baking.

The company started simply, by uploading short instructional videos on activities such as making Alfredo sauce and dips to its Web site—videos that eventually garnered about 250,000 downloads. After seeing such an "overwhelming" level of interest, Kraft created a social network and launched an engaging reality-style promotion—a contest—called "Real Women of Philadelphia," introduced and hosted by Food Network star Paula Deen. To call her video popular would be to completely understate its impact: The Paula Deen feature received over 10 million views. For the contest, home cooks prepared and submitted videos of their best Philly-inflected recipes for a chance to become a regularly featured cook on the Real Women of Philadelphia social network. Returns from the first two months showed that the content strategy was working and leading to sales. Video viewings on both YouTube and the official Web site generated more than 100 million gross campaign impressions, 3,600 uploads, and 550,000 unique visitors. The most valuable result, however, was that Philadelphia Cream Cheese sales increased by 8 percent, a substantial gain in a big money market (York 2010).

Kraft remains committed to growing Philly sales through Real Women of Philadelphia. Phase 2 of the initiative, underway in late 2010, centered on weekly competitions that showcased the Philly brand, and focused on solving specific problems or developing dishes for particular occasions, such as "side dish—time crunch" (Kraft 2010). Kraft listens constantly and pays attention to the conversation threads, recipe submissions, comments, and site search trends in order to sense change and stay on top of consumer mood, tailor features, select contest topics, and optimize content for Real Women of Philadelphia visitors and members. Kraft could have simply run a single, very successful contest by any measure; but by making it a marketing program rather than a promotional stunt, it put Philly in a position to reap long-term gains.

Listening Level: Advanced (Social research and social media monitoring)

LISTENING IN THE CONSUMER'S BACKYARD

Let's turn to another food example: a case where a company is attempting to grow by letting consumers know that its product—a condiment—is a great choice to include in food preparation, as well as to use as a topping. Where Kraft centered its listening and program on a brand-controlled Web site, this case covered a variety of environments, including social networks, forums, blogs, and Twitter. We will focus on the ways social media listening guided the company's social media marketing program, which had a recipe contest as a core element. The condiment company retained full-service vendor 360i for its project (Bird 2010). Their research effort closely follows the principles of effective listening research outlined and discussed in Part I:

1. Conduct a social media audit for the condiment category and brand, to uncover the following information:
   - Where conversations about condiments occur
   - Occasions of usage for the condiment type
   - Common uses in recipes
   - Ratio of branded to unbranded conversations
   - Competitor mentions
2. Analyze the target market (moms 25–54 who cooked frequently) with the aim of drawing digital and social profiles from third-party data that revealed their most frequently visited social channels and engagement preferences.

3. Draw implications for strategy and develop programs for customer engagement, blogger outreach, and recipe syndication.
4. Monitor and measure results.

Listening research enabled the condiment manufacturer to sense where the strategic opportunities lay:

- Recipes factored strongly in conversations, whereas product names were seldom mentioned. This created an opportunity to make the brand's name more central to the conversation, emphasize recipes, and leverage the contest as a launching pad.
- It was vital to narrow down the recipes to the most popular foods discussed. Conversation analysis showed that condiment-as-ingredient uses were frequently mentioned in chicken, salad dressings, seafood, and pasta dishes.
- The brand needed to select where to influence and engage online. Conversations occurred across a range of social media types, but blogs and Facebook accounted for the majority.

Listening insights furnished the basis for the social media marketing program:

- *Create a presence in the most relevant media; be where your customers are.* To do this, the condiment company focused on blogs and Facebook. On Facebook, for example, it created a page for sharing recipes, contest information, and special live chat sessions with the head chef of the company's test kitchen, which focused on the most popular recipes.
- *Engage influencers to multiply the message and stimulate interest.* The company reached out to popular mom bloggers, encouraging them to enter and post about contests. By doing so, they engaged a network that created both long-form recipes, to post on their own sites, and short 140-character recipes to post on Twitter.
- *Reach customers in their communities.* The agency created branded profiles on five different user-generated recipe communities. A branded profile is similar to a personal profile, except that it is a company or product profile that people follow, "friend," or look up. These profiles posted recipes and used optimized search tags and language to increase findability in those communities and in search engines.

Available social media metrics from agency 360i tell us that the listening-led program succeeded in the social realm in the following ways:

- *Referrals increased.* Traffic referrals from Facebook more than doubled during the campaign's run.

- *Awareness and visibility increased.* The company secured hundreds of permanent placements across user-generated recipe sites, appeared in the first results page for numerous relevant recipe searches on those sites, and elicited dozens of positive comments.
- *Influencer programs extended reach and generated favorable messages.* Numerous placements on mom blogs and twitter feeds, all with branded recipes, performed above benchmarks for reach and positive sentiment toward the product.

The social media numbers suggest a favorable impact on sales. Unfortunately, sales results were not available at the time of this writing, but the contribution of listening to the success of the social media strategy is firmly established.

Listening Level: Intermediate (Social media monitoring)

SELECTIVELY ADD PRODUCT FEATURES

Because it's the new "new" thing, many brands want to get some social media action going. However, after creating a fan page, opening a Twitter account, or adding social networking to their Web sites, many soon discover they lack a business-building strategy. They really don't know whether their customers want these features, and, if they do, how they want to use them. Yet there are companies further along the social media adoption curve, like ESPN, that have learned to listen and plan accordingly.

Founded by Bill Rasmussen in 1978, ESPN started out as a single brand on a single cable channel. In the early days of using satellites to distribute cable programming, the industry was far less sophisticated than it is today. In fact, Rasmussen paid for his leased satellite time from RCA with a credit card. Programming was novel, too; ESPN's first televised event was a slow-pitch World Series softball game between the Milwaukee Schlitz's and the Kentucky Bourbons. At launch, ESPN reached about 1 million homes and had ad revenues in the single-digit millions.

Today's picture is considerably sharper. ESPN is a diversified media company that is received in millions of homes in the US and abroad, has an array of brands, and enjoys billions in revenue from advertising and fees (Wikipedia 2009). Apart from its success as a company, sports media is a brutally competitive category, so keeping viewers, building their audience, and improving fan experience are keys to growth and profitability.

ESPN, therefore, regularly scrutinizes its properties for opportunities and improvements. For example, ESPN looked at its online SportsNation brand in an attempt to answer a few basic questions about its future business potential: Would SportsNation fans like it extended to TV? Which community features, such as Twitter, live chats, or polls, did they desire? In which ways would fans want to participate, by doing things like incorporate their own live game experiences? The answers to these questions would guide ESPN's decisions about going to TV, improving the branded experience, and generating new revenue.

ESPN listens to its fans through a private community and panels. For this particular research, it used a mix of listening and asking (survey) methods to develop insights and estimates that eventually shaped the company's decisions. ESPN's Director of Advertising Analytics, Julie Propper, told us that there was interest in the TV show, and that fans enjoyed sharing their voices with ESPN and others. However, further probing sensed a big "but": Fans wanted participation "as a complement to the experts, not as a replacement." Acting on these insights, ESPN green-lighted the TV show *SportsNation*, which now airs on ESPN2, and balances the voices of ESPN talent with those of fans (Propper (2009).

Listening Level: Advanced (Social research)

CREATE LINE EXTENSIONS

Companies looking for growth often consider providing extensions of product lines they already have. Among the very sound reasons for doing so are to: gain more customers, increase product variety, achieve greater marketing efficiency, pay lower promotional costs, and enjoy increased profits. It's no surprise that over 50 percent of all new products introduced are line extensions. It's also no surprise that a number of line extensions fail or drastically underperform. Marketers and advertisers can increase their chances for success in extending product lines by utilizing social media listening; doing so will allow them to see whether consumers have substantial enough interest in the extensions to warrant their launch.

Craft and hobby manufacturer and global distributor Provo Craft provides a telling example. The brand's leading product, Cricut, is a personal electronic paper cutter that slices paper and vinyl into all sorts of shapes and letters for scrapbooking, school projects, card making, and so on. Cricut expands the variety of shapes available by offering cartridges that owners can swap in and out of the machine. Growth comes from sales of Cricut machines and, afterward, the purchase of cartridges. It a "razor and blades" business.

Since innovative cartridge ideas for new crafting purposes are critical to the company's growth, it's essential that Provo Craft tune into the right signals from customers. The brand's product development typically started with consumer interviews, primarily through focus group research. However, like many companies, Provo Craft was intrigued by the social network-based conversations people were having around crafts, and wanted to listen in to take advantage of those discussions. Market Research Director Denise Rolfe explained why the company didn't use the more traditional focus groups: "While focus groups can provide valuable insights, they leave you vulnerable to early information leaks about your products, and don't always represent participants' true opinions" (quoted in Crimson Hexagon 2010).

Provo Craft's listening effort followed along the lines of the listening research prinicples outlined in Part I. It recognized that figuring out *where* to
listen was a crucial first step and major concern. The company's initial thought
was to start listening to the customer conversations taking place in its support
forum; however, it ran into a very typical problem: organizational silos. Provo
Craft's technical team managed the forum and "owned" the data, and refused
to provide it to the marketing and product groups. "It was as if we were unable
to hear valuable conversations that were occurring in our own backyard,"
Rolfe explained. So, instead, the company listened to customers and crafters
on forums, blogs, and social networks.

Provo Craft set out to understand how its marketing approach—infomer-
cials—resonated with customers and prospects. Its analysis confirmed that the
approach, infomercial content, and key messages were appropriate—important information to know, since it demonstrated the tight fit between the company's communications strategy and its customers.

Like most of the discussions people have, social media conversations are not
strictly limited to a specific topic. People conversing about marketing are also
talking about their experiences, innovations they've made or want, new solutions, or problems they'd like solved. For this reason, companies analyzing listening data need to keep their minds wide open, dispose of preconceived
notions, and incorporate the perspectives of different departments or responsibilities. Doing so ensures that the company extracts the sharpest insights from
the data collected (see Chapter 3 for a related discussion on analytic strategy).

By approaching its data openly, Provo Craft sensed that its customers used
Cricut in novel ways that the company had never considered before. Upon
looking more deeply, its analysis identified new applications; Provo Craft
responded by extending its product line with new application-specific cartridges for kitchen, bath, and home decorating, and by updating its messaging
to inform customers about them.

Additionally, Provo Craft's experience with social media listening increased
its confidence in using social media for marketing, advertising, and promotion.
For example, the company launched Gypsy, a handheld cutter tool, through
social-media networks, and ran a 24-hour challenge across Facebook, Twitter,
blogs, and even e-mail to generate awareness and purchase interest (Crimson
Hexagon 2010; Provo Craft 2009).

In a sense, social media listening became a Trojan horse for teaching the
value of social media marketing, and maximizing its value, to Provo Craft.
While many companies display genuine interest in social media marketing and
run pilots or toe-dip, they're often stymied by how to make it a true business
process part of everyday operations. One reason for this is measurement.
Social media metrics are typically activity-based, tracking such behaviors as
time spent, visiting patterns, or posting. They do not usually provide insight
into what people are thinking, doing, or feeling about life, interests, categories,
or individual products or services—which is where social media listening
makes its contributions. Sharing listening data and insights with colleagues

and across business functions can help companies move their social media marketing from the experimental stage to become a sustainable, long-term business contribution. (For more on this idea of gaining adoption, see Manila Austin and Britta C. Ware's essay in Chapter 21, and the vitaminwater case in Chapter 6.)

Listening Level: Intermediate (Social research)

EXPAND BUSINESS LINE

Single-product companies face a conundrum: Be known and respected for one go-to product, or expand outward to capture more sales and build business. Companies with only one product that has many potential uses can also be very successful. Lubricant WD-40 is an excellent example of this. The product line consists of different-sized aerosol spray cans, straws for squirting, and a pen format—just three items. Yet the company promotes more than 2,000 uses for its products, everything from lubricating to removing gum from hair, and stays fresh by actively soliciting new recommendations from its customers, all of which make it a versatile product that just about anyone can use.

Some companies, however, have a single product with just one or a very limited number of uses. Those firms often need to expand their business lines, and to do it in ways that their consumers track with and find valuable. Case in point: Trek Light Hammocks.

In 2010, this small Colorado-based company decided to explore new product categories for its camping supply line, which featured lightweight hammocks and related accessories. To help with the decision, Trek Light wanted to gauge what consumers thought of the brand and what they wanted from the camping industry, so it turned to a crowdsourcing agency called Napkin Labs. Crowdsourcing involves speaking with and garnering information from communities in a series of exercises that eventually generate, rate, and recommend ideas for development. Napkin Labs consulted a community of campers to learn about the camping gear industry in general, and explored specific areas like personal camping experiences and potential unmet needs for equipment.

Lively discussion ensued from these interactions, and led to two critical findings: Trek Light was not merely a "one-trick pony" hammock company so much as a lifestyle company with which people identified. For that reason, the community felt that Trek Light Hammocks should expand its business and introduce new products. Trek Light Hammocks decided to rebrand itself as Trek Light Gear to convey these notions, and reflected these changes on its Web site. As this book went to press, the company was in the final stages of selecting which new product areas it should offer (Richard 2010; Gibson 2010).

Social media listening can effectively "outsource" some of a company's business planning to its customers. This brings customers' voices into the company as partners, and enables them to tell you how you and your products or services can best serve them. Companies should take the listening findings as essential input, but under advisement: The business must evaluate, select, and prioritize requests, and figure out how to respond, market, advertise, and sell profitably. There's a line between reacting to customer requests and applying your resources wisely to chart and then stay on a course of business growth.

Listening Level: Intermediate (Social research)

INCREASE LOYALTY

Knitting and crafting are often social activities wherein people gather to work on a single project or enjoy one another's company while working on individual projects. Established in 1878, Lion Brand Yarn, a venerable manufacturer of yarns and crafting supplies, wanted to attract and connect with passionate needlers and hookers, and, like *Ladies' Home Journal*, sought to bring younger people into the fold (see Chapter 11).

Working with social media listening partner Converseon, Lion Brand identified and mapped key topics, themes, and activities of interest, and located authoritative individuals. Their analysis enabled them to create "an authentic and relevant online voice and identify engagement opportunities" (Young 2009). Lion Brand Yarn acted on these insights to create its podcast series, "Yarncraft" (also available through iTunes and as a CD) and "Lion Brand Notebook," its blog with community and social networking features (see Figure 10.1). To stay authentic, Lion Brand had company employees run the podcasts and site content.

Site-led "knit-alongs" and "crochet-alongs" engage community members in a virtual club. Each of these events focuses on a single project with its own required yarns and materials. These have not only proved to be popular; they also measurably drive sales of project-related items, as correlations show.

By creating a community and introducing topics and activities based on social media listening insights, Lion Brand enjoyed benefits well beyond a few additional yarn and supply sales. Lion Brand's VP of Marketing, Ilana Rabinowitz, advises that listening to those passionate about crafts allowed the company to meet both measurable and soft goals, namely: customer-guided marketing and product development; image management; bringing younger crafters into the fold; employee satisfaction increases; promotion on other blogs and podcasts; and becoming a meaningful part of crafters' lives.

Media patterns, customer impacts, and financial results bear out these points. Lion Brand Yarn was listed as "one of the 2009 Internet Retailer's 'Hot 100 Retail Web sites,' gathering more than 2 million visits a month. Podcast downloads number about 15,000 to 20,000 monthly." Its blogs enjoy readership in the tens of thousands per month, and customers participating with the brand through social media are 83 percent more likely to describe themselves as "very brand loyal." They're advocates and promoters, being several times more likely to recommend the brand to others (Rabinowitz and Young 2009).

Figure 10.1
Lion Brand Yarns created a social media strategy based on insights generated through its social media listening program. Lion Brand Network offers community and social networking features.

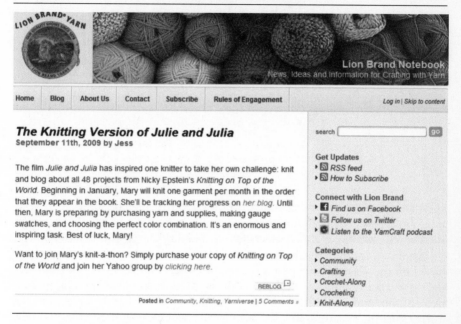

Site traffic generated from social media converts at higher rates than other sources, such as e-mail and banner ads, and average order value is higher. Looking at the month from June 16–July 16, 2009, traffic from Lion Brand's blog to its e-commerce site converted at a rate 41 percent greater than the brand's average traffic, and the order size was roughly 40 percent greater than the average ticket.

Listening Level: Intermediate (Social research)

SUMMARY

Social media listening helps companies grow business by sensing change, and then developing and acting on forward-looking consumer insights. When applied to proven tactics—which include capitalizing on consumer excitement, championing new product uses, creating line extensions, expanding business lines, and creating communities—companies are better able to compete in the present and create advantage.

CHAPTER 11

REBRAND AND REPOSITION PRODUCTS AND SERVICES

Rebranding and repositioning helps companies achieve a number of important goals that directly affect their revenues and profitability. Some of these include enhancing or renewing image, staying relevant to key stakeholders, and expanding the customer base.

Listening enables marketers and advertisers to rebrand or reposition based on the ways people perceive their products and services, the language they use, their emotions, and the conversational contexts that shape those perceptions and feelings. By doing so, they are better able to match and mirror customers' mind-sets, be more easily and clearly understood by customers, and be able to avoid the pitfall of forcing their branding or positionings onto customers. We are in an era of person-centered branding and positioning.

The cases reviewed later in this chapter will show that companies taking direction from the "people's positioning and branding" frequently benefit, and those that do not can produce the opposite scenario, wherein they're able to learn from their failures.

Although this chapter is concerned with the "re" prefix attached to "branding" and "positioning," the winning plays and tactics we present apply equally when developing original go-to-market branding and positioning strategies.

WINNING PLAYS FOR REBRANDING AND REPOSITIONING PRODUCTS AND SERVICES

Businesses use social media listening techniques and analysis to study the language, meanings, and contexts people use when talking about companies, product categories, individual products, or concepts. We identified four winning plays to develop compelling, people-led rebranding and repositioning from our case study analysis:

- *Listen to relevant voices.* Companies that limit whom they listen to risk positioning or branding in too narrow a space, and thereby jeopardize their ability to develop a positioning or branding relevant to all their customers. Publishing giant Meredith's repositioning of the magazine *Ladies' Home Journal* managed to strike this balance by adjusting the interests of older core customers *and* younger prospects. Social media listening enabled the company to research and learn which features were valuable to both groups, and which of the new features would be accepted and highly attractive to the younger group (see "Attract New Customers While Keeping Core Customers," later in the chapter). Had Meredith only listened to one group, the magazine's repositioning might have alienated the other and been less successful. Refer to Chapter 1 for a research-oriented discussion of the principle of selecting the right voices.

- *Listen across a range of contexts.* Always consider context—the frame within which people converse or experience—when evaluating positioning or branding concepts. The meanings people have for branding or positioning ideas will be different as contexts change. A broadband vendor, for example, learned that people have four different meanings for the term, depending on where they are talking about it (see Chapter 16). Don't make assumptions. Contexts we as marketers and advertisers think are most important going in, like health, may not be to customers, who have other more important interests, such as relationships and food, as the example of CPG Co. teaches (discussed later in this chapter). Although it might not seem obvious to do so, companies with highly specialized products or services also should listen *across* contexts, as by doing so they might uncover a related usage or meaning that will serve their branding and positioning.

- *Reflect "people-centered" rebranding and repositioning.* Leverage a penetrating consumer insight that melds with people's core beliefs or mental models. Dove's Campaign for Real Beauty centered on two of these attitudes: that 98 percent of women did not consider themselves to be beautiful, and 80 percent agreed that the media bombarded them with unattainable images of beauty. Dove successfully repositioned the brand as a means to help women resolve these issues, eventually creating an engaging social movement in which listening and social media strategy played vital roles in moving the cause forward. People-centeredness contributes to forging emotional bonds that enhance marketing effectiveness (see "Frame Products in the Context of Important Issues").

- *Do not impose a rebranding or repositioning, listen first.* Jumping into this process by gathering facts first before listening to learn the people's positioning and branding can lead to bad decisions. The Tropicana and CPG Co. cases provide examples of this, but had markedly different outcomes. Both started with a predetermined strategy rooted in third-party research and recommendations from top-notch consul-tants, but the CPG company listened to test the third-party ideas, whereas Tropicana did not. Tropicana's rebranding failed partly be-cause its strategy was set to focus on product purity and health bene-fits. Had Tropicana listened for the people's positioning, it would have learned which of the new positioning ideas might have taken, and which of the old positioning should be retained. In contrast, CPG Co. rejected their consultant's recommended positioning strategy after doing listening research. It found that customers held richer and more varied concepts about the positioning idea and then revised it accordingly. Allow listening data to challenge others' suggestions, re-main open-minded, and be bold.

Our case study research uncovered three tactics that lead to successful rebranding and repositioning:

- Express positioning in "people's words."
- Frame products in light of issues that are important to people.
- Attract new customers while solidifying the core customer base.

EXPRESS POSITIONING IN "PEOPLE'S WORDS"

Word meanings vary, depending on the people speaking them and the situa-tions in which they are spoken. This is especially true for words and concepts with broad meanings, such as "green" or "wellness," that have become widely used. Think for a moment about the various ways that people use these two terms. Community builder Communispace researched "wellness" and told us that it encompasses five contexts; while physical health is important, so are the emotional, mental, financial, and spiritual realms (Communispace 2010). This one word has five different meanings.

When positioning products, services, or companies, marketers and adver-tisers look to differentiate their offerings, and/or themselves, from their com-petition in meaningful ways. However, firms frequently use their own language, instead of their consumers', which results in positioning that does not resonate with people. We interviewed a CPG insights chief who studied the use of the word "sustainability" by listening to company sources and social media. Research uncovered that although the term figured prominently in the corporate setting, it did not come up often in people's conversations. Instead, they gravitated towards different terms entirely like "values" and "ethics" to describe corporate behavior. Context matters.

The importance of understanding words and their contexts is shown in two cases: one by a major CPG marketer, which did, the other by Tropicana Pure Premium Orange Juice, which did not.

Listen in Many Contexts

CPG Co. retained a leading branding agency to create and execute its new positioning. The agency's recommendation built on the company's established heritage; both organizations believed this would help align the firm's many brands under the umbrella positioning of "good for you."

Prior to making an all-out commitment, CPG Co.'s global insights leader suggested exploring the "good for you" concept to find out just how people thought about it in different contexts, such as religion, food, personal lives, even entertainment. This executive knew that exploring multiple areas would both lead to analytic richness and avoid the silo trap.

The firm's listening research focused on answering several central questions, which it tackled by using advanced text analytics and services from its partner, J.D. Power and Associates Web Intelligence (2010). In particular, the firm explored the use of a key term related to the positioning by studying blog posts and message boards over a six-month period. For proprietary reasons, we cannot reveal the exact term so we use instead "awesomeness." The research primarily concentrated on:

- *Context*: In which contexts do consumers currently use the key term "awesomeness"?
- *Meaning*: What does the "awesomeness" concept currently mean to consumers?
- *Segments*: How do different generational segments use and define this key concept term?
- *Brands*: Do other companies use the same positioning concept?

CPG Co. came to learn that people used "awesomeness" in several different contexts, including the following three examples—food, relationships, and health:

- *Relationship context*: People used "awesomeness" most often in relation to religion, the human spirit, bonds among people, kindness and caring, and even to convey sexual appeal and tension.
- *Food context*: People frequently framed "awesomeness" hedonistically, to refer positively to indulgent or traditionally "bad for you" foods, and to express enjoyment and satisfaction.
- *Health context*: Much to the firm's surprise, the concept was used *least* in the healthy, wholesome, "good for you" sense that was originally believed to be the main interpretation of "awesomeness."

Listening research opened the researchers' minds and uncovered uses not previously considered, and that went against the grain. Not only were these unexpected and surprising, they exposed weaknesses in the original concept that, if executed, might have misfired.

Research also found generational differences in "awesomeness," and that no other company appeared to have a viable positioning based on the term. Text analytics inferred generational differences from language patterns used by boomers, Gen X, and Gen Y that, while not exact, provide guidance. Generational contrasts were important to understand; since nearly all households purchase CPG Co.'s iconic brands, it needed to know if segmented positioning messages were necessary.

After evaluating and considering the findings, CPG Co. decided to deep-six the initial agency recommendation and develop an enhanced, more nuanced positioning instead, one that fit the various ways people think about and use "awesomeness," and delivered messaging that resonated with customers. As we went to press, in late 2010, CPG Co. was testing a variety of concepts and communications in a number of markets. Even as we await the outcome, we can already say this is a very good example of how social media listening insights provide alternative viewpoints to the accepted wisdom, which, when carefully considered and boldly acted upon, help companies change direction the right way—closer to their customers.

Listening Level: Advanced (Social research)

Do Not Restrict Context to One Area

CPG Co. was able to align its positioning squarely against its customers by listening to the right social media voices across contexts. As we pointed out, if it had failed to do so, its positioning might have been way off the mark. Tropicana's experience demonstrates how listening to only one context can lead to decisions that backfire in the marketplace.

Number-one-selling Tropicana Pure Premium orange juice sought to revamp its marketing as part of a broader initiative that parent company PepsiCo set out for its big-beverage brands, including Gatorade and Pepsi-Cola. Tropicana's effort involved launching a new ad campaign entitled "Squeeze," in early 2009, and replacing its iconic orange-and-straw image with a glass of juice. Six weeks later, a firestorm of protest erupted online and off, prompting Tropicana to pull the new packaging and return the old (see Figure 11.1). What happened?

Answering this question, Tropicana's president admitted, "We underestimated the deep emotional bond our most loyal customers had with the original packaging. That wasn't something that came out of the research," which used focus groups and design tests (quoted in Elliott 2009).

One reason Tropicana failed to recognize that passion was that its focus was on imposing a revamped marketing strategy, not determining whether customers even wanted it. Listen to how Peter Arnell, renowned brand expert and architect of Tropicana's multifaceted marketing and advertising campaign, described the company's strategy and rebranding in a press release (2009):

Figure 11.1
Rebranded Tropicana (right) led customers to protest the new design, online and offline, which resulted in a quick about-face. The old carton returned six weeks later.

It's time to remind consumers that Tropicana Pure Premium is pure, natural, and squeezed from fresh oranges. In order to reinforce this message, we focused on the health benefits of the juice but showed it in a more emotional way than ever before in this category. We want to remind consumers how it should feel to drink this juice every morning.

Is that what consumers want to be reminded of?

Tropicana and its agency appear to have fallen into the trap that CPG Co. avoided: namely, making assumptions about the context customers consider most important in relation to their product. Recall that CPG Co. learned that the recommended healthy positioning initially turned out to be the least-used context, whereas others, like "relationships," were much more frequent. Being single-minded about the health benefits most likely narrowed and skewed its analysis. Had Tropicana listened more broadly, and engaged customers and loyalists early on, it might well have developed a richer, more nuanced understanding of the contexts that are the most important. This probably would have let the company discern which aspects of the redesign plan resonated and which did not, while gaining valuable guidance on making the brand and its packaging even more relevant.

Ironically, Tropicana's advertising suggested that the company might have been able to do this, after all. One spot showed the relationship between a father and son, suggesting that the company had a bead on the emotional connections in which its juice played a part. However, the new carton did not accommodate that because of the decision to emphasize health.

While unfavorable and critical postlaunch comments helped Tropicana eventually set the brand straight, it came at the cost of some embarrassment—along with the need to spend hard-earned dollars twice on such things as package design, manufacture, and switching/remaking commercials. All of these activities affect reputation, expense, and bottom lines. For Tropicana and other companies experiencing a rebrand failure (recall New Coke, for example) it seems that switching to the old symbolism or formula quiets the storm. However, it also raises the questions: Are the companies, at best, only recapturing their old markets? Or by utilizing social media listening and engaging customers, could they discover new contexts through which to connect and grow their brands?

Listening Level: Intermediate (Social research)

FRAME PRODUCTS IN THE CONTEXT OF ISSUES IMPORTANT TO PEOPLE

Launched in 2004, Dove's Campaign for Real Beauty may be one of the best-known social media listening success stories. It builds on the lessons from the cases we've already reviewed, while also focusing on using a personal and social issue for positioning.

The Dove campaign is rooted in very astute research insights, initially developed through a multinational study that probed the relationship women have with beauty. The study explored their definitions of beauty, levels of satisfaction with beauty, the impact of beauty on self-esteem, as well as mass media and pop culture views on beauty. Two key insights emerged: that only 2 percent of the women considered themselves beautiful; and that 80 percent felt that the media set standards for beauty that "real women" could not achieve. These results helped to establish the campaign's mission: to make more women everywhere feel beautiful, every day, by widening today's stereotypical view of beauty, and inspiring women to take better care of themselves.

Well-known for imagery of women in all their forms, the campaign is tightly issue-focused, dedicated to stimulating discussion and debate and driving women to the Dove Campaign for Real Beauty Web site and Facebook group. Social media features enable them to comment and engage with women like themselves, with Dove's experts, and with brand advocates, while furnishing Dove with a listening post (see Figure 11.2).

What may be a lesser-known fact about the campaign is that it unfolded in stages, driven by new social media listening research. Since the first

Figure 11.2
Dove's Campaign for Real Beauty stimulated discussion about beauty, and
directed women to the brand's Web site. Social media features allow them
to post, comment, and engage with other women—and the brand.

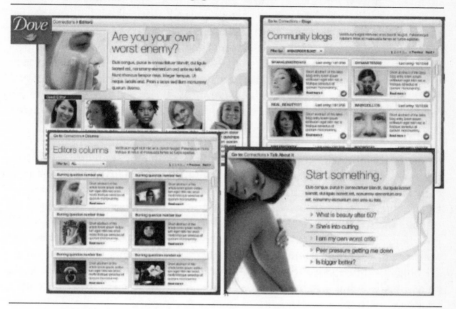

study in 2004, "The Real Truth about Beauty: A Global Report," subsequent research tackled different aspects, to capture a more complete picture (Dove 2004). "Beyond Stereotypes: Rebuilding the Foundation of Beauty Beliefs" (Dove 2006) explored self-esteem in 10 countries; it found that overwhelming majorities of girls and women wanted to change something about themselves, and that two-thirds actually avoided some social situations because of how they felt about themselves. "Beauty Comes of Age" (Dove 2006) looked into beauty and aging among women 50-plus in nine countries, revealing that nearly all believed that society looked less favorably on their appearance—especially their bodies—as they grew older. "Real Girls, Real Pressure: A National Report on the State of Self-Esteem" (Dove 2008) explored self-esteem in girls aged 8 to 17 and discovered that 70 percent felt they "don't measure up" in areas like their looks, schoolwork, or relationships with friends and family.

Today, Dove's evolving campaign focuses on addressing girls' self-esteem. Building off of the latest research, Dove founded the Dove Self-Esteem Fund and added a girls-only self-esteem zone, complete with social media tools, to the site. The forum offers content and experiences revolving around understanding, improving, and promoting positive self-esteem.

The Dove Campaign for Real Beauty is a microsite on Dove.com. While Dove.com has a tab for products, the campaign influences the entire site, with self-esteem-related content featured prominently throughout. True to its mission, Dove puts women with "real beauty" in advice and commercial roles.

From a business standpoint, the campaign and its social media listening-led initiatives not only resonate with and engage women (nearly 3 million have been involved with the Dove Self-Esteem Fund), but translate into brand performance, as well. Data available from 2004 revealed a very attractive impact: Global sales exceeded $1 billion, far surpassing company expectations. Annual 2009 sales, reported on Unilever's corporate Web site, showed Dove was the top cleansing brand worldwide, with sales over €2.5 billion in 80 countries (Unilever 2009).

Dove's campaign provides a potent illustration of a brand igniting and listening to social media conversations that are capable of changing social perceptions. The brand touched and improved the lives of many women and girls in fundamental and dramatic ways. Had Dove simply treated the campaign as a marketing exercise, chances are that it would not have been so successful. By framing the self-esteem issue through research, Dove recognized and respected the uniqueness of all participants: It enabled girls and women to express and share their own ideas, comments, and suggestions to address self-esteem issues. Through listening, Dove took actions that moved the campaign along in ways guided by listening insights. And, as the results show, the company benefitted by indirectly shaping preference and stimulating sales.

Listening Level: Advanced (Social research)

ATTRACT NEW CUSTOMERS WHILE KEEPING CORE CUSTOMERS

Companies with established product franchises eventually face the issue of bringing in new blood to overcome drops or flat lines in their customer base. Media and marketing powerhouse Meredith's renewal of celebrated magazine *Ladies' Home Journal* (*LHJ*) drew heavily upon social media listening to ensure that its repositioning reflected previous and new customer interests.

While ad sales and readership for this classic publication were breaking down, other horses in Meredith's stable—like *Better Homes and Gardens* and *Parents*—were running well. Despite a loyal readership, company research showed that satisfaction drivers among younger readers (for example, relevant content) were declining. Facing an aging-out problem, the company realized that long-term growth would come from bringing younger women into the franchise and, eventually, evolving with them in order to keep them.

Britta C. Ware, Meredith's research head, explained to us that the team had to walk a tightrope between satisfying the magazine's faithful core customers and energizing the editorial content to attract future subscribers. And, of course, as an advertiser-supported publication, they also had to signal the new direction without alienating current advertisers while simultaneously increasing their interest in a revamped *LHJ*. The economic recession was in full swing, and the researchers had from September to December 2008 to finish their work. The new issue had to be on the racks in February 2009. Pressure, anyone?

We discussed in our earlier review of Meredith's MixingBowl.com launch (see Chapter 6) that the company's Research Services group listens to its private community, Real Women Talking, for guidance. Naturally, the researchers wanted to leverage the community for the relaunch; however, they first had to persuade a new editor that Real Women Talking was up to the task. Even when some staff members or departments regularly employ a resource, that resource can often be unfamiliar or unknown to those in other functions. For that reason, getting buy-in from internal customers requires conversation, tact, and proof that it works. In this case, Research Services had to demonstrate that women in the community matched the *LHJ*'s core and intended audiences, and that reams of research conducted to date would be consulted. Fortunately, the mission was accomplished, and the community was brought into play.

As they had done with MixingBowl.com, the editorial team developed a vision for the redesign. They then crystallized this as a minimagazine for community discussion and feedback, in the form of a questionnaire and follow-up live chat facilitated by Real Women Talking operator Communispace. Survey responses indicated that both prospective and current readers felt generally positive toward the new design. The chat aimed to get current readers' views by asking them to expand on points needed to finalize editorial direction and design. Asking eliciting questions like: "How do you feel about the tone of magazine?" "Should there be a bigger focus on parenting?" prompted free-flowing conversation and comments.

The last question proved to be pivotal, and perhaps even internally challenging. The magazine's newly appointed editor had recently moved from running the very successful *Parents* magazine at Meredith. Would she and the redesign team be open to the answers they got for a question, even if the answer was no? As it happened, the women's comments were not really supportive of this topic; they questioned the need for yet another source of parenting advice, especially those who had kids in their teens. However, one woman's request to see more "family" articles changed the conversation. Other women rallied around the thought, expanded it, and gave examples of stories they would like to see, especially those of how other families meet challenges and overcome hardships. Meredith listened and acted on the conversations.

Research head Ware adds that just one round of feedback allowed them "to test the new design and trust they were headed in the right direction—as guided by Real Women Talking (see Figure 11.3). The new magazine should engage younger women and stay sufficiently consistent with the brand to hold onto loyal readers."

Figure 11.3
Ladies' Home Journal revitalized its publication by listening to guidance from
Meredith's private online community, Real Women Talking. It struck the important
balance of attracting new younger readers, while keeping loyal readers satisfied.

As they had with MixingBowl.com, the ad sales teams were able to convey
readers' enthusiasm for the new design and draw upon compelling quotes to
help make their case. Ware relates that initial results "suggest the redesign was
indeed successful; advertisers have described the new look as 'more modern,'
'more relevant,' and 'fresher.' February 2009 reports for the inaugural issue
indicated that revenue was up 25 percent over last year." More specifically,
business is growing in key categories like beauty, and magazine leadership feels
that growth will take off even more intensely when the economy rebounds
(Ware and Austin 2008).

The two Meredith cases—one for launching a new product, the other for
repositioning a classic brand—demonstrate the value that companies can gain
by employing a continuous, consistent, disciplined approach to leveraging listening resources and engaging with their communities.

Before leaving this case, it's important to note that many companies
experience "politics" over listening, as Meredith did. Social media listening is still new; it requires people to leave their comfort zones and base
decisions on unfamiliar methods, data, and findings. My experiences leading listening workshops and strategy sessions at some of the world's best
marketing, advertising, and research companies remind me how difficult
that is, and how important it is to couple listening with a change management initiative.

Listening Level: Advanced (Social research)

SUMMARY

Businesses that successfully rebrand or reposition their company, products, and services do so by listening to the right voices, listening across conversational contexts to understand the range of meanings or preferences people have, reflect a "people's positioning and branding," and avoid imposing a company-centric branding or positioning onto customers. Because data from social media listening is still new and unfamiliar at most companies, organizations may sense risk and be reluctant to make decisions based on listening findings, especially when they challenge conventional wisdom or past experience. For that reason, listeners need to build trust yet be persuasive.

CHAPTER 12

MANAGE REPUTATION

Not so long ago PR firms listened by monitoring mass media sources, like print pieces and broadcast transcripts. Their efforts relied on rudimentary techniques, such as clipping books, human analysis, and basic reports on the volume of coverage, themes, and their sentiments. This all changed when these firms realized that ordinary people were holding conversations online. What had been water-cooler chats, sideline banter at soccer games, and Q and A's with local experts on some product or other moved to social spaces via keyboard presses and Internet connections.

Upon looking into online word of mouth, marketers and agencies recognized that it combined details and opinions about product features, plans, and experiences, and, importantly, the companies themselves. They saw how those conversations could bring Olympian companies to their knees, as famously happened to Dell, or to elevate niche players, like Zappos, to the pantheon.

Social media is more than a place for chitchat; social networks and their communications tools enable people to coordinate pressure tactics aimed to persuade companies to take actions they desire. Moreover, such movements do not need centralized leadership or control as they once did, since information sharing is continuous, handheld, and global. These developments place companies (and many institutions) in unfamiliar and potentially vulnerable positions, due to the intensity and speed with which their products, business practices, and/or executives can appear in opponents' crosshairs, as the Nestlé episode amply demonstrates later in this chapter. Old-school control strategies—like taking down information, or closing access—no longer work and, typically, backfire.

Listening is critical to protecting, repairing and building reputation. The bone-shaking impacts of external events on the corporation as a whole mean that listening insights are relevant and need to be shared throughout. Consequently, the sharp lines dividing PR from other business functions like advertising, marketing, operations, product development, legal counsel, and customer support have blurred. Reputation management has become a shared responsibility throughout organizations.

WINNING PLAYS TO MANAGE REPUTATION

This chapter examines reputation management in the social media era. The case studies we analyzed, from both small and large companies, revealed the following six winning plays:

- *Anticipate issues and concerns.* Help your company gain valuable lead time by adopting "always-on" social media listening tactics. Regularly monitor key sites that customers, prospects, and relevant stakeholders visit frequently to tune into and follow their conversations. Steve Rubel, Edelman Digital's Senior Vice President and Director of Insights, talks about this within the context of awareness. Companies need to develop foresight, to know what is happening around them, and to be aware of what key people are doing, thinking, and feeling about companies, products, and services (Rubel 2010).

  For example, routine surveillance led toy and board game maker Hasbro to discover an Amazon review that referenced the death of a young child attributed to playing with one of the company's popular toys (detailed in the "Discover Product Threats" section later in the chapter). This event prompted Hasbro to undertake a full-fledged social media listening project, the insights from which guided its very disciplined and effective customer-centric response. Commit to a listening program to help your company avoid nasty surprises and lower the risk of significant or lasting reputation damage.

- *Understand the voices in the conversation and evaluate their positions.* Issue positions are seldom only two-sided, pitting customers against companies. They usually involve multiple stakeholders. Apple's "antenna-gate" issue, where the phone was faulted for dropping calls when held a certain way, was a three-way affair that involved Apple, iPhone customers, and the tech/consumer electronics media. Apple realized that consumers and the media held different positions: Customers considered the problem minor, whereas the media thought it major. Apple's response had to and did address and satisfy the opposing concerns of both groups. Keep in mind that stakeholder groups may not be homogeneous in their outlooks; people within them may hold different opinions and viewpoints. Analyze social media conversations to discover and dissect areas of interest, to ensure that all relevant perspectives are addressed.

- *Bring together complementary sources of data to develop a full picture.* Do not rely on social media listening data alone; use triangulation, a method of using a variety of data sources to tell a rich story. See Chapter 3 for a discussion of triangulation. Apple listened to social media conversations and consulted its own records, which included product sales trends, return rates, and call center logs. By examining customer behavior, Apple enhanced its confidence in the conclusion that customers did not find the antenna issue nearly as critical as the media commentators. That insight influenced Apple's communications strategies for customers and the media, as well as its resolution policies (see "Understand Which Voices Are Driving Comments").

- *Engage stakeholders to help enhance or restore reputation, both internally and externally.* Leverage social media listening insights for reputation management strategy, but directly engage with stakeholders to bring about change. Every case we reviewed showcased the different ways companies remedied their situations. One small Web services firm intercepted disgruntled customers to resolve its problems quickly. Food product giant Nestlé changed suppliers for one of its most essential ingredients, in an attempt to satisfy the environmental demands of interest groups, customers, and other interested parties (read "Engage in Social and Environmental Issues"). Electronic game maker EA Sports rebutted a programming error made public through YouTube by submitting its own entertaining and creative video that generated much goodwill among gamers (described in the "Convert Negative Sentiment" section).

- *Involve related business functions or units when engaging and responding.* Hasbro's toy recall didn't involve only the communications disciplines; it also engaged the operations and legal departments. Share listening data across your organization to achieve a common understanding of the issues and insights, and present them in a framework to which colleagues can relate. Prepare engagement plans as far in advance as possible to cope with various potential scenarios of unfolding events and threats. Companies that are caught flat-footed in a crisis, like Nestlé was, can appear tone-deaf and inadvertently fan the flames of discontent. (To Nestlé's credit, the company managed to pull a 180 by moving from good, old-fashioned control-oriented defense to eventually joining the conversation and engaging sincerely with consumers.) In contrast, brands that are able to appraise the situation, bring resources to bear, and deal with troublesome matters in ways customers want—as Hulu did—can strengthen relationships while repairing, and possibly improving, their image (see "Share Listening Insights with Business Partners"). The best plan may be to head off controversy in the first place by taking an early and visible role in important issues.

- *Expand foresight for more sophisticated preparedness.* Most of the examples we cover portray a sudden crisis around a product or service issue with which companies grappled short term. Given the intangible value of reputation, it's in most companies' intermediate and longer-term interests to respond to reputation problems adroitly, confidently, and effectively. Instead of making it up as you go along or doing a hasty search for guidance, institute a set of principles relevant to your company or product. Use social media listening to explore potentially reputation-threatening events, and pay careful attention to social media activity, the different voices, and their tactics. Assess the ways in which companies—perhaps your own—got a handle on the problems, attempted to resolve them, and evaluated their level of success. The next time listening signals tell you trouble is brewing, you will already be ahead of the game, when every second counts.

Companies use a variety of tactics to manage their reputations. Our case study analysis revealed six that we examine through case studies:

- Discover product threats.
- Listen to all relevant voices, not just some.
- Understand which voices are driving discussion.
- Listen to customer dissatisfaction.
- Convert negative sentiment.
- Engage in social and environmental issues.

DISCOVER PRODUCT THREATS

Not too long ago, regulatory agencies and companies themselves announced when product issues affected consumer safety. But social media has changed this, along with so many other things. Today's online conversations include product reviews and forums that enable customers and prospects to review, rate, discuss, and alert readers to benefits and problems alike. In fact, ratings and reviews are a big business in and of themselves, with vendors such as BazaarVoice (www.bazaarvoice.com) providing turnkey solutions that post reviews and comments on product or retailer Web sites. They also extend the reviews' reach by syndicating them across different sites, thereby allowing people to easily locate them through Web searches. These developments have enabled product news and reviews to spread nearly instantaneously, making social media listening a priority for those companies committed to managing their reputations. Organizations that remain proactive through regular social media listening improve their chances of dealing effectively with good and bad news. Hasbro's case demonstrates this point.

During the 2006 holiday selling season, a Hasbro employee performing a routine check of Amazon product reviews discovered a comment no manufacturer wants to read. A toddler had died playing with one of Hasbro's products, a toy bench and workshop complete with tools, screws, and nails. The toy maker immediately contacted the Consumer Product Safety Commission, which found upon investigation that the nails were only suitable for children three years or older, and found that the product labeling was correct. "The toy without the nails does not present a hazard," Consumer Product Safety Commission spokeswoman Julie Vallese told the *Washington Post*: "Parents don't have to take the entire toy away; they just have to remove the nails."

Hasbro voluntarily recalled the product and offered a gift certificate to product owners in exchange for nails they returned (quoted in Shin 2006).

Parents' concerns and anxieties can reach fever pitch when their children's safety is at risk, and especially when putting lots of thought into the perfect holiday present. News of product recalls tends to generate widespread media coverage, giving consumers a great deal to say on blogs, message boards, and review sites. The choice to manage its response required that Hasbro do a lot more than check a review site. The company had to monitor and analyze substantial numbers of posts and comments. To do so, it worked with full-service social media listening vendor TNS Cymfony to identify and track themes, analyze consumer reaction, evaluate Hasbro's response, and monitor the progress of the crisis. Hasbro learned that the major conversation drivers centered on safety and foreign production of toys, and that specific concerns were directed toward two specific brands, but not the Hasbro brand overall. These insights shaped Hasbro's communications and response, and ensured that it directly addressed customer concerns.

The responsibility of managing recalls is spread out across different departments. Products need to be taken off store shelves; customer service has to ramp up; legal strategy must be developed; and government relations need to be opened. Hasbro involved consumer insights, senior management, marketing, PR, and operations to share the social media listening results and evaluate how best to act on them from their functional perspectives.

The results were positive. Post volume dropped by 75 percent after the first week, signifying that the communications and response were calming the situation. The way that Hasbro handled this crisis earned 42 percent more positive mentions than negative ones, and the company "was able to address specific product issues and concerns in a timely manner and maintain consumer confidence." One consumer statement summed it up pretty well: "I have bought in confidence this year in light of the recalls. I think it's unfortunate [that] they happened, but I have to say that my confidence has not been compromised. They were extremely proactive in getting toys off the shelves" (TNS Cymfony 2009). Social media listening enabled Hasbro to address specific consumer concerns in close to real time; its insights contributed to an authoritative response and headed off damage to its image.

Listening Level: Intermediate (Social media monitoring)

LISTEN TO ALL RELEVANT SOCIAL MEDIA SOURCES, NOT JUST SOME

Listening to appropriate sources for social media listening lets companies hear the "right" voices, as well as the full spectrum of conversation topics. This is essential to achieving constructive data, and directly influences the quality and utility of listening insights derived from data analysis. Assembling a family of relevant social media sources assures completeness; in contrast, failing to include important sources risks missing important discussions, skews investigations, and results in misleading insights, since source data is incomplete. (See Chapter 1 for a discussion on voices.) An experience American Airlines (AA) had with a service interruption teaches us about the problems of relying on limited sources.

There are certainly legitimate reasons for airlines canceling and rescheduling flights, such as poor weather conditions. Travelers deal with these from time to time, and while they aren't happy about it, the sting is somewhat relieved by knowing the cause is a just one. It's an entirely different matter when airlines cancel flights and disrupt travel for reasons completely *within* their control. Such an event occurred with American when the airline halted all its MD80 flights over four days in 2008 because it had neglected to comply with an engineering compliance/change order on wire bundles, as ordered by the Federal Aviation Administration (FAA). According to a representative, the airline "used every communication channel available to stay in contact with people and let them know what was going on." After monitoring comments, AA "felt that the information was generally correct and balanced enough to where we didn't have to get involved in the conversation. Some of the comments were tough to take, and on some blogs people were actually defending us."

Customers, however, were furious, not only at the delays, but at the company and its executives. Comments responding to the news on popular blog PlaneBuzz asked: "OK, so would it be tacky to bring up the issue of executive bonuses right now?" Another: "Why would you think the CEO would have any morals or ethics?"

Blog analytics company Hitwise revealed that Web site complaints about the airline went up 25 percent over the same time a year earlier. Instead of having a response mechanism in place to address customers in a timely manner, AA instructed travelers to e-mail their opinions, which resulted in a 13 percent spike. But the next stat was eyepopping: About 75 percent went to social networking site MySpace to vent their frustrations (Qualman 2009).

This case sharply outlines the perils of limiting the social media sources to which a company listens. American Airlines fell short in a number of key ways:

- First, it was not thorough. Although AA claimed to use "all communication channels," its online monitoring appeared to be limited to the blogosphere, as there were no mentions of any other social media.
- Second, AA failed to scrutinize social networks. People use social media for different purposes: Blogging and social networking are not equivalent, and it's a mistake to assume that they are. Consequently, AA could not get to the specifics of comments expressing anger, frustration, or support about delays or the airline. It certainly would have been instructive to learn what travelers thought about AA's maintenance practices, and their perceptions on booking future trips. Such insights could rebuild trust and confidence.

- Third, AA missed valuable opportunities to engage with its customers. By failing to join the conversation, the company wasn't able to support defenders. It also missed the chance to confirm, deny, or help affected travelers with issues, which allowed the back-and-forth to continue, with no apparent end to the storm—other than time and the unknown, likely detrimental impacts on the brand.

Listening Level: Intermediate (Social media monitoring)

UNDERSTAND WHICH VOICES ARE DRIVING COMMENTS

Should, as the saying goes, "the squeaky wheel get the grease?" In other words, should marketers and advertisers pay the most attention to the loudest voices?

Social media is rife with voices clamoring for attention, essentially shouting, "Listen to me! I have something to say." It's important to know which voices to heed, and understand what they are saying. At times, these voices can be at odds with one another, which presents companies with the problem of evaluating them, judging their merits, and deciding on a course of action. Apple iPhone 4's "antenna-gate" is one example.

Encouraged largely by unrelenting conventional and social media attention to what was perceived as a major product misstep—a faulty antenna implementation on its newly launched iPhone 4 that caused dropped calls if held a certain way—Apple was hammered by authoritative voices for its slow and poorly executed progression of responses to resolve it. The company initially blamed users for holding the phone incorrectly; it then claimed that a software glitch caused the problem and promised a patch to fix it. However, Apple's deeper investigation revealed that there was some truth to the holding issue—primarily affecting people who held the phone in their left hand—but the software problem related to another matter. Apple CEO Steve Jobs eventually held a press conference announcing a solution: free phone cases to remedy the holding/dropped call problem. Jobs also detailed factual data that helped put the matter in perspective, and made it clear that the problem was not Apple's alone; other carriers experienced similar problems, which they documented on their Web site.

Jobs also made a significant point based on insights gleaned from social media listening, which were then triangulated with Apple's own records (see Chapter 3 for a discussion of triangulation). Customers, Apple found, were not nearly as lathered up about the issue as the journalists, pundits, and gurus. Jobs documented that logged calls into AppleCare for the antenna problem amounted to only about one-half of 1 percent of all calls for the iPhone 4; sales kept exploding, and the product return rate was under 2 percent, well below the 6 percent of the previous iPhone model.

In short, his conference worked: Google search levels, which serve as a proxy for interest, spiked on the day of the press conference, and then quickly tapered off to lower levels as people considered and apparently approved of Apple's response (Rappaport 2010).

Apple's appraisal of these voices and their different positions toward the iPhone validated the company's approach to resolving the issue. The brand maintained positive views among customers by fixing the problem for the small number of people experiencing it, and shifting the negative sentiment expressed by the authorities to neutral or better by countering with the facts. Apple successfully balanced expectations or demands for immediate and expensive remedies, such as a wholesale product recall, with getting the facts out and establishing a basis for their actions (Cooper 2010; German and Ogg 2010; Winterfeld 2010; Google Insights for Search 2010).

Listening Level: Intermediate (Social media monitoring)

LISTEN TO CUSTOMER DISSATISFACTION

Customer dissatisfaction can potentially lead to customer loss and impaired ability to attract new purchasers. Companies must understand the reasons underlying dissatisfaction to develop insights for reversing the sentiment and help keep them on a growth path. The two companies we discuss next experienced high levels of dissatisfaction: The first was caused by a failure to tune into customers; the second was caused by a service change. We'll look at the social media listening-inspired strategies they employed to turn their situations around.

Tune into Customers

"My Dell Hell," the classic case of a prominent blogger who lambasted Dell's customer service, opened the industry's eyes to the importance of blogger relations and engaging with customers. Dell famously responded with DirectToDell and Dell Ideastorm, the latter driven by none other than Michael Dell himself, remaking the company inside to match its world outside.

Portland-based Internet marketer and software solutions provider NetBiz encountered a similar situation to Dell's. Despite the fact that some of its 12,000 small business clients were loudly complaining on blogs, Twitter, LinkedIn, and other social networks, the company didn't know it, because it wasn't listening to social media. After NetBiz finally caught on, the provider realized that although there was truth to some of the comments, plenty of them were inaccurate or distorted. Taking a page from Dell's playbook, NetBiz decided to turn the situation around and smash its "wall of silence" by social media listening, engaging, and providing service in new ways. Its actions can serve to instruct companies of all sizes.

Starting with social media listening, NetBiz used a combination of free tools, like Google Alerts, and low-cost services, and created a presence on key social media sites to pick up the conversation. Now, when company listeners encounter dissatisfied customers, they escalate to direct engagements by approaching individuals to understand the reasons they're unhappy. They then work jointly toward finding solutions. Developing relationships with prominent small business and search bloggers allows NetBiz to tap into their expertise and guidance. Together, all of these activities help the company develop deeper insights into customers and prospects.

Also seeking to become more transparent, NetBiz started a blog that showcased customer successes, a very active Q&A section concerning all matters related to Internet and small business marketing, and stories about its charitable and community-based activities (see Figure 12.1).

The company created a branded community on Facebook to have another social media listening post, to educate, engage, and develop new insights. NetBiz shows companies that are in the process of determining how to implement social media listening with modest budgets and goals that it can indeed be done—and done well.

Listening Level: Fundamental (Social media monitoring)

Figure 12.1
NetBiz listened to customer complaints and responded
with a program modeled on Dell's.

SHARE LISTENING INSIGHTS WITH BUSINESS PARTNERS

Online video streaming Web site Hulu licenses selected content from hundreds of sources, such as TV networks, movie studios, cable properties, and Web sites. The TV networks dictate which programs Hulu can stream; for example, in 2009, when FX asked Hulu to remove episodes of the popular series *It's Always Sunny in Philadelphia* from the site immediately, Hulu complied. A short time later, Hulu users expressed their outrage across social media, airing frustration at the lack of warning and explanation for the removal of the series. Gathering and analyzing the content and sentiments in Twitter updates, complaint e-mails, and blog posts regarding the issue, Hulu CEO Jason Kilar consulted with FX to craft an acceptable solution. Together they agreed that episodes could run for two weeks, and then be removed. Kilar then conveyed the news in a letter, along with an apology to users for the poor way in which his company handled the show's removal. This quick, smart response stopped the snowballing negative sentiment toward Hulu in its tracks. Numerous blogs republished Kilar's letter, which was received warmly by Hulu-ians for the company's honesty in admitting fault and for giving users another chance to watch the show (Kilar 2009; Saleem 2009).

Listening Level: Fundamental (Social media monitoring)

CONVERT NEGATIVE SENTIMENT

Customers will take companies to task over small and large problems alike if they affect enjoyment or detract from the product experience. The "holy grail" turns the words of naysayers, complainers, or smart-alecks around to create positive results that engage a community. EA Sports' example shows us how this was done with humor and style.

Can Tiger Woods really walk on water? One fan of Electronic Arts' popular Tiger Woods PGA Tour 08 game, Levinator25, thought otherwise. He even went so far as posting a video on YouTube calling out a glitch in the game: Tiger striding across a water hazard and hitting his ball seemingly from a perfect lie.

EA Sports, the game's maker, regularly monitors its discussion boards and noticed references to the video. Companies facing this kind of publicity might expect an uproar from their core audiences, especially when they are so passionate. Comments on the Tiger Woods forum show just how deep they run; every feature is scrutinized, analyzed, and commented upon. Here's an example:

> In regards to this flagstick hitting issue, am I the only one who thinks the sound of the impact needs work? Really, it sounds more like hitting a mud wall than a metal or fiberglass flagstick. Minor point, but again it would lend it more towards the "sim factor."

One reply: "It just happened to me on the first hole at Wolfcreek—from maybe 3 inches up the pole right into the sand trap 15 yards away—very unrealistic if you hit it almost at bottom level.

Let's remind ourselves: They're talking about a *video* game.

A company that's been in business for many years, it's safe to say EA Sports understands its audience, due to the social media listening it has done in its "brand backyard," from sources like user forums, and "consumer backyard" sources, where gamers congregate (see Chapter 1 for more detail on backyards). EA also gleaned from game designers that players love "Easter eggs" and other hidden features and surprises they can uncover.

Rather than responding conventionally, EA Sports—as the old software saying goes—"treated the bug as a feature." The brand publicly responded a short while later to Levinator25 and its community with a YouTube video featuring the "glitch," followed by the real Tiger Woods making the shot.

Rather than describe the video, you can view it on YouTube; just type this link into your browser: www.bitly.com/eavideo_woods.

Gamers really appreciated EA Sports' effort. The brand not only countered the "glitch" comment; it generated enviable levels of engagement that strengthened connections between players and the game. In September 2010, YouTube viewing stats showed Levinator25's video getting a tad over 1 million views; EA Sports reply video, over 5 million YouTube views—and viewers commented and rated the video at higher rates. EA Sports built upon the buzz around the video response for marketing the game's 2009 edition (YouTube 2010).

Listening Level: Fundamental (Social media monitoring)

Figure 12.2
Responding to a negative video criticism of its popular Tiger Woods game, EA Sports created its own YouTube video, which not only defused the point, but was warmly embraced by its community.

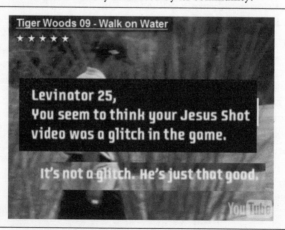

ENGAGE IN SOCIAL AND ENVIRONMENTAL ISSUES

People look for companies to address social and environmental concerns that arise from their own, or from their industry, profession, or business. This has been true since the publication of Rachel Carson's landmark book *Silent Spring* in 1962, which documented the effects of the widespread use of synthetic pesticide DDT. Global warming, habitat destruction, and sustainability are just three hot topics many companies face today. Worldwide sensitivities to these and other issues continue to increase, spurred by globalization and companies scouring the world for supplies and finding ways to produce or secure them. How companies manage and communicate such issues has a considerable effect on the marketplace: Customers and prospects use them to assess company reputations and their purchase decisions, while regulators and interest groups may launch investigations, demand accountability, or give praise.

Managing reputation requires companies to act and engage in social and environmental issues, not just listen passively to social media conversations about them. Companies can be reactive or proactive. We'll examine two cases: a reactive one featuring Nestlé, and a proactive one launched by P&G in 2010.

Embrace Engagement

Nestlé's case differs from most others discussed earlier because the food manufacturer was targeted by special-interest group Greenpeace for its environmental practices. In March 2010, Nestlé came under fire for buying some of its palm oil supply—a key ingredient in its popular Kit Kat bar—from a firm that had been accused of repeatedly destroying Indonesia's rainforest to plant palm trees. In an act to protect Indonesia's rainforest and endangered orangutans and other rare animals, Greenpeace unleashed a global social media protest that spawned from a video that went viral. The video depicted an office worker biting in to a "Killer" bar, packaged identically to Nestlé's Kit Kat, and finding an orangutan's finger. The gruesome and bloody video satire sparked massive consumer outrage about Nestlé's palm oil sourcing in thousands of postings, tweets, and uploads to blogs, Facebook, Twitter, and YouTube.

Nestlé listened to the online protest, but was unsure of how to conduct an appropriate social media response. Initial attempts to neutralize the complaints were naïve and defensive because the company did not understand the value of engagement and conversation at that time. Nestlé's traditional command-and-control communication tactics and censorship enraged people. The company had the Greenpeace video removed from YouTube, citing copyright infringement. This backfired by prompting even more curiosity about the video and increasing anti-Nestlé sentiment. Nestlé's Facebook page filled with criticism, to which it responded by furiously hitting "delete" on all negative comments concerning the palm oil debate. Its online reputation took a hit, with people describing the situation using words like "disaster," "nightmare," "meltdown," and the cleverly wordsmithed "kitkatastrophe" (Hickman 2010; Infegy.com 2010; Greenpeace.org 2010).

Nestlé started learning how to display more open-minded behavior and begin addressing the problems head-on. The company apologized on its Facebook page and opened itself up to discussing the issues and stating its case: It explained that it had already ceased operations with the criticized palm oil firm, and noted it only ever purchased 1.25 percent of its supply from them.

Not long after the release of the Greenpeace video, Nestlé announced a "zero deforestation" policy, and partnered with the Forest Trust to monitor its conduct. Greenpeace extolled Nestlé's policy adoption and commitment to sustainable palm oil production as an important victory.

Nestlé's case highlights a few additional points worth discussing. First, Greenpeace gave a lot of credit to people around the world for participating through social media and taking their own initiatives. In the organization's words, "People are awesome!" Greenpeace viewed its role as offering guidelines for citizen action but not masterminding or scripting every move; it trusted that people would use measured judgment, coordinate among themselves via social tools, and do good things. Second, the campaign started and ended in just 10 weeks. That's less than one business quarter, and a time frame within which few executives have experience for making big market-influencing changes. For contrast, another earlier successful Greenpeace campaign for infant formula took 10 years. Last, several of the tactics Greenpeace used overwhelmed Nestlé to such an extent that the company did not have adequate response plans. For example, Greenpeace encouraged people to friend Nestlé's Facebook site, switch their avatar pictures to the "Killer" logo, and negatively comment on palm oil. More than 20,000 did (Social Media Club of Sydney 2010). We can expect that high-pressure global social media campaigns will become more prevalent as greater numbers of people join social networks.

Listening Level: Intermediate (Social media monitoring)

Align the Company

Companies like Procter & Gamble have proactively made large-scale commitments to social issues. P&G's global focus on sustainability, for example, intends to position the company as out in front of the issue, shape positive images, win new customers, and avoid reputation-harming protests and citizen actions. Here's how CEO Bob McDonald explains it:

> Consumers are more skeptical today and more cynical than ever before, and want to know what they're buying into. When we do the right thing, consumers give us the benefit of the doubt and help us win at the first moment of truth, when they're

in front of a shelf, or in front of the Internet, buying a product. I think when you do the right thing, *with social networks the way they are today*, the business just takes off (quoted in WARC 2010, emphasis added).

However, sustainability entails more than a single company deciding on good innovation, production, and marketing practices, which are then communicated to consumers. That is outdated paternalistic strategy. Sustainability requires an evolving dialog and adaptation in which companies, consumers, scientists, and governments collaborate over time. It also means continuously gathering and interpreting early signals through worldwide social media listening, in order to understand the conversations, what's working, what's not, where new interests lie, and adjusting accordingly.

SUMMARY

Managing reputation in the social media era presents companies with unfamiliar challenges and vulnerabilities. We must recognize that companies are no longer separate from customers, but rather part of their conversations— a trend that can quickly turn positive or negative, and impact marketplace performance accordingly. Brands need to anticipate those turns in order to confidently and effectively plan, engage, and respond. Social media listening provides companies with insight from marketplace signals for doing so.

CHAPTER 13

COMPETE STRATEGICALLY

Sizing up your company's own products or services alongside your competitor's offerings is fundamental to developing a competitive strategy. Social media listening provides businesses with ways to make comparisons. Analyzing online conversations uncovers specifics like the level of interest people express in particular products, their features and benefits; the emotions, likes and dislikes they convey; and how they position them in their minds. Experienced strategists will recognize that these types of data resemble those in a standard SWOT analysis, used for discovering and evaluating company or product strengths, weaknesses, opportunities, and threats.

WINNING PLAYS TO COMPETE STRATEGICALLY

The following five winning plays for competing strategically emerged from our review of these case studies:

- *Use social media listening to find areas of competitive opportunity.* Determine where competing will make a difference in performance. In an era of parity products, choosing the basis upon which to compete is critical. Products perceived as essentially similar have a difficult time battling based on features or performance. Advantage often needs to come from elsewhere, such as meeting needs better or some other aspect of the marketing mix. For example, Kraft, whose Tassimo pod coffeemaker is considered on par with market leader Keurig, looked into search trends to gauge interest in its product. Kraft unexpectedly discovered that interest in Tassimo was geographical, concentrated on the East Coast, especially in the Northeast. Marketers at the company realized that they could generate new sales by adopting a listening-inspired strategy to improve distribution and retail marketing in those areas, thereby making it easier for potential customers to find and purchase the product (see "Identify Competitive Strengths" later in the chapter).

- *Understand the "people's positioning"* for your product or service. Derive the people's positioning of your product or service from social media listening, and compare it to your product's "official" positioning through a map-and-gap analysis. Mappings between the two indicate that positioning is resonating, whereas gaps reveal areas of disconnect. Evaluate any disparities for opportunities to correct misperceptions or adjust positioning, and to ensure that products remain in tune with customers and prospects. For example, if your product positioning stresses functional superiority, but customers view your product as providing a specific emotional benefit, eliminating that discrepancy helps the product map its perception. Marketers and advertisers who align their strategies with customer positioning are more likely to be successful (Ries and Trout 1981).

- *Continually evaluate position in relation to business events, and adjust as necessary.* Because competition occurs constantly, the people's positioning of products and services can change at any time, thereby affecting the competitive viability of your offerings. Social media listening offers marketers and advertisers the extraordinary capability to stress testing positioning in near-real time, to gauge its effectiveness. Here's how to do it: First, listen continuously for the people's positioning. Second, track how this positioning changes over time in response to the stress from competitive or marketplace events, such as new product introductions, recalls, or environmental damage. Last, consider whether you need to make listening-inspired adjustments to resync the product with the people's positioning. The Tylenol and Kindle cases, described in this chapter, are examples of two products that experienced bone-rattling events and effectively responded by using social media listening insights.

- *Leverage social media listening insights and include multiple viewpoints in competitive response.* Incorporate social media insights into competitive strategies. For instance, social media listening enabled one household products manufacturer to evaluate the threat posed by a new competitor from the customer's perspective, and then take action that proved effective for the company's product. In contrast, Scrabble licensees shut down a wildly popular derivative game played on Facebook that it viewed as an infringing competitor. Although the game maker came out with its own replacement, it alienated a passionate fan base and failed to generate much interest, as many people lost interest and just stopped playing (see "Handle Changes to the Core Brand").

When planning a competitive response, be open to findings that challenge the corporate mental model and make sure to draw upon multiple viewpoints. In Scrabble's case, legal considerations appeared to trump player concerns revealed through social media listening; apparently, they were strong enough to beat back any challenge to their mind-set and strategic choices. Had the Scrabble licensees abandoned their "command and control" company-first approach and offered solutions that engaged fans, everyone involved might have enjoyed more successful outcomes.

- *Consider making a commitment to performing retrospective analyses using historical social media listening data to develop your own competitive playbook.* Go back in time and immediately run through the steps just outlined. What events did your company or product experience? How did customers respond? What actions did you take? How effective were they? What did competitors do for their own products, and against yours? Answering questions like these can help compile an invaluable reference that equips your company to handle events and unfolding circumstances more confidently. Coupled with the foresight that social media listening signals provide, your company should be better prepared to anticipate change and compete more effectively. See the discussion of backcasting on p. 6.

We identified five tactics companies used that contributed to their competitive strategy:

- Identify leverageable competitive strengths.
- Understand product positioning in customer terms.
- Keep company and customer product positioning in alignment.
- Interpret competitor risk from the customer's perspective.
- Handle challenges to the core brand.

IDENTIFY LEVERAGEABLE COMPETITIVE STRENGTHS

Marketers pit products and services against one another on several dimensions, such as price, superiority, image, or meeting customer needs. Figuring out which of these areas matter most to customers and prospects is both an essential marketing function and a critical challenge. This becomes especially important when prospects perceive competing products as nearly identical or equivalent. Marketers need to know which levers they can push that will improve sales for their brands. Social media listening helps identify those levers, as the Kraft Foods example shows.

Kraft Foods' Tassimo (single-serving pod coffeemaker) shares the podium with category leader Keurig. Seeking to increase sales and share, Kraft turned to a mix of free and paid tools to discover where a competitive opportunity might lie (Cotignola 2010). The brand's investigation unfolded quite clearly, and answered these questions:

- What are the relative conversation volumes for Tassimo and Keurig?
- What do people like and dislike about each brand?
- What are the behaviors and emotions people express about each brand?
- How interested are people in each brand right now?

If you look at these questions again, you'll probably realize that they are in line with our earlier discussion of analytic strategy (Chapter 3), and that they are some of the most familiar and standardized market research questions asked when analyzing situations and looking for relative strengths and weaknesses. Companies that use social media listening do not need to ask different questions or frame them differently; the only variation lies in the methods and data used to answer them (see Part I for more discussion about research methods).

Kraft used three tools from its box to answer the questions: no-cost Google Insights for Search (an analytic tool for search queries), Twitter Venn (a tool that analyzes the co-occurrence of terms used in tweets), and ConsumerBase, a social media analysis tool from NetBase. (See the entries for Google Insights and NetBase in the Appendix for product details.)

Using these tools, the company's research:

- Searched for terms "Keurig" and "Tassimo" in NetBase's database of social media conversations, and plotted the trends over one year. They found that while people talked actively about both brands, Keurig conversation levels were double those of Tassimo. Finding: Clearly, share of voice reflected Keurig's leadership position. (Note: See Chapter 17 for a full discussion about share of voice and market share.)
- Looked into "likes" and "dislikes" as reported by NetBase and represented in "word clouds." They discovered that customers liked both brands a lot, as the ratio of dislikes to likes was less than 5 percent. They also found that the features and benefits people liked or disliked for each brand were nearly identical; they saw the convenience and brew quality as positive elements, and considered broken machines or overly expensive prices as drawbacks. Finding: Both brands were well-liked and perceived as parity products.
- Examined behavior and emotions through NetBase reports. They observed that positive behaviors like buying, wanting, or purchasing outweighed negative behaviors such as not using or not wanting. Emotions that supported the behavior clustered around love, like, and need. Finding: People were interested in purchasing Tassimo, and held favorable views. Tassimo was competitive.
- Estimated consumer interest in each brand by running queries and interpreting reports from Twitter Venn and Google Insights for Search. (Twitter Venn analyzes Twitter topics to determine how often they occur individually and how often they overlap, as in a conventional Venn diagram.) After looking at a period of roughly seven years, results showed that search trends exhibited strong seasonal preference for both brands, which peaked in the winter holiday season. Keurig's marketing appeared to be more effective in stimulating search; its search volumes climbed year after year while Tassimo's remained constant. Looking at Twitter updates to learn how often people talked about the brands recently,

Figure 13.1
Tassimo discovered that product interest centered on the East Coast.

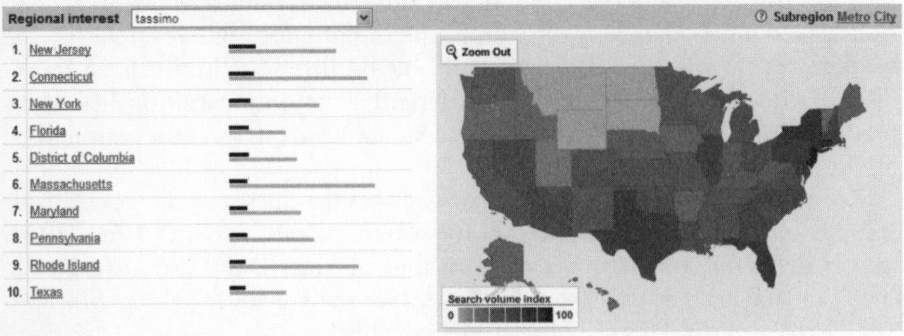

Source: Google Insights for Search, September 30, 2010. Used with permission.

Keurig conversations occurred seven times as often. People tweeted about one brand or another, but not both.

Google Insights for Search provides some very valuable ways to slice and dice its search data beyond simple search trend. For retailers, "regional interest" (a breakdown of search volume by states) sheds light on the geography of demand. Here, Kraft discovered something previously unknown: Interest in Tassimo was concentrated on the East Coast, with the top 10 states in the Middle Atlantic and New England regions (see Figure 13.1). Finding: Although Keurig had more consumer interest and word of mouth, people considered the brands separately, and geography played an important role in Tassimo's appeal.

This chain of analysis showed Kraft that Tassimo was well regarded among potential consumers who were open to purchasing it. While Keurig currently dominated, its product did not hold any outright advantages. For that reason, Kraft reasoned that it could derive competitive advantage from leveraging the geography finding—the key insight—and recommended that Tassimo marketing initiatives hit hard in East Coast markets.

Listening Level: Intermediate (Social media monitoring)

UNDERSTAND PRODUCT POSITIONING IN CUSTOMER TERMS

Products fight it out in the marketplace by adopting and supporting positions believed to give them competitive advantage. Product positioning refers to "consumers' perceptions of a product's attributes, uses, quality, and advantages and disadvantages relative to competing brands" (Boone and Kurtz 2006). Product positionings are mental models designed to help customers and prospects understand what they are about, what they do, what benefits they provide, and why they should be preferred and purchased. Positioning influences essential marketing decisions, such as communications, packaging, pricing, or sales channel programs.

Marketers and advertisers access an arsenal of research tools for positioning. Several frequently used techniques include perceptual mapping, trade-off analysis (technically known as "conjoint"), focus groups, and surveys. Social media listening offers an alternative approach by revealing how people in target markets position a product, rather than the way a product wants to position itself.

Text analytics company Crimson Hexagon explored the way people talked about two analgesics, Advil and Tylenol, on blogs, forums, and publicly available Facebook and MySpace pages over a five-month period (Crimson Hexagon 2009). Utilizing its software's automated capability to identify conversation themes, Crimson Hexagon discovered that people talked about each product differently: Advil for pain, and Tylenol for safety and children (see Figure 13.2 for details on the conversation themes).

This research uncovered that people hold nuanced understandings of these products. Most seemed to recognize that each one's active ingredient carries some risk, but only Tylenol sparked conversation about safety, gentleness, and

Figure 13.2
People talk about Tylenol and Advil differently:
Tylenol for safety and Advil for pain relief.

Themes in Online Conversation: Tylenol & Advil

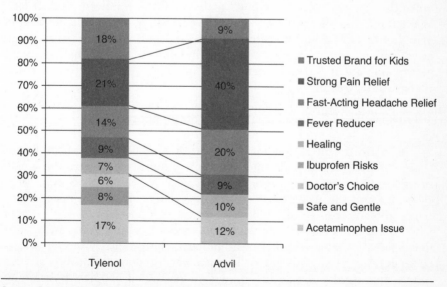

Source: Crimson Hexagon, 2009. Used with permission.

doctors' recommendations. The key point here is that Crimson Hexagon did not structure its research categories on the basis of brand marketing. Instead, the firm captured the ways people positioned the products in their minds according to their understanding and experiences.

Listening Level: Intermediate (Social research)

KEEP COMPANY PRODUCT POSITIONING AND CUSTOMER'S PRODUCT POSITIONING IN ALIGNMENT

Marketers and advertisers who understand the ways that people position their products receive valuable signals about how to stay in sync with customers and prospects. That is especially important when events occur that can alter product positioning and its brand health, such as new product introductions, recalls, or product safety issues. The Tylenol and Amazon Kindle cases we'll examine demonstrate how events impact consumer perception, and how insights can shape competitive strategy.

Because Tylenol's active ingredient, acetaminophen, had been linked to liver damage at certain dosages, an FDA advisory committee seeking to protect the public announced restrictions on acetaminophen products (Paddock 2009). Researchers noted a related spike in conversation when this occurred, as people wanted to know what the news was; however, it quickly returned to normal. The reason may be that, while liver damage was a risk, people talking about Tylenol read past the headlines to the facts. The FDA report noted that the risk was "very low" for people who followed product label instructions, and that acetaminophen played an "important role" in treating pain and fever. Tylenol withstood a potential business threat because the news, initially framed as negative, actually reinforced deeply held customer perceptions about Tylenol safety. Consequently, Tylenol did not have to change strategy at all.

Listening Level: Intermediate (Social media monitoring)

It was a different matter for the Amazon Kindle. The company had to change strategy or risk decline. As many people are aware, the Kindle ruled the e-book roost for several years and was beginning to seem invincible . . . until the Apple iPad came along. Think of the way people perceived the Amazon Kindle before the iPad introduction ("killer"; "must have") and immediately afterward (doomed, also-ran). Amazon realized that Kindle's strategy needed overhauling if the product's success was to continue. A company known for its customer listening, Amazon is successfully remaking the Kindle in line with a revamped people's positioning, highlighted by the following elements:

- Affordable pricing for travel and gift-giving purchases
- Ability to access a library of unparalleled size
- Improved reading features
- Enhanced connectivity and broader capabilities, like games
- Avoidance of the additional expenses and reading downsides the iPad introduced

The result: Kindle 3 models sold out immediately, making it a bigger success than any of its "predecessors" (Agnello 2010; Hurst 2010).

Listening Level: Intermediate (Social media monitoring)

INTERPRET COMPETITOR RISK IN CUSTOMER TERMS

Brand strategy bears some similarity to basketball: One team has to defend against another team, which is constantly attacking and adjusting, and success can come from any individual on the floor. How brands assess and counter their competition impacts their brand health. What do they do, for example, when an innovative new team comes into their house?

One particular leading household product faced this situation when a new item with a "distinct, novel form" was about to roll out. Partnering with J.D. Power and Associates Web Intelligence, the company launched a social media listening project to monitor and track conversations. Similar to the Tylenol/ Advil case just discussed, they identified and monitored discussions relating to the competitor's form, price, and advertising, and learned that consumers did not think well of the new rival. They expressed beliefs that the product was clumsy and unattractive, and criticized it for its high price point. As a result, the household product maker did not take any direct or defensive actions, like increasing spending on marketing, or reducing price. It simply kept abreast of the situation through continuous social media listening (J.D. Power and Associates, undated). Social media listening insights allowed for a type of expert counsel that gave the company valuable guidance, and credit should be given to the managers in charge for acting prudently and wisely on it. It took excellent judgment—and great confidence in the listening data—to resist the temptation to join the fight and call attention to their opponent's features and benefits. Moreover, the company enhanced its ability to maintain its competitive edge by listening for signals of change that, when strong enough, would bring forth a swift and strategic marketing response.

Companies vary in their capacity to respond to social media listening. Mindset is a governing factor because it influences the way companies interpret marketplace signals—as shown especially clearly in the Scrabble case, described next.

Listening Level: Intermediate (Social media monitoring)

HANDLE CHALLENGES TO THE CORE BRAND

Brand health is easily affected in the digital world, given the rampant copying, borrowing, and sampling that takes place. How should brands react when their intellectual property and distinguishing features are copied and extended—and then become very popular in someone else's application, program, or product? Business futures can hang in the balance, as this example from Scrabble shows.

Jayant and Rajatj Agarwalla, two software developers from Calcutta, India, developed a Facebook application called Scrabulous that became wildly successful. Modeled on Scrabble, right down to the board colors, the app added all sorts of social networking features and enhanced capabilities.

Scrabble licenses rights to two companies: Hasbro in the United States and Canada, and Mattel everywhere else. Both of these companies took notice of the popularity of Scrabulous, and both filed a copyright infringement suit against the Agarwalla brothers. At the time, Scrabulous had about 600,000 daily players and nearly 4 million active users—a significantly large community of interest (Knowledge@Wharton 2008; Eldon 2009).

Once the legal action was underway, Scrabulous was removed from Facebook, and passionate Scrabulists lit up the site. Determined to fill the void, Hasbro partnered with Electronic Arts to create Scrabble Beta for the United States and Canada. Mattel, together with RealNetworks, released Scrabble Worldwide, excluding the United States and Canada. Later, an Indian court ruled that only the name was in violation, *not* the game. The Agarwalla brothers released an updated, renamed version of Scrabulous called Wordscraper quickly thereafter.

At the end of September 2010, Scrabble had 907,765 active monthly users; Scrabble Worldwide had 589,491 monthly active users; and Wordscraper clocked in at just 98,875 monthly active users (Allfacebook.com 2010). Both individually and collectively, the number of active users did not come remotely close to that of Scrabulous in its heyday. One reason for the drop: There were now incompatible Scrabble versions, where before, Scrabulous had been a single game. Due to geographic licensing restrictions—and also because Hasbro and Mattel developed their games differently—players using one version could not play with players using a different version. An American could play with a Canadian Scrabble player, but not with a Greek friend, or anyone else in the rest of the world, for that matter. This did not sit well with most gamers, who wanted to play well with others, no matter their location.

Interested observers, like Wharton professors Peter Fader and Kevin Werbach, raised questions about the merits of Hasbro's decisions. Hasbro knew how popular Scrabulous was, based on size alone; even a cursory scan of comments revealed the depth of player passions. But was Scrabulous a threat to Scrabble? After all, people loved Scrabulous because they loved Scrabble. Even with new bells and whistles, Wordscraper's failure to catch on as Scrabulous had was due to the fact that it had shed its Scrabble-ness (Knowledge@Wharton 2008).

This episode reflects the limitations of company mind-sets and their impact on decisions. It is apparent that both Hasbro and Mattel looked at Scrabulous as a competitor and license infringer, capable of devaluing the Scrabble brand, with which they enjoyed success. Both took action, mostly legal, to eliminate the threat—a classic command-and-control response. Yet the community was sending an entirely different signal: We want Scrabulous to stay; please work it out.

Though Hasbro and Mattel may have heard Scrabulists' pleas, and recognized their passion, we can conclude that they did not, in the end, listen openly and without bias. The companies might have considered other options to address players' concerns: They might have licensed and modified Scrabulous; worked with Scrabulous to make a universal version, allowing anyone to play with anyone else; or involved the Agarwalla brothers in their Facebook version development.

The irony here is that by failing to incorporate listening insights that brought players into their versions, Hasbro and Mattel created only mildly successful online brands. Their tactics ended up alienating a large, engaged community that should have been a key asset and source for growth.

Listening Level: Fundamental (Social media monitoring)

SUMMARY

Companies can use social media listening insights to inform a wide variety of competitive strategies, ranging from identifying specific product strengths to handling full-frontal assaults. Successful organizations center their strategies on customer and prospect perceptions of their own products, as well as those of their competitors. Companies that fail to bring people's voices into their brands risk alienating their customers and prospects, which can lead to weakened competitive viability and diminished performance.

CHAPTER 14

PROVIDE CUSTOMER CARE AND INCREASE CUSTOMER SATISFACTION

Social media listening is a customer care game-changer. Some advocates, like Zappos CEO Tony Hsieh, believe it should go further: "Customer service shouldn't be a department," he claims. "It should be the entire company." Hsieh took his own advice, building Zappos on a culture of social media listening and engagement. The company grew from zero sales in 2000 to $1 billion in just eight years (Fresh Networks 2008). That stellar achievement led Amazon to acquire Zappos, and confirmed Hsieh's reputation as a business model innovator and management icon. Zappos' strategy of listening to market signals serves as a blueprint for many young companies that see outstanding service, engagement, and transparency as the path to growth and profits.

Social media listening-based customer care is growing; companies large and small, local and global, handle customer complaints, take suggestions, answer questions, and provide information with little more than a free Twitter account or Facebook presence. Southwest Airlines, Comcast, Whole Foods, L.L. Bean, neighborhood coffee shops like Groundz, San Antonio's Maggiano's restaurant, and New York City food trucks are just a few examples.

Social media listening-powered services not only help with traditional inbound needs, like taking a call or replying to an e-mail; they also enable businesses to follow and continuously monitor their customers in near-real time. A new breed of software that combines social media management with workflow and collaboration tools allows companies to listen for concerns, reach out to the people voicing them, and engage with them as appropriate, and then analyze and report their customer care activities. For example, when reps from organic grocery chain Whole Foods spot customers tweeting about what to make for dinner, they can make general suggestions to them. They can even go a step further by consulting the tweeter's profile and past tweets and make truly relevant recommendations that are tied to their preferences—say, for fish or certain flavors.

The cases we review in this chapter highlight a key difference between traditional customer service and the growing "social service" movement: Relationships are not just private two-way conversations between a company and customer. Nowadays, they take place in the public square. A single tweet, post, or wall scribble can quickly ripple through and across blogs, review sites, and social networks in ways that influence brand preference and perception, for not just one person, but for their entire social graph—even people they don't know, as the following findings show (Barnes 2008):

- People choose companies or brands based on their customer care experiences (95 percent).
- People choose companies or brands based on the customer care experiences that others share online (74 percent).
- People believe that blogs, rating systems, and discussion forums can give consumers a greater voice in effecting changes in customer care (81 percent).
- People do not believe that companies take their opinions seriously (70 percent).
- When asked, people claimed that "protecting others" was one of their motivations for sharing their customer service experiences online.

Getting customer care "right" in the social media era is essential for sustaining customer relationships and contributing to business growth. Social media listening signals help steer companies in the right direction. The following company examples will lead the way.

WINNING PLAYS FOR CUSTOMER CARE AND CUSTOMER SATISFACTION

The tactics and company cases we reviewed led us to develop five winning plays:

- *Align goals that social media listening approaches can achieve for customer service.* Companies that garner value from social customer service began their mission by stating clear goals. Zappos viewed service as a pillar supporting its entire business. AT&T sought to mollify Apple iPhone customers disappointed in its wireless service and keep them until new infrastructure went online. Comcast wanted to overcome the negative perception that it didn't care for its customers. In addition to their clarity, these goals were well suited to a social approach because they involved the emotional aspects of products and services, as well as people's opinions of companies.
- *Supplement traditional customer service with social media listening customer service.* Utilize multiple channels. Even companies known for their

social media listening customer care prowess have phone centers and e-mail/chat support; handle mail correspondence; and sometimes host and participate in support forums, where customers are encouraged to help each other. For most companies, social media is a small but important part of the mix. For example, cable provider Comcast's e-mail volume is more than three times that of its tweet management on a daily basis, and in-bound phone calls are 99 times greater than e-mail (see the "Manage Customer Expectations" section).

The question of scale is one that every company needs to address. Organizations must balance their tactics appropriately for the quality and level of service they want to provide. Figuring out how to do this involves more than financial analysis. Businesses also need to consider their company culture: whether it's appropriate to engage with customers through social media, and whether these operations can, or should be, outsourced as customer demand increases. Almost every company will need to make that decision: Half of all Americans and two-thirds of people 25–34 belong to at least one social network (Pick 2010).

- *Leverage social media support to shape customer perception toward your company, products, or services.* Although social media volume is typically lower than other channels, it's also much more visible. These customer care communications occur in full view of other customers, and are often accessible through search engines. Whenever possible, businesses should recognize this opportunity to demonstrate their efforts, responsiveness, and satisfactory problem solving for the individuals seeking assistance—but also with a view to their larger customer communities. Comcast repaired its image and Zappos built a successful company this way.
- *Engage with permission—respectfully, civilly, ethically, and transparently.* Customer service requires that engagement between companies and individuals succeed. Precisely because these conversations are public, organizations that participate in them need to hold themselves to a high standard, for all to see. The examples from JetBlue, discussed later in the chapter, show that companies must secure permission from customers. With permission, JetBlue delivered great service in one case. In a second instance, however, it did not receive advance permission, and by failing to do so, inadvertently ended up with a disgruntled flyer and raised a secondary issue, which the airline then needed to address. Wine retailer Naked Wines handled a difficult customer on its Facebook presence by outlining every step it took to resolve the issues at hand, which resulted in a vote of support from the company's Facebook friends. Because of its open nature, direct engagement is new for many companies, and potentially affects company perception and reputation, both negatively and positively. It's vital to develop policies that guide employees, as retailer Nordstrom did, to govern the way they connect with your customers and share information.

- *Mine and leverage customer support interactions to provide insight and share within customer service and across the company.* Derive greater value and listening power from social media customer service by analyzing the marketplace signals that agents aggregate and filter. Take advantage of the number-crunching and reporting tools available in monitoring software to identify trends that highlight important service issues. At a minimum, let your company's traditional support operations know about these; go further, and share them with departments like marketing, sales, retail, purchasing, and product development. Doing so will both promote acceptance of social media data and provide your colleagues with the kind of customer insight capable of helping the entire organization satisfy customers. For example, if Whole Foods found itself answering a torrent of questions about the spicy condiment sambal oelek, it could feature the ingredient in its magazine's recipes, feature it throughout the store with displays and sampling, or offer dishes including it in the prepared food section.

The winning plays we recognized were derived from four tactics:

- Listen, assist, and engage in near-real time.
- Engage openly, respectfully, ethically, and civilly.
- Manage customer expectations.
- Make sure solutions satisfy customers.

Let's look at each of these tactics, and the companies that used them so successfully, in more detail.

LISTEN, ASSIST, AND ENGAGE IN NEAR-REAL TIME

Using a Twitter search several years ago, JetBlue's communications chief, Morgan Johnston, found that some people were asking questions, and others were making inaccurate statements. Wanting to set the record straight, Johnston (with JetBlue's approval) created the company's corporate Twitter account, in 2007. The airline's Twitter page establishes the value proposition up front, in its bio: "Have a question? Follow us and let us help!" It also personalizes the account by naming the staffers on duty.

Travelers responded enthusiastically to JetBlue's initiative. By early October 2010, the airline had attracted 1.6 million followers, and was following back 115,000 of its customers (Twitter 2009a; Twitter 2010). Johnston and his team use commercial off-the-shelf software to schedule tweets for known events, like announcements and fare deals; respond to inbound tweets expressing questions or concerns; and listen and respond to their Twitter "waterfall."

Figure 14.1
JetBlue responded to an after-midnight tweet regarding an
overheated cabin within two minutes after receiving it.

@jetblue...you Need to turn down the
heat on your 7:55pm flight from Boston
to Den ver. It was rough.

12:32 AM Dec 15th, 2008 from Twittelator in reply to JetBlue

 JetBlue Thanks for the heads up! (sometimes flight crews
get overzealous traveling from cold to cold!) *12:34 AM Dec 15th,
2008*

Their software provides a rich set of tools for collaboration and teamwork.
They are able to profile authors through their conversation history, follower/
followed status, and other measures that establish a person's authority or
influence. Many other companies have followed in JetBlue's footsteps, with
such varied examples as Virgin Trains, I Can Has Cheezburger, the *Martha
Stewart Show*, and the White House.

A quick glance at JetBlue's Twitter account while writing this chapter
showed tweets providing service, information on destinations served, updates
on weather affecting travel, promotions, charity events, instructions on checking flight status, and resolutions to ticket issues ("We will honor the lower air-
fare and issue you a JB credit if your flight prices drop before departure").
Specific details of customer service issues are typically handled by direct tweets
off the main page. There were also some JetBlue customers who used the airline's Twitter account to meet up and pass time with one another before their
flights. ("Stop by if you're in SF! RT @xyzzname @jetblue @nikewmsmara-
thon sitting in a JetBlue seat waiting for a free manicure.")

JetBlue customers use Twitter to get help just when they need it. The screenshot in Figure 14.1, from Dave Raffaele's 2009 blog post titled "How JetBlue
Used Twitter to Treat Me like a Human" provides two very good examples of
what can be done for a traveler on a single journey. First up, a complaint
regarding an overheated cabin.

Raffaele made it clear how much he appreciated being listened to, so much
so that he became motivated to share the positive response he received:

In under 2 minutes, JetBlue responded with this tweet acknowledging my concern. It may seem like a small thing, but think about it. Here is a huge organization listening to me complain about the temperature on their plane over a channel
that is far from mainstream. Even more impressive is that it was not an automated response. There was a real person writing that little note. It may not sell
more plane tickets, but it definitely made me want to tell this story.

Figure 14.2
JetBlue responded to a service-related complaint at an airport by explaining the reasons, sizing up the situation, and then involving the local general manager and supervisors in its resolution.

@jetblue **In denver and want to check my bag but there us no one at the counter. What's wrong with this picture?**

10:39 PM Dec 16th, 2008 from Twittelator in reply to JetBlue

sogrady: @daveraffaele: the JetBlue crew in Denver's usually only there ~2 hrs before the flight. you'll probably have to wait 30-45 minutes.
about 1 month ago · Reply · View Tweet · Show Conversation

JetBlue @sogrady is a step ahead of me – but sending a note to the GM and Supes as a heads up anyway. Are there many waiting? *10:46 PM Dec 16th, 2008*

daveraffaele: @JetBlue There are probably 5 or 6 people waiting. Not too bad
about 1 month ago · Reply · View Tweet · Show Conversation

JetBlue sent a note to Theresa our General Manager out there *11:08 PM Dec 16th, 2008*

JetBlue you should see some Crewmembers showing up shortly – our offices in DEN are away from the ticket counter. *11:15 PM Dec 16th, 2008*

daveraffaele: @JetBlue, @sogrady Thanks for the tag team action. @michellebb and I will just hang out in Hudson news for a while. :)

Raffaele was actively tweeting during his return trip, as well, when he arrived early at the airport and wanted to check luggage, but no one was around to help him. He fired off the tweet shown in Figure 14.2.

JetBlue's response was thorough, as Figure 14.2 shows; but another aspect of the experience really impressed Raffaele—community involvement:

> Not only did JetBlue respond to me directly, but other folks who follow me on Twitter also gave me insight based on their own experience. With the help of the crowd, [JetBlue] was again able to turn a situation that would have normally annoyed me into one of understanding and outstanding customer experience.

Assuming Raffaele represents a certain type of traveler, these excerpts show that he, and others like him, not only expect great service and prompt resolution to problems, but that JetBlue is dedicated to his well-being by constantly monitoring his "traveling EKG" and engaging in an appropriate way at any time. This example also sheds light on another aspect of customer care: the fact that it is a community activity. While brands need to listen to customers, they also need to listen to how customers interact with and help one another, and make it easy for the community to do so. This creates another source of insights, such as learning the rules of thumb, tips, and tricks customers use to accomplish some task that suggests new ways of doing things or confirming/debunking the merits of various company approaches.

Listening Level: Intermediate (Social media monitoring)

ENGAGE OPENLY, RESPECTFULLY, ETHICALLY, AND CIVILLY

Of course, people and their preferences differ vastly. For every Dave Raffaele who is comfortable with benign surveillance, there are others who may find it unnerving when companies start to "follow" them. Brands seek connection for all types of reasons, so it's up to them and their individual customers to agree on the relationship type that fits best. This may well mean *no* relationship, and the consensus is that brands must be ethical in these matters, transparent in their aims and benefits, and authentic in their voice. If all goes well, transparency leads to openness and, eventually, to trust. Historically, ethical practices for online communications emerged in the early days of e-mail, and have since been codified into features like permissions and unsubscribe options. But friending, following, and adding contacts are fairly new business practices, so companies are still working on proper techniques.

To begin here, we'll stick with JetBlue and take the example of two friends conversing on Twitter one evening. After mentioning JetBlue during their conversation, they soon received e-mails notifying them that they were being followed by JetBlue. The friends found this to be a bit spooky, and one suggested that the airline was using bots to do updates—far from a personal approach. A few minutes later, one of the friends and a social media consultant, Joel Postman, received this post on his blog (shown in Figure 14.3), explaining JetBlue's motivation and agreeing to their unfollow requests.

JetBlue's response clarified things for Postman, and also gave him a deep appreciation for the airline's willingness to adjust based on social media listening. Postman's take on the interaction is shown in Figure 14.4.

JetBlue's action may appear to be just a personal reply, but there's reason to believe that the response served a larger strategic purpose: to spread the word about JetBlue's actions and the reasoning behind them. Recall our mention of the software a few minutes ago; JetBlue used its author profiling feature to quickly see that Postman had some authority on Twitter. Around that time, Postman's followers/followed ratio was 8,632/8,222, and he had tweeted 12,203 times (Twitter 2009b). Further, by posting on Postman's blog, JetBlue helped ensure that its response would be available outside of Twitter. The reason: Although Twitter was not indexed by all leading search engines at the time, most blogs were. So if someone does a search for "JetBlue following" or something of the sort, the searcher would find JetBlue's post in Postman's blog.

JetBlue used listening to anticipate and respond to important concerns that Postman shared with others, and set wrong-headed opinions straight that

Figure 14.3
JetBlue responds to a customer's concern over Twitter following,
by posting a comment on the customer's blog.

Hi Joel,
Sorry if we [spooked] you or your friend by following you on twitter. @JetBlue isn't
a bot; it's merely me and my team keeping our ears to the ground and listening to
our customers talk in open forums so we can improve ours service to them. It's not
marketing; it's trying to engage on a level other than mass broadcasts, something I
personally believe more companies should try to do.
Because corporate involvement in social media is a new and evolving discipline, I
also take a specific interest on conversations revolving around our role here. I'd
have DM'd you and Lisa directly if you allowed DMs, so please also forgive me for
following the link on your twitter page here to send you this note. [Note: a DM is a
private one-to-one message on Twitter].
You and Lisa are no longer being 'followed' as you seem to indicate.
Again, my apologies
Morgan Johnston
Corporate Communications
JetBlue Airways

Figure 14.4
After JetBlue explained its actions, the affected customer wrote an appreciative
blog post (Postman 2008). Subsequently that post was indexed by search engines
and commented upon by other bloggers, which extended the reach and visibility
of JetBlue's position.

Morgan and I exchanged a few emails, and I learned that [he – not a bot –] is behind
JetBlue's tweets . . . Morgan is very well informed on social media ethics and
aware that corporate use of Twitter can be tricky. I am impressed that Morgan was
watching Twitter closely enough to sense an issue, responded quickly, apologized,
and removed the two of us from @JetBlue's list. This served as a demonstration of
the company's active participation in the Twitter conversation, its willingness to
course-correct, and of the new speed of social media with which corporations have
to contend.
Not every corporate social media initiative will be satisfied with engagement alone.
JetBlue is in uncharted skies. Morgan and JetBlue have shown a true willingness to
engage in a real conversation alongside the company's promotional tweets, and I
think that's how successful corporate social media has to play out.

might have escalated into large-scale concerns across social media. Giving a thoughtful response to an influential person like Joel Postman—and, by extension, his entire network—allowed JetBlue to explain its position in a way that would help maintain a favorable brand perception.

Listening Level: Intermediate (Social media monitoring)

Engage with Civility

The JetBlue examples show respect to customer conversations and to their authors. But there are some scenarios in which people are downright ornery, mean, or insulting—behaviors that can bring out the worst in a company's social media voices. Doug Zanger tells a story of how one cranky listener's comments on Portland's alternative station, 94/7, escalated into a nasty series of personalized remarks that could impact its business (Zanger 2009):

> Whoever was at the wheel decided to get a little personal, and it made the station look really bad. This station prided itself on getting feedback across the board and, in one swing of the tweet, completely abandoned [their approach] because [they] didn't like what [they] heard. Firstly, this episode should remind us [that] ill will could rub off on advertisers. Secondly, and more important[ly], if you have someone officially Twittering on behalf of your agency, you must remember at all times that everyone is watching.

This is an assertion that startup online wine shop Naked Wines completely understands. Its example shows that respectfully dealing with a challenging customer not only can lead to a satisfactory outcome, it can have a positive effect on the entire brand's community (Charlton 2009).

A customer complained on Naked Wines' Facebook page about a delivery that did not arrive. The company initially tried to resolve the problem offline, by calling the customer and offering a full refund. For whatever reason, the customer went back to complaining online. After some back and forth in public view, the company outlined everything it did to resolve the situation, including refunding all the money the customer had ever spent with Naked Wines.

Facebook fans supported the company, which strengthened Naked Wines' image and may even have won over some new customers, as we see in the thread shown in Figure 14.5.

Listening Level: Fundamental (Social media monitoring)

Develop Policies for Engagement

The radio station and wine company examples underscore a point made earlier in both the introduction and JetBlue case study: Customer service and

Figure 14.5
Naked Wines' Facebook fans expressed support for the way the company handled a
difficult customer.

> *"can't keep all of the people happy all of the time. Personally I think NW are doing great
> things for the online wine game – certainly keeping most of the people happy ALL of the
> time!"*

> *"I am actually tempted to try Naked Wines because of the way they deal with...
> SHOUTING IN CAPITALS........They seem very reasonable while she doesn't....."*

> *"what a sad misunderstanding .. I can vouch that customer services at Naked Wines are
> extremely customer oriented .."*

satisfaction conversations are held in public, and exposed to interested parties. Before the advent of social media, customer service was essentially a series of one-on-one encounters with anonymous agents in a call center. Today, it's not only the quality of the problem's resolution that matters to customers. They also take careful notice of a company's conduct and etiquette throughout the entire process.

This is why so many companies have developed explicit social networking policies that encourage their employees to connect with customers to deliver information they are seeking, and to do it in a manner the company has deemed acceptable and proper. Most of these guidelines advise employees to act in ways that seem like common sense: Use good judgment, and be respectful, transparent, humble, human, and good listeners. Policies like these also serve to protect confidential, private, and personal information; safeguard intellectual property belonging to others; and prevent linking to unknown or unreliable online resources (Nordstrom 2010). If your organization does not have such guidelines in place, or if you simply want to do some benchmarking, you might take a look at Chris Boudreaux's (2009) analysis of 46 social media policy documents. It provides helpful guidelines for organizations that are just beginning to become active in social media or are old hands.

MANAGE CUSTOMER EXPECTATIONS

When large companies with hundreds of thousands or millions of customers encounter a product or service issue, they usually feel the brunt of their customers' dissatisfaction in short order. Their opinions and problems spread swiftly through social media. In many instances, the primary job of customer service representatives is twofold: tactical (assuage customers), and strategic (establish a level of goodwill that will carry the company through until it can make changes and offer solutions). We'll see this in the AT&T example we now discuss.

People who want an Apple iPhone have only one place to go (at the time of writing): exclusive mobile provider AT&T. Apple's attractive, capable, coveted mobile device has legions of loyal users, who value its simplicity, design, features, and apps. However, many of these same users are extremely dissatisfied with AT&T's network quality. They experience nagging problems like dropped calls and interrupted Internet service, and complain that AT&T's Web site services break when demand is high. They won't leave for another carrier because the cost of giving up the iPhone and switching to another provider is too great. So they stay and turn to social media to vent and commiserate with one another—which they do quite frequently. The company racks up about 10,000 mentions per day, a number that can skyrocket when there is important product or service news.

AT&T decided to counter dissatisfaction by forming a dedicated team to monitor comments and respond to them on Twitter, YouTube, and Facebook. Almost half of the people reached by AT&T's social media reps take the time to engage with someone on the 20-member team. Heavy demand puts a lot of pressure on the staff: By June 2010, the number of service tickets was running about 32,000 per month. The team acts as a concierge, handling some requests and making connections to other departments that can resolve the issues.

The reality is that networks need to invest in infrastructure in order to solve their problems. AT&T took that step by budgeting nearly $20 billion dollars to improve both its wired and wireless infrastructure. The company's social customer service aims to keep subscribers reasonably satisfied until the fix is in place, and to stave off defections when contracts expire. Team leader Shawn McPike explained, "From a care perspective, I don't worry about [the network complaints] from day to day. What we worry about is that there are customers out there who have problems. We need to at least get them engaged to show that we're listening, and that may turn the tide over time" (quoted in Patel 2010).

Listening Level: Advanced (Social media monitoring)

Commitments to outreach through social media listening do pay off. Comcast's Twitter-based effort, @ComcastCares, responded to customer problems and complaints seven days a week. The program was the brainchild of then-Comcast executive Frank Eliason, and it worked to change—and markedly improve—Comcast's reputation for service. It's important to note that Comcast's social media customer service, like that of AT&T and other companies, supplements traditional channels like e-mail, chat, and the call center. E-mail, in fact, is the most active channel in Comcast's support operation.

According to Comcast CEO Brian Roberts, Comcast receives 300 million calls per year—more than 800,000 on a daily basis. In contrast, the social media group receives about 2,000 tweets per day; reaches out to about 600 people per day; and engages with about 200 to 300 people per day (Kawasaki 2010).

Comcast shows that adding social media listening can be a judolike strategy, one that enables companies to leverage a small fraction of the customer base to repair broken reputations. As a result, social media listening for customer service has strong business appeal. Although Comcast does not report hard metrics of success, the company claims that bringing the customer's voice into the company has value. Comcast CEO Brian Roberts provides a ringing endorsement, publicly claiming that "Twitter changed our company" (ForaTV 2009; Solis 2008).

Listening Level: Intermediate (Social Media Monitoring)

MAKE SURE SOLUTIONS SATISFY CUSTOMERS

Using social media listening, furnishings retailer Crate & Barrel discovered that one of its products—a $400 children's table—was too soft, and easily damaged by a child's normal use. Wanting to correct the problem, Crate & Barrel redesigned the product and offered replacements to owners of the faulty design. Kudos, right?

Well, not exactly.

In order to get the new model, owners had to disassemble and return the old table, a process that rendered returns and exchanges minimal. By keeping its social media listening ears open, Crate & Barrel learned that taking apart, boxing up, and shipping a "clunky table" was just too much hassle for most consumers. However, the retailer did not act on these insights and, as a result, the number of returns simply did not increase. We can assume that most parents just threw up their hands and hung on to the original (Klaassen 2009a). Not only did the lingering dissatisfaction throw these parents' future purchases from the company into question; it also exposed a vulnerability that competitors took the chance to seize.

Here's a case where social media listening might best be considered "hearing." Diane Hessan, CEO of online consumer insight company Communispace, counsels: "'Social media listening' doesn't mean getting one small piece of data and taking action. Sometimes it means getting a piece of data and probing it further" (quoted in Klaassen 2009b). For example, Crate & Barrel could have listened for possible solutions that came up in discussions, such as: "Yeah, it's a hassle, but if they only . . . [insert potential consumer suggestions]." Had the company engaged in conversation with owners, it might have learned of some tried-and-true return methods that manufacturers and suppliers use to appeal to customers. For example, instead of sending back the whole table, would owners have been open to sending in a receipt or credit card statement? What about some other proof of purchase, like a UPC code, manufacturer's lot number, or even a minor piece of the table? How about sending a box and shipping label, and then arranging for a package pickup, at owners' convenience? If the company had listened, drilled down, and explored, it might have come up with a workable solution that was best for their customers—and, therefore, their brand.

Different business functions need to be coordinated in support of serving customers, especially at companies that deal with physical items. It is a holistic company response, not the province of a single department. Crate & Barrel probably made its decision in this case based on input from marketing, legal, customer service, manufacturing, and shipping and receiving departments. The policy requiring customers to return the complete table was a company decision, which apparently could not be changed, even in light of the guidance social media listening offered, and could have provided, had Crate & Barrel continued to listen to the returns "conversation." This is another clear example of how effective customer service responses depend on fully engaged organizations and "always on" listening.

Listening Level: Fundamental (Social media monitoring)

SUMMARY

Companies use social media listening-based customer service best when it is matched to the right goals. Social support should supplement other forms of support, in order for companies to meet customer needs as customers would like. Companies must realize that social support is often carried out openly, which means that their response timeliness, quality, and "human-ness" influence not one individual but a community of customers, with the perception of a company in the balance.

PART III

LISTENING-LED
MARKETING AND
MEDIA INNOVATIONS

Ask the average marketing person what social media listening is best suited for, and you'll hear "insights and customer service—it's the world's largest focus group!" That's only partially true, of course, and we hope it's a notion this book has already dispelled. What is considerably lesser known is our ability to use listening to transform soft conversations into hard data, as well as for a wider variety of business-building purposes. The four chapters in this part analyze innovative applications for listening data in media and marketing:

Social TV Measurement (Chapter 15) has been developed to evaluate viewer interest in programs. These go beyond measuring mere audience size to assessing audience engagement and intention for media strategy, planning, and buying. These tools are already changing ideas about the programs in which brands should advertise or use for product placement.

Listening-Based Targeting (Chapter 16) uses people's conversations and media behavior to identify potential audiences via techniques like text mining, content analysis, and trend watching. These methods are especially valuable for uncovering multicultural markets, locating people who discuss common interests, and developing language-based segmentations.

Achieve Share of Market Goals (Chapter 17) explores the relationship between share of conversational voice and share of market. This approach aspires to extend the traditional advertising voice/share of market into the social media realm, and understand it through listening. Although it's clearly still an emerging area, the evidence we've gathered suggests that market share and conversational share of voice are correlated: Leading brands have the largest share of voice; the second brand has the

161

second largest; and so on. Just as conventional research does, this trend may provide advertisers and marketers with guidelines for maintaining or growing market share and developing strategy and budget. It can also allow brands to reap the benefits inherent in larger market shares, such as greater cost-efficiency, customer preference, and trade clout.

Listening-Based Sales Predictions (Chapter 18) reflect new approaches to forecasting near-term changes in sales. This chapter goes into detail on the many conversation factors that impact sales, and the various types of predictive models that were built from those elements. Instead of just being number generators for CFOs, the models become templates for planning and strategy because they reflect what is important to people buying particular products and services. Features that improve sales in prediction models are factors that companies can optimize in marketing and advertising. This could be thought of as suggesting a new marketing discipline: "prediction-led strategy."

Of one thing we can be certain: these four applications are only a beginning.

CHAPTER 15

SOCIAL TV MEASUREMENT

Despite the attention online video receives daily, broadcast television remains the most important advertising medium. TV's share of worldwide ad dollars jumped from 38 to 46 percent over the last decade; Americans log 36 hours of tube time per week, versus 1.6 hours weekly for the streaming stuff watched on computer monitors and mobile screens (Fulgoni 2010).

TV's "king of the hill" status results from a growing and almost adulatory appreciation of its value to advertisers in today's media landscape: its unrivalled power to attract audiences. To paraphrase Mark Twain, "The report of television's death was an exaggeration."

Although people watch more TV than ever before, viewership for almost every program is smaller than years ago, due to the 500-plus channel universe available through cable, satellite, and the Web. Watching TV resembles the modern family dinner: Members rarely sit down at the same time; rather, each eats according to his or her own schedule and tastes. What, when, where, and how to watch shows is a personal programming exercise that regularly involves the use of DVRs and on-demand services, which liberate people from the rigidly scheduled activity television watching once was. The days are long gone when the CBS, ABC, and NBC television networks controlled America's viewing and organized our lives.

In today's TV world, there are two factors worth noting about the viewing experience. First, people often use multiple forms of media simultaneously. It wasn't so long ago that people read the newspaper or flipped through magazines while watching TV; it was on as background. Today, television viewing and Internet use go together like iPods and iTunes. Three out of four Americans use the Internet and TV at the same time—and this number is growing every day. In fact, major TV manufacturers are pushing this trend along by offering Internet-enabled sets. When using the Internet, viewers mostly interact with friends on Facebook and Twitter, or look up search terms on Google (Yahoo 2010). This combination of social media and television is creating a "worldwide living room," where people chat about programs, stars, and ads easily with their online friends and networks (Poniewozik 2010). And since Internet use is increasingly mobile, this "living room" is really anywhere and everywhere the viewer is located.

The second element to note is that enjoying television is an important part of our social lives. Think back to the 2010 World Cup: There were countless stories about the many restaurants and bars that capitalized on soccer fans who gathered to watch, eat, drink, and celebrate or commiserate together. On most days, many of us talk about TV shows, YouTube videos, MySpace music, books, and all types of media content with family, friends, colleagues, and associates, at home, at the football game, around the water cooler, and online. Conversations about TV act as social lubricants and give us a common topic to discuss.

Consequently, TV outlets are looking to have their shows attract and engage very social viewers, and hold onto them over time; and advertisers are looking to be in shows that people seek out. Both groups are supplementing eyeball-based ratings with measures that offer insights from listening to social media conversations. Several research companies have begun to develop social TV ratings grounded in listening, the subject of this chapter.

SOCIAL TV RATINGS

To appreciate the innovations in social TV ratings, we'll begin with a quick overview of the conventional ratings business. Over the last 50 years, media measurement companies calculated program and commercial ratings from diaries, surveys, set-top boxes, or metered samples. These were computed at overall levels such as "Adults 18-plus" or "all U.S. households," and the demographics of audiences "reading print media titles," "watching TV shows," "listening to radio programs," and "using the Web or Web-based services."

The ratings business evolved in the mass media era to support the notion that marketers should reach the audiences with the largest numbers of consumers targeted for their advertising. Along with that, the media industry developed measures like gross rating points, cost-per-thousand, and cost-per-point, to plan, buy, and negotiate media. That data guided marketers to choose shows where their products' advertising should be placed. It estimated how many people they could expect to reach, how frequently the ads would be seen, how cost-efficient the buy was, and the audience it delivered postrun. Most practices designed for mass media found their way into the digital realm, as well; as a result, media planning and buying still looks very much the way it did at the height of the mass media era. (As an aside, the merit of measuring digital media in traditional media terms has been an important long-running debate in the industry. It is beyond the scope of this book to explore, but a very interesting topic if it relates to your work or responsibilities.)

Social TV ratings supplement and enrich traditional ratings. Several companies today—including Collective Intellect, General Sentiment, and Networked Insights—offer these services. Although each company's ratings computations differ, there are some similarities in their methods, such as:

- *Social Media Source selection*: Research identifies locations online where viewers hold conversations and comment on TV programs. These sources include official show sites, fan pages, unofficial fan sites, specialized blogs and forums, and social networks.
- *Conversation collection*: Marketers develop rules for extracting relevant information that they use to create search queries that retrieve the conversations.
- *Conversation analysis*: Measures of engagement or involvement—especially the volumes of posts, comments, and reads—are central to the process of computing social TV ratings. Additional analytics provide enhanced detail and more granular analysis, such as the strength of the bond between viewer and show, themes, brands, characters and plots, and the sentiment expressed about them.
- *Reporting*: Vendors provide custom and syndicated reports, as well as dashboards that track trends and display key indicators like volume, sentiment, themes, or word clouds. Some offerings incorporate third-party data sources, such as Quantcast, for demographic information.

Social TV ratings have started hinting that the way people bring the programs into their lives differs from their general popularity as measured by conventional ratings. To take one example, Networked Insights computed social ratings for the top 75 Nielsen-rated shows over the February through April 2010 period. As shown in Table 15.1, social ratings and Nielsen ratings for the top 20 socially rated programs highlight the differences between them. Several shows rated low by conventional methods were very successful in the social realm.

Comparing the two ratings approaches, the results showed that while there was agreement on two of the top shows—*American Idol* and *Glee*—only seven of the top-rated Nielsen programs appeared in the top 20 socially ranked shows. Unsung programs like *Heroes, Saturday Night Live*, and *Cold Case* had social rankings ranging from sixth to eleventh place, whereas they brought up only the distant rear of Nielsen's rankings. In other words, shows with low conventional ratings can be huge successes in terms of their social popularity (Networked Insights 2010).

In addition to ratings, companies measure the strength of the bond between viewers and programs by factoring in sentiment, affinity, and intention to stick with the program. Collective Intellect, for example, develops an "audience viewing intention" score that sheds light on viewers' plans to watch programs,

TABLE 15.1   Top 20 Network TV Shows Ranked by Social Rating

SOCIAL RANK	NIELSEN RANK	PROGRAM	SOCIAL INDEX
1	10	Lost	131.4
2	1	American Idol	126.5
3	4	Glee	60.5
4	44	The Simpsons	55.9
5	*	Heroes	55.1
6	3	Dancing with the Stars	51.4
7	20	House	51.1
8	24	CSI: Miami	48.5
9	*	Saturday Night Live	47.6
10	35	30 Rock	45.4
11	*	Cold Case	41
12	40	Family Guy	40.5
13	25	The Office	39.5
14	27	Bones	38.9
15	18	NCIS: Los Angeles	37.9
16	*	So You Think You Can Dance	35.2
17	*	Chuck	34.9
18	11	CSI	34.5
19	13	Survivor	34.4
20	*	How I Met Your Mother	32.2

*Indicates very low Nielsen rating.
Source: Networked Insights (2010). Used with permission.

and whether they'll watch it live. Jointly, ratings and bond strength reveal the ways programs do, and don't, resonate with viewers.

EMERGING PLAYS FOR SOCIAL TV RATINGS

Because these companies analyze conversational substance, they leverage listening-based insights to help users of their ratings gain business advantages in ways that go beyond the "horse race" ratings, by incorporating them into planning media strategy, message creative, and media content. We see four plays emerging from developments in social TV ratings:

- *Improve media planning and targeting.* Locate the shows whose viewers talk about specific product categories and use that as a basis to integrate them into media plans. Doing so increases the odds that messages will reach not only the right people, but highly engaged ones. Combine that with analysis of the sources where conversations take place to develop a strategy that integrates Web sites, forums, and social networks into the media plan. Vet them for quality and conversational fit (Key 2009).

Additionally, enhance ratings forecasts by building listening data into models. (See Chapter 18 for a related discussion focused on sales forecasting.) One valuable use is to refine ratings trends predictions for on-air programs, or for prototyping ratings for new programs not yet aired that may be considered for media plans. Boosting forecast accuracy will lead to better media strategy and tactics.

- *Make smarter media buys.* Companies that buy on the spread between conventional and social media ratings may be able to purchase time more cost-effectively, especially for low-rated programs whose audiences concentrate highly engaged customers and prospects for specific products. Even when buying time in premium properties, those with higher social ratings will deliver more highly engaged audiences. Purchasing on the basis of social ratings can give companies a competitive advantage over rivals that do not.

- *Provide creative input that syncs with viewer interest.* Use the conversational themes, people's likes and dislikes, and their sentiments uncovered through listening analysis in order to give direction to creative development, for messaging, and the product itself. Broadcaster RTL Nederland tweaked its version of talent show *X Factor* on a weekly basis to keep it in step with audience buzz. Through listening-derived insights, the show made regular changes, modified its format, and opened itself up for greater audience participation by satisfying the desire for behind-the-scenes looks at contestants; it even brought back an immensely popular singer who had been sent home (Verhaege et al. 2009). Here in the States, Bravo network president Frances Berwick told the *New York Times* that, "We get a lot of information about story lines, and the different people, and what they want to see more of" (Quenqua 2010).

- *Don't stop with television programs; extend the social ratings concept to all media.* All media that companies use in their plans should benefit from social media listening insights. It is entirely possible to profile media such as magazines, radio stations, or Web properties the same way as described for television programs. You can rate them on engagement and conversation fit, and integrate that knowledge into the media plans. Similarly, you can leverage creative insights to ensure that communications address customers' deep interests.

Listening-led actions inspired by social TV ratings like those described here may substantially increase the effectiveness of marketing and advertising. Social ratings are still very new, and companies using them are probably keeping mum about how they are using them and what they've learned. But we'll be listening—and you should, too.

SUMMARY

Social media listening is ushering in new ways of measuring the appeal of television programs, by gauging them on their level of audience engagement. Using listening-based measures, businesses can delve deeply into conversation analysis, with implications for media planning, buying, creative executions, and television programs themselves, which, in combination, may lead to more effective engagement and communications.

CHAPTER 16

LISTENING-BASED TARGETING

Social media listening provides new tools to help companies locate people who talk about their categories, products, or services. Interest in listening-based targeting strategies is growing because of increased social media adoption, and, as we discussed in Chapter 4, markets are becoming more precisely defined these days in terms of mind-sets, shared concerns, activities, and lifestyles reflected in conversations, and less so by straight conventional descriptors like demographics, geographies and dayparts. Recall the "sandwich situation" case in Chapter 4; it focused not on a generation, but on multigenerations of caregivers from Gen Y to baby boomers. As conversations broaden to become more "multi," it will become more important to use listening techniques to deeply understand and leverage them for targeting purposes.

Our review of case studies and research methods uncovered four emerging approaches to develop targeting strategies that link listening to:

- Behavior
- Gender; multicultural; and lesbian, gay, bisexual, and transgender (LGBT) conversations
- Offline word of mouth
- The different contexts in which conversations take place, to pick up the signals

We'll break each of these down, in turn, in the following sections.

BEHAVIORAL LISTENING

This method uncovers clues about customers and prospects by listening to their behavior, as noticed in patterns, statistics, and trends. We discussed two cases that used this approach in Chapter 5, one for Hennessy Cognac, the other for Suzuki's Hayabusa motorcycle. In both instances, the companies discovered completely "hidden" markets by listening to the behavior of drinkers and riders. Hennessy exposed a passionate cognac-loving market by recognizing linking patterns in its Web server logs from a third-party Web site to its own. This kind of linking indicates interest, affinity, and connection. Suzuki looked at purchase behavior that was buried in sales reports. Both companies conducted additional research to learn about these prospective customers and evaluate their business potential, and each completely revamped its marketing strategy to focus on these new markets. Importantly, these were not merely tactical changes, but rather long-term commitments. The strategies have been in play for several years, and evolve as each brand's market does.

These are only two examples of behavioral listening that lead to targeting strategies. Virtually every business can look into its own customer records and interactions to detect changing patterns about customers, their needs, and interests; they then can listen to and utilize that information to target insights.

GENDER, MULTICULTURAL, AND LGBT LISTENING

Research conducted by Johnson and Lai (2010) revealed five factors that influence listening to multicultural consumers, and which apply to any diverse group:

- *Generation*: First, second, and following generations exhibit differences as they experience American culture. Different age groups interpret historical events—such as the Cuban revolution, the Stonewall riots, or the emergence of feminism—from their own generational perspectives. Those perceptions color their worldviews and produce variety in values, interests, and behavior.
- *Culture*: Groups have values, tastes, and preferences they share among themselves and, at times, with the broader culture. The meanings they hold, though, may be somewhat or quite different, depending on the person holding them.
- *Language*: Words do not mean the same thing when their cultural context changes, as many groups have their own terms and vernacular.
- *Lifestyle*: How we live our lives varies from culture to culture and person to person.
- *Digital usage*: Differences between "digital natives" and "digital immigrants" shape options for work and leisure.

The important point is to always be aware of and appreciate diversity. There are countless forms of meaning and expression within and across cultural groups. It's often a challenge to recognize and evaluate these various meanings, and listen to these signals authentically, without bias or agendas, as

Dagny Scott points out in her essay in Chapter 19. Yet doing so is vital for bringing all relevant voices into businesses and brands. The result is that companies bring products and services to market that reflect the people they serve. They're also able to remain on a business growth path that keeps up with, and even stays a little ahead of, the people they're serving. Let's take a quick look at three examples.

- *Gender listening*: We discussed a case in Chapter 5 in which one electronic game maker noticed a trend: more female-authored posts and comments on forums. That early warning alerted the publisher to emerging market opportunities, which gave the company lead time to develop a successful line of games for females—and to do so before its competition did. P&G's BeingGirl.com case provides another excellent example (Chapter 8).
- *Multicultural listening*: As just mentioned, attending to multicultural voices revealed new markets for Hennessy and Suzuki to target; likewise, in Chapter 5, a direct marketer of health and beauty products.
- *LGBT listening*: Companies like Southwest Airlines and Subaru, brands like Absolut vodka, Barefoot Wines, and Pottery Barn furniture, and travel Web site Travelocity.com listen to the LGBT "market" to develop strategies, programs, and services explicitly for them. The word "market" appears in quotes to indicate the remarkable diversity of the LGBT community; the only feature that all members share is a sexual orientation other than heterosexual. Tom Roth, founder of Community Marketing, Inc., a leading gay and lesbian research firm, told a meeting of ARF's People Council (2010) that people identifying themselves as LGBT are included in every racial and ethnic group, religious affiliation, political party, age group, geographic region, income level, and occupation, and buy products in nearly every category.

OFFLINE CONVERSATION LISTENING

Viewers, listeners, or readers talk about brands, shows, characters, and advertising both online and offline. Word-of-mouth researcher Ed Keller explains that offline word of mouth accounts for roughly 90 percent of all conversations, with online covering only 10 percent (Keller 2008). Significant differences exist between the two. People perceive the face-to-face nature of offline conversations to be more credible, more positive, and more likely to inspire purchase. This is not to say that offline listening is hands-down superior to online, only that it is worth factoring when planning listening initiatives, as the following example shows.

Like many media companies, CNN studies its audience to learn about special qualities that help make its viewers especially attractive to particular advertisers. To deviate from the typically demographic-heavy audience surveys about product ownership and plans to buy, CNN decided to enrich its understanding by studying the audience's conversations, specifically in regard to the categories and products they discuss most. For instance, CNN found that its audience had more daily conversations about the Lexus brand than audiences on rival cable networks. To locate the highly engaged individuals who were doing most of this talking, CNN explored the media behavior of talkers across its cable and online properties. It eventually noticed that those who watched CNN programs *and* logged onto its Web sites chatted about Lexus automobiles four times as often as the total population. Quite unexpectedly, and to its benefit, CNN discovered it attracted a remarkably concentrated crowd of Lexus-talkers, which became recognized as fertile advertising ground for targeting owners and prospective buyers. Trade reports confirmed the Lexus commitment to targeting CNN's audiences across its online, mobile, and apps platforms. For example, Lexus, along with Chevron, bought the entire ad inventory on CNN's iPhone app when it launched (Butcher 2009).

People do not always talk about categories, products, or services equally online and offline. Keller's research cites examples of a new video game that was widely discussed online, and a national retailer that wasn't. For the retailer, and for companies whose categories, products, or services seldom appear in online conversations, offline listening provides a valuable source of customer insights and targeting strategies. Companies that enjoy healthy levels of online conversations can also benefit from offline listening, which can be used to validate insights and targeting strategies, and contribute to completeness in analysis by revealing aspects of conversations that were not part of the online discussions.

Although the cases described employed a variety of sophisticated techniques, any size organization can take advantage of offline listening through techniques as simple as suggestion boxes, comment cards, low-cost Web surveys, or honest discussions with customers and prospects. Don't just gloss over this feedback; take the time to read them and extract the topics, improvements, or innovations mentioned. Put these ideas into a spreadsheet. Once they're laid out in one place, themes are likely to emerge that will suggest targeting ideas (and probably others, as well).

LISTEN FOR LANGUAGE IN CONTEXT

Words have different meanings depending on their context. "Chair," for example, can mean a seat, a professorship, a corporate officer, an orchestra position (e.g., second violin), and even the electric chair. A case in Chapter 11 highlighted the different contexts in which people used a particular term that one consumer packaged goods (CPG) company considered for repositioning its business. Disguising the actual term as "awesomeness," for proprietary reasons, we saw that people used it in various ways to describe personal relationships, food, and health. The term "broadband," which is used generically to mean high-speed communications, is another one of these multiple-meaning words, as evidenced in the following example.

One broadband services marketer sought to understand the assorted ways people used the term so that the company could sharpen its targeting, communications, and engagement practices. The marketer retained full-service listening vendor Converseon and worked with researchers there to analyze conversations. They found that the term "broadband" was used frequently in four distinct contexts: the client brand, mobile broadband, fixed broadband, and high-definition television (HDTV) (Key 2009). Even though everyone was talking about the topic, there were four different discussions occurring. This required the company to target its efforts against four related but discrete groups. Listening provided an efficient and straightforward path to defining segments for targeting.

Let's take the example further to show how targeting insights can inform social media planning. Converseon's listening uncovered the social media sites where the different conversations took place, categorized them, and then graded them for quality and conversational fit. Thanks to this research, they learned where to communicate and engage, and found that forums are best suited for technical discussion around the brand, as well as mobile and fixed broadband. Consumer discussions around HDTV through broadband are suited for search-friendly blogs where enthusiasts congregate (see Figure 16.1). Using these results, Converseon's CEO Rob Key told us that because broadband availability

Figure 16.1
**Knowing where topical conversations take place, and grading
the locations, enables social media targeting.**

Conversation Top Domains March 2009

Brand Discussion		Mobile Broadband		Fixed Broadband		Hi-Def TV through Broadband	
Domain	Rank	Domain	Rank	Domain	Rank	Domain	Rank
twitter.com	A	howardforums.com	B	whirlpool.net.au	A	whirlpool.net.au	A
whirlpool.net.au	A	forums.dpreview.com	A	digg.com	A	dslreports.com	A
menstennisforums.com	C	whirlpool.net.au	A	hardforum.com	C	tgdaily.com	A
answers.yahoo.com	A	exetel.com.au	C	forum.lowyat.net	B	digitalhome.ca	B
forum.gsmhosting.com	A	evdoforums.com	C	p2pnet.net	A	twitter.com	A
forums.hardwarezone.com	C	forum.lowyat.net	B	3.8mustang.com	C	digitalspy.co.uk	B
wili.org	C	twitter.com	A	overclockers.co.uk	C	forum.videolan.org	A
forum.lowyat.net	B	mybroadband.com.za	C	forums.digitalpoint.com	A	webwire.com	A
megite.com	C	vodafone.co.uk	B	twitter.com	A	investorshub.advfn.com	A
eu.playstation.com	B	forums.crackberry.com	A	dslreports.com	A	tvover.net	C

Domain Influence Scores - Ranks:
A   Venue falls in the top 1% of highest trafficked, most influential sites
B   Venue falls in the top 10% of high trafficked sites
C   Venue falls in the bottom 90% of trafficked sites

■ Blog   Common top domains
■ Forum   ▨ Twitter.com
■ Micro-blogging platform   ▨ Whirlpool.net
■ Wiki   ▨ Forum.lowyat.net
■ News Aggregator   ▨ Dslreports.com

converseon

Source: Rob Key, Converseon (2009). Used with permission.

varies by provider and geography, top conversation venues tend to be specific to providers or locations.

EMERGING PLAYS FOR LISTENING-BASED TARGETING STRATEGIES

The four approaches to developing listening-based targeting reveal the following emerging plays:

- *Listen inclusively to capture and analyze a variety of voices, contexts, and their conversations to develop targeting insights.* People use language differently in various circumstances and contexts. Although we might assume that we can, we can never truly be sure of who is, or may be, interested in what we're offering. For example, about 25 years ago, New York City replaced the curbs in one neighborhood with an innovative new style using miniramps called "curb cuts." The motivation was to comply with the Americans with Disabilities Act (ADA) to make sidewalks more accessible. The City discovered not long afterward—unexpectedly, and to its delight—that these curb cuts appealed to a broader array of New Yorkers, such as cyclists, mothers with strollers and young children, the elderly, and shoppers wheeling groceries from store to apartment. What started out as a limited idea focused on one "market" turned out to be a universal solution that was attractive to individuals they hadn't previously considered. Listening to conversations and observing behavior allowed the City to expand its targeting by promoting the benefits of curb cuts to all New Yorkers, which led to greater utilization and pleasure for many more people than originally intended.

- *Combine listening-based techniques with conventional targeting to support marketing and advertising strategy.* Listening-based targeting appears to contribute most effectively when it is selected to support clear objectives, as was the case with CNN and the broadband marketer. Furthermore, this method is most successful when it's used as one component of a strategy that combines multiple targeting approaches. Incorporate listening-derived targeting with conventional targeting methods. For example, a quick-service restaurant might learn from listening to target people wanting a midafternoon pick-me-up, and then blend that with daypart and geographic targeting to reach people at the right time from coast to coast.

- *Listen openly, without bias or judgment.* Conversational listening often lets marketers and advertisers travel into new communities and hear different and unfamiliar voices. French-made Hennessy and Japan's Suzuki listened to African-American and urban cultures, respectively, in ways that later benefited them. Research results in Hennessy's case prompted one marketing executive to declare that the "brand vision was not necessarily ours, but this does not make it any less valid. The brand be-longs as much to its consumers as to its managers . . . . We must listen without prejudice" (Florès and Whiting 2005). Listening with that kind of openness allows companies to develop targeting strategies that are cul-turally relevant and respectful. Acting on them requires boldness and a commitment to making decisions that move business forward, instead of maintaining the status quo.

- *Develop segmentations based on conversations and context.* Look into the words or phrases people use, where they use them, and the meanings they give them. Take business, cultural, and media contexts into account when creating conversation-based targets—something we saw in the broadband, Hennessy, and CNN examples. Determine whether conversa-tions separate into two or more groups that require their own targeting ideas, as the broadband example showed. Evaluate the relative strength of conversation-based targeting compared to targeting currently used for a product or service, and go with the strongest one. Hennessy and Suzuki did this, and greatly enhanced their businesses.

SUMMARY

Listening-based targeting provides a new and complementary approach to more conventional targeting methods. Analyzing conversations and the con-texts in which they occur leads to insights for targeting and segmentation strat-egies that mirror customer and prospect interests. Remember to be inclusive when developing targeting strategies, and capture the diversity of voices inter-ested in categories, companies, products, or services. Consider integrating listening-based targeting with conventional targeting approaches to achieve business objectives.

CHAPTER 17

ACHIEVE SHARE OF
MARKET GOALS

$\mathbf{S}$etting an advertising budget to achieve a targeted share of advertising voice is one of the most critical decisions a brand has to make. The right share of voice protects and grows market share, while the wrong share of voice can cause the hold brands have on their market share to slip (Institute of Practitioners in Advertising (IPA) and Nielsen Analytic Partners 2009). As social media conversations supplement—and may even supplant—advertising, a new question emerges: Does a similar relationship exist between *conversational* share of voice and share of market? Can marketers and advertisers achieve a targeted market share by achieving a targeted share of conversational voice? The ability to answer that question can guide the ways in which companies budget, plan, and evaluate their media and marketing programs.

If this chapter were an episode of *MythBusters*, the answer to the "myth" of market share and social media conversation would be "probable." The evidence we have so far is suggestive, but not yet conclusive. However, it's certainly intriguing enough to discuss, and inspiring enough to warrant a deeper look.

Studies from full-service listening companies TNS Cymfony (2008), Keller Fay Group (Moore 2010), and Nielsen (Swedowsky 2009), all performed separately, show that the basic relationship between conversational share of voice and share of market appears to hold across ready-to-eat cereals, automobile brands, and warehouse clubs, respectively. The warehouse club findings shown in Figure 17.1 (Moore 2010) demonstrate the correlation.

A closer look at Costco's data reveals that its conversational share of voice is greater than its market share; that difference is what IPA/Nielsen calls an "excess share of voice." IPA/Nielsen's report concludes that excess share delivers growth: for every 10 percent of excess share, share of market generally increases by one-half of 1 percent. (The payoff is bigger for leading brands, whose gains could nearly triple to 1.4 percent.) If that relationship carries

Figure 17.1
Share of conversation parallels share of market among
warehouse clubs (Swedowsky 2009).

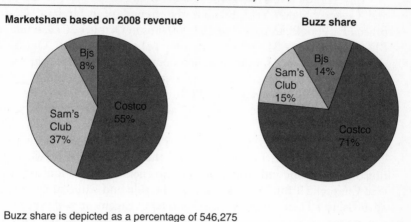

Buzz share is depicted as a percentage of 546,275
mentions of Costco, Sam's Club and Bj's in 2008

Source: Moore, 2009. Used with permission.

over, Costco's results suggest market share improvement arising from its 16 percent excess share of voice. Further empirical research is needed to determine if excess share of conversation voice works the same way as it does in advertising share of voice. If it does, then marketers and advertisers will have an additional tool at their disposal for budgeting and strategy.

Share of conversational voice differs from advertising voice in that advertising share of voice increases when advertisers purchase media impressions that raise or lower their relative share. Marketers and advertisers can influence their conversational share of voice—and potentially their market shares—through strategy and tactics that stimulate or depress conversation.

Four factors shown to affect conversation are customer passion, emotional engagement, marketing communications, and the media context in which ads appear. Let's look at each of these in detail.

- *Customer passion and advocacy*. To further examine the Costco example, Nielsen Online notes that the brand's disproportionate share of voice resulted from the extraordinary grassroots passion exhibited by the Costco community. Costco members think highly of the products, and especially its private-label brand—which, listening analysis showed, meets their expectations for "cheaper" and "less expensive" goods but with quality comparable to national brands. When digging into conversations across all the stores, only Costco's Kirkland brand was mentioned by name (Swedowsky 2009).

Conversation levels rise as the number of brand advocates rises; to that end, Costco's higher levels relate to the strength of its fan base. Costco's official Facebook fan page had 153,000 fans in October 2010, while rival BJ's page had only 21,000—a ratio of 7:1 (Facebook 2010). Outdistancing competitors on advocate numbers contributes to market share advantage, because of the advocates' activity levels and generally positive comments (Nail and Chapman 2008). Conversely, declines in advocates and their weight of influence can presage market share declines (Onalytica 2008).

- *Emotional engagement.* Dr. Carl Marci and his colleagues at neuromarketing research firm Innerscope study the relationships between emotional engagement and advertising effectiveness through biometric study. (See Chapter 19 for Marci's essay on the role and value of emotions in advertising.) Their research on emotional engagement with Super Bowl commercials shows that engagement levels "correlated significantly with the number of times the advertisements were downloaded and viewed online, as well as with the number of times the advertisements were commented on online in the general population at large" (Siefert et al. 2009). In other words, the more emotionally involved viewers are, the more downloads and buzz emerge, which contribute to online conversation volume and share of voice.
- *Marketing communications*, advertising, programming, publicity, and news give people plenty to talk about online and offline. Advertising weight changes and media scheduling raise the discussion level in social media. A TNS Cymfony analysis of flat-panel HDTV brands Sony and Samsung showed that outspending a rival and timing it to a key selling period—like the holiday season—can stimulate online conversations, change historical share of voice patterns, and give brands momentum (Nail and Chapman 2008).
- *Media context* influences word-of-mouth conversation about advertising. ESPN studied the relationship between ad exposure in NFL and college football programs (13 brands) on different sports platforms and word of mouth afterward. Using Keller Fay's TalkTrack (a nationally representative, weekly word-of-mouth survey), ESPN found that while word of mouth peaked on the days the ads aired, viewers continued to talk about them afterward, and at levels higher than nonviewers. Taking two brands and projecting their conversations nationally, Keller Fay estimated that each enjoyed conversation increases in the 80 to 90 million range. Additionally, the firm discovered an interaction effect: Viewers watching the game on both television and ESPN.com had higher word-of-mouth rates than users of either platform alone.

EMERGING PLAYS FOR ACHIEVING MARKET SHARE

That the historical correlation between share of voice and share of market holds, and that a number of factors have been shown to stimulate conversation, led us to develop three emerging plays:

- *Influence conversation levels through a combination of online and offline strategies and tactics.* Think of the four factors just discussed as levers for enhancing conversation levels and share of voice for companies, products, or services. Each brand will need to determine the best mix of conversation drivers for its marketing purposes and market share goals.
- *Leverage social media listening to track progress toward share of conversational voice goals, and use them to adjust programs in near-real time.* Use observations gleaned from listening in three ways:
  - Develop insights for conversation-generating programs.
  - Measure overall levels and patterns in conversation drivers that are important to your conversations, such as trends in advocates, postings, and reading activity and sentiment.
  - Keep tabs regularly on your share of voice and the relative shares of voice among competitors.

  Make timely budgetary, strategic, or tactical adjustments, as necessary, to keep your share of conversation voice where it needs to be. For example, if a competitor is gaining share, consider increasing activities to raise your voice in order to protect your market share and make other competitors vulnerable. A decrease in a major competitor's share of voice signals an opportunity to raise your own share and better your chances for growth. Also keep in mind that factors other than communication strategies influence market share. For that reason, always evaluate communications strategy effectiveness by including all other variables that affect market share, such as competitive changes, product innovations, promotions, or trade deals.

- *Add social media data into predictive models for market share.* TNS research head Larry Friedman told us in an interview that social media data should be strongly considered as input to market mix models. Referring to Bowman et al.'s modeling work (2010), he noted that "social media brings about market share changes that rival the changes one would see through changes in ad spend" (Friedman 2010). Social-media-enhanced models not only improve prediction, they can also enhance planning and lead to deeper insight by answering questions like: "What is causing positive/negative conversation that is affecting share? And what should we do to maximize/minimize its impacts?" This pioneering research needs to be expanded, and the impacts of positive and negative information need to be more generally understood. However, the promise of better business results through better planning and prediction is becoming a reality.

SUMMARY

A solid body of research validates the correlation between advertising share of voice and share of market. Early evidence suggests that the correlation holds between conversational share of voice in social media and market share. If that is the case, marketers and advertisers have an additional metric for setting their budgets and targeting conversational share of voice levels to achieve. Unlike share of advertising voice which is accomplished only through media buying, raising conversation levels results from at least four factors that can be influenced through marketing and advertising strategy, tactics, and programs. Share of conversational voice may also be used to evaluate marketing and advertising effectiveness and provide near real-time guidance for taking actions that maximize or correct them.

CHAPTER 18

LISTENING-BASED SALES PREDICTION

Social media listening provides us with signals that can be used to sense the near-term future. Our ability to improve foresight contributes to better and more desirable company futures (Johansen 2007). We are learning from diverse studies on product categories like entertainment and consumer electronics, or elections for public office, that social media listening data can accurately predict near-term results, such as changes in sales, or winning candidates. The research chiefs, advertisers, and vendors with whom we spoke welcome that power and see listening-based prediction as an emerging business tool. Networked Insights CEO Dan Neely captured that thought when he told us:

> Listening will help create models that can predict changes in markets and consumer trends. Most market research has a predictive element: We study the present and the past to inform what we will do in the future. But, the future will see predictive analytics that can match the vast data set of online conversation against an economic marker or other data set outside of social media—and predict business outcomes. (Neely 2010)

For almost all companies, the ability to anticipate change—even just a few days or weeks out—offers valuable guidance. Predicting the short-term future provides companies with closer-to-real-time data that factors into making marketing, operational, resources, and financial decisions that keep or sharpen competitive edges, and keep the company-customer relationship in sync. This chapter concerns the ways listening data contributes to predicting short-term sales and outlines the emerging plays that are beginning to shape strategy and influence positive business outcomes.

Sales forecasters nowadays possess sophisticated tools for estimation and analysis. Some of these include interviews with key buyers, customer surveys, and market-mix models. Some, the innovators, have recently turned to social media conversations as a source of data to use in straightforward and very sophisticated models to predict future sales within a narrow window of time. Here is a rundown of the types of social media data used to forecast sales:

- Post volumes
- Tweets and status updates
- Search trends
- Online advocacy
- Product reviews

The following pages discuss a variety of sales forecasting approaches using these data sources. You'll notice that most of them were conducted by academics or in company R&D labs on topics such as book sales, movie box office, DVDs, and consumer electronics. The primary reason for choosing these product categories is availability of data. Sources like Amazon provide a wealth of current and historical information on thousands of products, sales rankings, and publicly available consumer-generated content. Though we haven't yet seen research from companies exploring sales prediction yet, we expect that some of them have active research programs but are keeping these close to the vest for competitive reasons. We look forward to the time when their results become available, as their accessibility will stimulate interest in—and knowledge about—cutting-edge uses for social media listening-based sales predictions and their use in strategy.

POST VOLUMES

The study credited with popularizing listening-based prediction explored the question: Can online buzz predict book sales? Researcher Dan Gruhl and his colleagues at IBM's Almaden Research Center and at Google collected and analyzed about 500,000 sales-rank values for more than 2,000 books on Amazon over a four-month period (Gruhl et al. 2005). They then correlated the changes in sales rank for each book with online postings from a variety of relevant sources, and reached the following conclusions:

- Carefully hand-crafted search queries produced volumes of postings that predicted sales ranks—queries that, in many cases, could be automatically generated.
- Online discussion can successfully predict spikes in sales rank for individual titles.

This type of work, correlating post volumes to sales changes, remains popular today. Researchers have added refinements over the years, such as weighting posts according to factors like audience size, source authority (such as through Technorati rank), influence of the post's author, or sentiment. In the competitive marketplace of contact lens solutions, for example, the leading brand was forecast to lose share of category sales because its influence-adjusted share of the posts was declining over time (Onalytica 2009).

TWEETS AND STATUS UPDATES

Twitter's popularity, openness, and roots in broad public communication make it fertile research ground. Now that status updates can be posted on Twitter from popular social networks like Facebook and LinkedIn, tweets are becoming more reflective of the social networking population—and more valuable as a research source. For that reason, more and more market researchers have turned to Twitter to glean insights about what's on people's minds. October 2010 saw nearly 2.5 billion tweets posted on Twitter; that's about 80 million per day, or about 1,000 per second. And people don't just post; they search for what people are saying, 1,200 times per second (BuzzingUp 2010). Most of those posts will not be relevant to researching a specific category or product. But even if only 1/1000th of 1 percent of October's tweets are relevant, that's 25,000 comments and opinions—a substantial number, and one far larger than most surveys or focus groups would ever generate in a single month.

These stats portray active, engaged, chatty social networkers, and beg the question: Can Twitter activity be analyzed in a way that allows sales to be forecasted? Two researchers from HP Labs sought to answer this question for movie box office receipts (Asur and Huberman 2010). Movies generate research interest for several reasons: People avidly discuss them, both online and off; they have known release dates, which, therefore, permit before-and-after comparisons; and trade sources publish their gross revenues. Importantly, several services exist that forecast movie receipts, enabling comparisons of social-media-derived forecasts to competitors and to actual figures.

Asur and Huberman studied 24 movies over a three-month period, capturing and analyzing nearly 3 million tweets from 1.3 million people. Their analysis looked at the "tweet rate"—the number of tweets per hour—concerning a particular movie both before and during the first two weeks after its release. They studied the ratio of positive to negative sentiment (polarity) to determine its impact on predicting second-week sales. Briefly, their findings were:

- Tweet rate is the best predictor of box office sales in weeks one and two.
- Prior to release, tweets contain a higher proportion of links referencing the movie's publicity (trailers, photos, news, or blog posts, for example), but retweets are a minority. However, these do not predict the relative performance of the movie's box office.
- Following release, tweets become more subjective, as people write about their opinions and experiences. The ratio of positive to negative tweets made some improvements in forecasting sales, but "they were not as important as the rate of tweets themselves."

- Tweet rate predicted box office results better than the Hollywood Stock Exchange (HSX), a prediction market that's long been considered the gold standard. HSX is a virtual exchange where traders buy and sell shares in movies. The movie stock prices can predict box office results: lower prices, lower box office; higher prices, higher box office.
- Tweet rate not only predicted opening weekend numbers, but accurately forecasted the revenue for all movies in distribution, some of which were two months old.

Overall, the authors concluded that: "The results have shown that the buzz from social media can be accurate indicators of future outcomes. The power of social media is illustrated by the fact that a simple linear regression model considering only the rate of tweets on movies can perform better than artificial money markets."

The tweet rate method is applicable beyond movies, to just about any product or service actively discussed in online conversations, especially for those, like entertainment, cars, consumer electronics, or sports, that have an official launch, release, or event date.

SEARCH TRENDS

Many companies plan marketing and investment activities according to news about business conditions, such as monthly retail, auto, and home sales, reported by the government or other organizations. However, timeliness and accuracy are two inherent problems with the monthly releases, as the government issues reports about one to two weeks after the month ends. For example, June reports come out in mid-July. Even then, data may not be final, as it may be revised up to two times subsequently. Improving data by overcoming these issues can equip businesses and policymakers with more accurate, timelier information about the current business environment, and can, therefore, improve the quality of their decisions.

Google economists took up the challenge to "predict the present." While we know that search leads sales, these researchers sought to uncover whether search volumes on a particular category or brand would be helpful in predicting that category's or brand's monthly sales. To test that, Google economists Hal Varian and Hyunyoung Choi built two forecasting models to predict sales one month ahead. One model included Google Trends data; the other did not. Details on the models are available in Varian and Choi (2009). The models themselves are very straightforward; and, for those so inclined, the authors provide the software code to create them. Google Trends, available through Google, provides daily and weekly reports on query volumes related to most industries and individual brands. It is described more fully in the Appendix.

Varian and Choi's research analyzed areas like automobile sales and those of individual brands, home sales, and travel. After running its models many times, Google concluded that those that include relevant Google Trends data "tend to outperform" those that do not. In other words, Google Trends data leads to more accurate predictions of month-end sales. Ideally, Google's researchers state, prediction could be improved further by developing models that identify "turning points" in categories and brand sales within the month. That would give managers the ability to respond to real-time shifts in their market (Varian and Choi 2009).

ONLINE ADVOCACY

Advocates, those passionate people who champion companies or products, contribute substantially to sales and market share. In the HDTV market, Samsung's market share leadership over Sony was correlated with advocacy. Although more people are familiar with the Sony name, Samsung outscored it in terms of conversational volume and favorability during the key selling season. Why? Samsung had a greater number of advocates than Sony or other competitors (Nail 2009).

In order to be predictive, we need to model the relationship between advocacy and sales. One step in that direction comes from full-service listening vendor MotiveQuest, which created an online measure similar to the Net Promoter Score, called the Online Promoter Score. Net Promoter Score is calculated by using answers to a single question: How likely is it that you would recommend Company X to a friend or colleague? Researchers compute the score by subtracting the percentage of detractors from the percentage of promoters. The Net Promoter Score links to company revenue growth rates (Reicheld 2006). For its computation, the Online Promoter Score, developed in conjunction with leading academics, listens to and analyzes social media conversations and sentiment (MotiveQuest 2009).

MotiveQuest's work with the MINI automobile utilized the Online Promoter Score to gauge the effectiveness of the brand's communications programs in generating sales. Following a successful U.S. introduction, MINI did not have a new product for its second year—a serious hurdle in a marketplace where sales momentum and new-car sales are driven by introductions, relaunches, and updates. MINI's agency, BSSP, built and implemented a progressive three-pronged communications program based on listening insights from Motive-Quest research (see Chapter 9 for a full description of this case). As the campaign rolled out, MotiveQuest tracked the relationship between the Online Promoter Score and sales from January 2006 through April 2007. Its analysis revealed that changes in the Online Promoter Score predicted changes in sales about one month in advance. The direction and size of the sales changes were just as important: Sales increased or decreased by 53 percent of the change in the Online Promoter Score. If the score went up by, for instance, 10 percent, then sales would increase by 5.3 percent. While the percentage change in sales will likely differ depending on the industry and brand, one result that emerged from this study is clear: The value of advocacy on sales is measurable and can be used to develop and evaluate marketing and advertising.

PRODUCT REVIEWS

Product reviews feature prominently as a source of online conversation. Internet reviews influence purchase, and retailers such as Best Buy and sites like Bizrate.com encourage their visitors to post appraisals and evaluate products. Amazon is especially aggressive in this area, ceaselessly developing new ways for its community members to post, read, and engage with one another. The wealth of comments and ratings attracts researchers who want to learn if, and how, user-generated content influences sales.

The first wave of research focused on the ratings and volume of reviews, and it solidly supports the notion that reviews influence product sales, box office receipts, and TV show ratings (Chevalier and Mayzlin 2006, Hu et al. 2008). However, those early studies did not capture the dynamics of evaluation, reading, and acting upon reviews that take place within a virtual conversation; conversations in which people pay attention to the qualities of both the review and the person writing it. Readers are listening for clues, and this second wave of research is looking for those same clues and gauging their impact. Understanding which features of reviews influence customers gives companies additional insight for making decisions such as which reviews to promote, which product features to emphasize, or which keywords to buy for a search engine marketing program. The emerging picture is one where customers weigh good and bad news and act in accordance with the judgment; people are not responding in knee-jerk fashion to high ratings.

An analysis of the related literature uncovered the following factors as those that influence sales:

- *"Helpful" reviews*: Helpful ratings may be a stronger motivator to purchase than the overall "star" rating for a product. People judge reviews as helpful in two ways: One is that review readers actually mark them as helpful, which is feedback that the retail site then counts and displays. The second method is to use readers' own evaluations of the review's opinion (subjective) and factual (objective) statements.

  Reviews containing primarily objective comments are generally considered to be more helpful, while highly opinionated evaluations are usually less so—and have a downward impact on sales. However, the type of product makes a difference as to which kind of statements readers find most helpful. Readers value objective comments for feature-based products like electronics or washers, whereas more subjective statements are appreciated for experience-based products like DVDs. That makes sense, as the former relates to performance and the latter to how people felt about a movie (Chen et al. 2008, Ghose and Ipeirotis 2010). As more research is done in this area, marketers and advertisers will look forward to learning about the helpfulness of the mix of statements for products or services that combine experience and features in widely discussed categories such as autos, travel, and consumer electronics.

- *Reviewer characteristics*: There are differences between the top, or power, reviewers on sites and those who author individual posts. Two studies suggest that reviews by the top 1,000 reviewers are *not* important to people's purchase decisions. While it may be ego-gratifying to be designated as a "top reviewer," their impact on sales is not retailer-gratifying. Review readers value expertise, readability, and the right mix of subjective and objective content. The reviews that the community rates as helpful are the ones influencing sales, period. Amazon, for example, "spotlights" the two most helpful reviews for a product, and these "super-reviews" impact sales more strongly than the average of all the other helpful reviews. Those reviews serve as shortcuts, enabling people to reduce the time they spend searching and evaluating (Chen et al. 2008, Hu et al. 2008, Ghose and Ipeirotis 2010).
- *Product coverage*: Reviews of newly introduced products or those that did not garner many reviews have greater impact on sales than those for widely covered products. For example, the power of an individual review for a *Harry Potter* book is less than a review for a less popular title.
- *Sentiment*: The accepted wisdom is that unfavorable reviews depress sales and positive reviews increase sales, but the relationship is actually more nuanced than this. In fact, there are times when negative reviews spur sales, as well as instances in which both negative and positive sentiments have no impact.

Two factors appear to positively influence sales even when the reviews are less than favorable: product awareness and perceptions of review quality. Jonah Berger and his colleagues investigated awareness and found that while positive reviews increased book sales for *all* authors they studied, negative reviews affected authors differently. Specifically, the more critical assessments hurt the sales of well-known authors, but increased sales for lesser-known authors by raising their profiles and interest in their work. Berger theorizes that negative word of mouth may work in a similar way for lesser-known products or services (Berger et al. 2009).

Elements that indicate a quality review—one that is informative, fair, balanced, well-written, and spell-checked—are also associated with increased sales, even when the review itself is negative. Reviews that lay out the strengths and weaknesses provide information that readers use to evaluate the product from their perspective and interests. For example, a reviewer who claims that a particular product is difficult to hold in her small hands might not be a showstopper for someone with normal-sized hands. If criticisms or objections are not as important to the reader, increased sales can result (Ghose and Ipeirotis 2010).

There have been several studies of the effects of "buzz" on box office sales. Some of these indicate that the volume of postings or tweets about a movie impacts sales more powerfully than sentiment does. In other words, the mere fact that people are discussing a movie is often more important than the opinions expressed during these discussions. The reason may be, as noted earlier, that people are reading or discussing them for their helpfulness, balancing the pros and cons in light of their own specific interests and preferences.

- *Product features*: There's a new method that uses text mining on product reviews to extract the features discussed. It then estimates their importance to consumers and the opinion around them, and models their contribution to sales. For example, by studying camcorders and digital camera sales on Amazon, Archok and colleagues (2010) determined that discussion over features had the greatest impact on sales—far greater than factors like product price, product age, trends, seasonal effects, and the volume and sentiment of reviews. What's especially interesting is the ability to include subjective features like "ease of use" and "design" into the models; these terms capture intangible qualities that influence decisions but have been hard to explain in a quantitative way. By including product features from the posts, researchers were able to build accurate predictive models of near-term future changes in sales.

- *Passage of time*: Reviews lose their influence over time; the early ones have the most substantial impact on sales. This is presumably because people have additional information available to them as time passes (Hu et al. 2008). Jonah Berger found that although the impact of negative reviews on lesser-known authors diminished over time, this was not the case for established authors. The reason: People may be more willing to buy afterward because the negative review raised awareness of the author—which correlates with purchase—and their memory of the review's disparaging tone had faded. In other words, when a famous author comes out with a clunker, people write it off and look forward to the next one; but when a book by an emerging or promising author comes out and gets a negative review, buyers think more about the author than they do the specifics of what reviewers did not like.

Emerging Plays to Predict Changes in Sales

We identified four emerging plays that aid in predicting changes in sales:

- *Match the sales prediction approach to the type of product or service marketed, as well your organization's capabilities.* Sales prediction methods will continue to be tested and improved, and new ones will appear as the discipline evolves. We have already learned that, one, all social media sources are not alike; two, types of products or services, such as functional or hedonic products, generate a variety of discussions and are evaluated differently; and, three, that accurate predictions can use simple trends, like the tweet rate, or combine very sophisticated text mining and econometric modeling. Increase your brand's confidence in listening-based sales predictions by triangulating; utilize and compare several listening-based approaches and/or combine them with traditional sales predictions.

Companies of all sizes can conduct sales forecasting; several of the methods described in this chapter can be adapted by even the smallest business. Predictive approaches grounded in analyzing volumes are applicable and, importantly, relatively easy to do well. For example, every company should take advantage of programs like Google Trends or Google Insights for Search, free tools that provide reports and downloadable data on current and historical trends in search terms.

By importing the search data into a spreadsheet and adding a column for sales, users can discern lead-and-lag relationships among search volumes and sales—no special expertise or additional investment required. To add a little more insight, integrate search volumes for competitors, to learn how competitive searching affects your search volumes and sales. You can also perform similar analyses when people tweet, blog, or otherwise discuss your category, brand, product, or service in public places.

- *Leverage sales predictions and develop strategy linked to sales drivers.* Sales prediction models reflect people's behavior, the way they interpret discussions, and how they act. Use those listening-based insights to give clear, specific directions for tailoring or adjusting marketing and advertising strategy to grow sales. Consider some of the strategic and tactical guidance available from our review:
  - Detect and respond to changes in demand in near-real time.
  - Identify and promote the most helpful reviews.
  - Emphasize the features people value most highly.
  - Match emotional and rational messaging to reflect the product or service type.
  - Select "hot button" terms for search engine marketing keyword purchases.
  - Reach out to the right people for direct engagement.

  Designing strategy and implementing tactics that are grounded in factors that motivate sales promises to bring about greater coherence in marketing and advertising. You'll want to predict and adapt continuously as goals, programs, peoples, and resources become more closely aligned.

- *Challenge the conventional wisdom around ratings, influence, and sentiment.* People do not blindly respond to high ratings, influential reviewers, or positive buzz. Research shows that they instead take a more balanced approach to conversation content; they weigh the pros and cons, and take the writer or speaker into account. Even negative reviews do not always lead to negative outcomes, and can actually stimulate sales under certain circumstances. For these reasons, question the received wisdom about influencers, ratings, and sentiment, and determine whether, and how, it applies to marketing and advertising your products and services.

For example, Amazon's elite top 1,000 reviewers have shown to be unimportant to book sales, whereas a reviewer that the community had deemed "helpful" can inspire sales. Companies that are tempted to base an influencer social media strategy on such lists may find their programs underperforming. The key seems to be locating those individuals the community regards as influential, not choosing reviewers based on their volume of activity.

- *Share the predictions with colleagues and management.* Predicting sales changes from listening data transforms conversation into valuable management metrics and points the way to the near-term future that colleagues and senior management readily grasp. The sales prediction is a common currency. As valuable as consumer insights are for the marketing and advertising functions, their power is often unrecognized or underappreciated by the C suite. However, executives and higher-ups will see the connection of listening-based sales predictions to the bottom line right away. Communicate predictions throughout the company, to open possibilities for more shared understanding of customers, greater collaboration, better strategy and tactical programs, and more concerted action for building business.

SUMMARY

Social media listening data is being used to accurately predict sales in the short term, providing businesses with signals about their current environment. These forecasts allow companies to take action by responding to expected changes in demand. Initially based on buzz volume, prediction models have matured to capture the content and characteristics of online discussion that drive sales. Marketers and advertisers can leverage those qualities to create and implement strategies and tactics that resonate with customers and link directly to revenue growth.

Because customers and prospects are not automatons, you must carefully consider the pros and cons in discussions, consider the writer's or speaker's perspective, and act according to their judgment. Conventional notions of the impact of influence, sentiment, and product ratings do not apply across the board, and companies need to reflect upon the applicability of these ideas to their specific situations. Last, listening-based sales predictions provide measures that nearly every function appreciates and understands. Sharing them across your organization can bring the value of listening to the entire enterprise.

PART IV

LISTENING'S NEW FRONTIERS

Up until now, lessons from contemporary research and cases provided guidance based on the best of what is known about social media listening. As a young and still emerging field, listening is evolving and pushing boundaries. To understand what lies ahead, we consulted the Lewis and Clarks, experts actively exploring and mapping listening's new frontiers. This part's five chapters bring together 15 contributions from 18 leaders who grapple each day with listening and its business value for companies, their brands, and their products and services.

Rooted in their real-world experiences and presented from their perspectives, the essays of these leaders are remarkable, for their focus on issues central to business building, their specificity, and the strength of their prescriptions. There is, however, one overarching theme and directive that connects them all: Expand your thinking about listening and the ways you can apply it. Future contributions rest upon listening to new signals; diving into deeper levels of analysis and insight; basing decisions on listening data; and reinventing media and marketing as social processes centered on engagement. Companies need to become listening organizations through and through, if they are to achieve listening's goal: to sense, respond, and act in a timely customer-centered manner that mutually benefits their business and the people they serve.

Five winning plays were derived from these essays and each is covered in turn in Chapters 19 to 23. Here are the plays, with very high-level summaries. The chapters will provide a more detailed discussion of key themes.

- *Listen to new signals.* Not all listening signals come from conversation; some can be found in the silent signals of emotions. Listen openly, without preconceived notions and without prejudice in order to hear what people are really saying or expressing.
- *Focus on culture.* Deeper insight comes from understanding people in all of their cultural contexts. Listening is more than recognizing what people

say; it includes understanding the values, motivations, meanings, and relationships that help explain why people speak and act as they do.

- *Change the research paradigm.* Social media listening research should bring about an era of real-time data that anticipates change and can be used to visualize and create a rewarding business future. For that to happen, data quality needs to improve; companies need to ensure that their people develop and work with quality data; and organizations need to effectively communicate the insights from this data throughout their enterprises.

- *Rethink marketing, advertising, and media.* Conversations are being considered like media. This change challenges conventional notions of what advertising is, how it is planned and bought, how it is consumed, and how it is evaluated. One controversial scenario outlined describes an emerging world where advertisers pay people for conversations that ripple through social networks, instead of paying media companies for ad placements as often as they used to. Conversations, engagement, and mobility are creating a globe-circling "people's network," with new rules for effective and successful marketing.

- *Become a listening organization.* Productive listening requires that you have the right organizational structure and executive support—something many companies often lack. We need to view and implement social media listening strategically, with an eye toward improving business processes and driving company culture. Organizations must embrace a new "mental model" for listening, one that is capable of sustainably creating value for the enterprise.

Now, onward to the future of listening.

CHAPTER 19

LISTEN TO NEW SIGNALS

Conversations are the raw materials of almost all listening research. Yet companies pushing listening's boundaries do more than listen to conversations; they also pay attention to the silent signals of behavior and emotions that potential customers offer. Observing what people do and understanding how they feel leads to insights that may be less apparent when we rely solely on what people say.

We caught a glimpse of behavioral listening in the Hennessy and Suzuki Hayabusa cases in Chapter 6, and again during the discussion on targeting in Chapter 16. Behavioral listening recognizes patterns or trends from observations or data, which become springboards for deeper investigation. For example, trends in Web site linking tipped Hennessy Cognac onto a hidden market of passionate African-American consumers. From a standard sales report, motorcycle maker Suzuki noticed that a substantial percentage of its high-end Hayabusa buyers were urban and multicultural, an unexpected finding that ran counter to its conventional target market notions of racing and performance enthusiasts. Each company followed up on the behavioral clues it received by conducting listening, ethnographic, and market research to refine its understanding and develop insights. Both brands completely revamped their marketing strategies with successful results. The key takeaway here: Companies must listen openly, without presumption or judgment, and avoid imposing their views. Dagny Scott, head of cultural and business insights for advertising and design firm Crispin, Porter + Bogusky, explains why in her essay, which follows.

Neuroscientist Carl Marci focused on listening to the unconscious emotions of audiences as measured through biometric signals, a kind of listening that lets businesses anticipate what consumers will think and feel, even when they're unable to express these emotions consciously. For example, companies might expose potential consumers to media advertising or in-store experiences, and then measure their responses. In his essay here, Marci's real-world examples show the various ways that brands use biometric listening insights for a variety of purposes, including marketing strategy and testing advertising creative.

Listen Openly to Signals

Dagny Scott, Director of Cultural and Business Insights,
Crispin, Porter + Bogusky

When I was a young woman taking some time to vagabond around the country after graduate school, I worked as a waitress. Amid the din of the morning rush of a Santa Fe café, I would make the rounds refilling coffee cups, a pot in each hand, asking "regular or decaf?" It was the simplest of questions, begging the simplest of answers. Yet I realized instantly on many occasions after the customer had answered that I had no idea which pot to pour from. Because the question had become robotic—asked dozens of times over the course of the morning—I simply didn't hear the answer. In short, I was no longer listening.

That is a scenario to which many of us can relate. And here's another one: Who hasn't been speaking with a partner or colleague when conversation gets heated? You may be acting like you're listening, but you're simply using the time to rehearse in your mind exactly what you are going to say the moment he or she finishes. Any listening that's being done at that point is an act of gymnastics, in which you twist and turn the incoming words to confirm or deny your own worldview.

Most of us tend to think of listening as a passive activity. However, it is not. We also tend to think that listening occurs without judgment; that it is an objective, factual reception of information. On this count, too, we often fool ourselves. Our ears are not receptacles, and words are not facts. Listening, in fact, takes work.

What does all this have to do with our industry? Everything. While listening now refers to something specific in terms of brand conversations and communications, it must be rooted in the very human principle from which the word originated for it to function meaningfully. And frankly, we're pretty lousy at that. So it stands to reason that we might not be as great at the advertising application of listening, either.

This is not a new problem by any means. A century ago, Pulitzer Prize-winning author Upton Sinclair wrote about the difficulty of getting a man to see truth when his salary relies upon his not seeing it. Likewise, today, it is difficult for corporate players to truly listen when their business model relies on legacy practices, their performance is measured by old metrics, and their bonuses are predicated upon short-term gain that discourages making course changes.

We see what passes for listening all the time, but it's a thin brew, watered down with preconceived notions, previously whittled-down questions, a narrowly construed set of concepts, and an outcome in which the interest is already vested. Discovery—true discovery, borne of open-ended listening—is rare indeed. That's because the upshot is often hard work, work that might overturn those notions, upset those plans, and force a recasting of goals.

On the other side of the equation is the environment in which we attempt to listen. With chatter and noise growing ever louder, it's hard to recognize the core of what's being said. We live amid a relentless torrent of headlines—no longer printed, of course, and generated by everyone. Gravitas and goofiness alike are mashed and flattened into one indiscriminate ticker tape of bits: An earthquake devastates Haiti. A boy floats away in a balloon. The markets are up. A video goes viral. Jobs are lost. An affair is revealed. The markets are down. The images and headlines beget the next moment's images and headlines. The news of the day, large and small, comes and goes; it's always something else tomorrow, though it's always somewhat the same, too. Each screen flickers and dies, flickers and dies, one spot in the great pointillism that is culture today. New networks form, the swarm moves. You must get in. You must be big. You must know what's happening. You can't miss this wave. Wait, never mind; it's something else already.

The headlines, the fragments, and the connections combine, filling our world, *becoming* our world itself. The noise grows louder. But we confuse the rise of Twitter and the fall of Hummer with the real news. So we race to "get in" on Twitter, not realizing that by the time we do, something else will have taken its place. We fail to see that Twitter is a symptom, an advantageous play at the intersection of larger forces—instead of the force itself. Not realizing that we have confused listening with reacting.

To truly listen implies no presumption, nor any judgment. However, it is not an empty act. To truly listen is the hard, Zen work of actively creating and maintaining a beginner's mind. To listen, one should be prepared to do something that does not come naturally: Be open to feeling uncomfortable. Try as you might to remember this when you claim to be "listening" to the consumer and to culture. Remember the lessons you have learned, from your partner, your child, your friends, your life. Remember what it means to listen first as a human being.

Biometrics: Source for Listening Insights

Carl D. Marci, MD, Co-founder, CEO, and Chief Science Officer, Innerscope Research, Inc.

There is an interesting dichotomy around using biometric tools for listening in the market research industry right now. Some brands and companies consider this kind of research to be a future tool for tomorrow, while others view it as a reality occurring today. The latter group is collaborating with companies like Innerscope Research to listen to unconscious emotional responses in order to brand messages across a variety of stimuli.

Most Fortune 100 companies have adopted biometric research to some degree, and are testing throughout the world. Since these study results are regarded as a competitive advantage, many have opted not to publicize their findings yet. However, the power of this listening approach should be accessible to all researchers. My views on the role of neuroscience-based tools for listening are grounded in my experience leading Innerscope, an active and growing

(*continued*)

(continued)

company with over five years working in the market with many large businesses and brands.

Innerscope listens to the biologically based signals of the unconscious in order to gain a better understanding of consumer engagement with brands and marketing messages on any platform. These signals are the embodiment of emotional response, generating signature responses that are direct outputs from the brain.

Our brains are the ultimate multitaskers; they're constantly doing multiple things at the same time. The explosion of knowledge that has recently emerged from multiple scientific fields—especially affective neuroscience—is more than relevant to how business can listen even more closely to emotional experience. The lessons we've learned form the foundation of new approaches to measuring the unconscious. Some key tenets include:

- *Emotions are the primary drivers of human behavior.* This is due in large part to the fact that the brain's emotional centers process information before it reaches cognitive areas. As a result, unconscious emotional responses significantly influence conscious thinking.
- *Emotions efficiently tell us which bits of information to engage and which to ignore.* The bits we emotionally engage are the most relevant on an unconscious level. Emotional processing directs attention, enhances learning, and influences memory.
- *There are no direct connections between the emotional centers and the language centers of the brain, so it is difficult for people to accurately report their emotional experiences consciously.* By listening to unconscious emotional engagement through biological responses, we eliminate conscious biases from the research process altogether.

Using our biometric technology platform in combination with eye tracking, Innerscope measures these subtle, unconscious responses as they occur, by processing signals of heart rate, respiration, skin sweat, motion, and visual attention.

However, you also need to understand what you hear, and put that listening effort to work. Every Innerscope study has yielded new insight for us, and actionable direction for the businesses listening with us. Some of my personal favorites include our Super Bowl studies and our work with the Campbell Soup Company.

An earlier reference in Chapter 18 to the results of our 2008 Super Bowl study mentioned one of our findings: that the greater the emotional engagement, the more downloads and comments an ad contributed to online share of voice. We have run the study each year since, in an effort to keep the research fresh.

A unique finding from the 2009 Super Bowl centered on the economy. Historically, ads using economic themes had never scored particularly high in emotional engagement across our ad database. Yet during the very early stages of the great recession in February 2009, people were already showing signs of sensitivity to the economy in their unconscious emotional responses. Our top Super Bowl ads were Careerbuilder.com (need a new job?) and Cash4gold.com (need to liquidate some assets?). While people were not able to verbalize the anxiety that the burgeoning economic situation caused, their biometric responses were communicating it clearly. This adds to the considerable scientific literature supporting how the unconscious subtly affects behavior long before we are able to consciously identify that an effect occurs or express why it is taking place.

For the Super Bowl in 2010, Innerscope partnered with *Wired* magazine for an "ultra geeky Super Bowl party" that married studying the ads with a party for loyal readers. Listening to this specific audience segment was not going to provide a representation of the general public; however, it would tell us what was most relevant to the trendy, tech-savvy, digitally conscious millennial generation. Our Top Ten list did not look anything like the other lists in circulation. *Wired* readers were most engaged with ads for video games, gadgets, free food, and Google, findings that make sense in the context of listening to this target audience.

More specifically, our top-performing ad for Electronic Art's video game Dante's Inferno was listed as one of the "weakest ads" in rankings from other measurement services. Importantly, the game itself had received weak reviews from other gamers at the time of its initial release. After the Super Bowl ad aired, the game became the top-selling original-title video game for the first quarter of 2010. Again, it makes sense that *Wired*'s readership would respond emotionally to an ad that was relevant to them, and that this group represents a sample of the population that propelled game sales early in the year.

Another example of how listening to biometric signals translates into actionable insights for businesses can be seen in our recent work with the Campbell Soup Company. The company embarked on a multiyear research exploration of consumer experiences of Campbell's products, both in the home and the grocery store soup aisle. By listening to how the customer interacts with the soup aisle from a biometric and eye-tracking perspective, Innerscope helped Campbell Soup determine new ways to organize the category and shelves for easier navigation of core products. New ideas about clustering product options around benefits leverage the way people are naturally inclined to search for soup. Given that a lot of shoppers make grocery store purchases on impulse, this is a critical area for insights into what is going on unconsciously during those moments.

One of the greatest advantages of biometric research and listening to unconscious signals is that business is able to anticipate what consumers are going to think and do based on how they feel—even though customers are not able to consciously express it. This applies to questions at any level, from basic decisions of "go or no go" for ad creative to the complexities of "where do we go from here" marketing strategy. By drawing on a variety of lessons and best practices on unconscious responses to television, print, radio, online, and out-of-home, Innerscope is developing models of advertising effectiveness that are relevant for the ever-evolving media landscape.

The future of biometric research itself is all about listening to the consumer's unconscious, and connecting the dots to business decision making. Studies in both market research and academia have shown that emotional responses have a stronger relationship to brand attitudes and purchase intent than other more cognitively based measures of advertising effectiveness. Innerscope's own work

(continued)

(continued)

with clients has also provided examples of our unconscious emotional engagement metric clearly linked to all stages of the path to purchase, from attracting
attention to seeking new information to purchase behavior. Market and media
research is truly on the front lines of discovery and has just started work to
uncover the relationships between biometrics and other critical business metrics.

The lesson here? Make listening on multiple levels the core of what you do.
With each opportunity to listen to what consumers feel and engage in, use the
evolving conscious measurement tools and the new tools of unconscious biometric measurement to become savvier marketers with a greater appreciation for the
true consumer experience.

CHAPTER 20

FOCUS ON CULTURE

The hallmarks of social media, interaction, and communication should focus our attention on *culture*—the behaviors, values, and meanings people express and share. Culture provides the context through which people are able to understand one another. Just think about what it's like when you visit an unfamiliar part of the country or the world. Before you even travel, you want to find out about your destination's culture. This information will give you important clues about how to go about your business or leisure enjoyably and successfully.

Too many marketers and advertisers listening to social media conversations focus on the superficial aspects—that is, the words—without paying enough attention to the cultural context in which those conversations occur. They understand some things, but they still miss a lot. After all, what good does it do us to know that moms talk about a diaper's performance when it's not informed by the way moms view their role, and the emotional underpinnings of their infant care? Or that people are more frequently searching for terms like "foreclosure" or "consumer debt" without knowing what they are thinking about and how they are coping with changes in the economy, their jobs, and their families?

The matter of culture becomes more important when a company's social media use moves from being a superficial add-on to a primary method for doing business. Companies participating and engaging more often need to be culturally literate in order to understand, engage with, and serve the people within their communities, and able to develop and leverage cultural insights. These cultural insights may well become the "new demography" and replace broad and inflexible characterizations of consumers with nuanced understandings of people.

Professor and social media research authority Robert Kozinets's discourse on digital ethnography (called "netnography"), along with a second piece from Columbia Business School's Joe Plummer and pollster John Zogby on "neo-tribes," highlight two productive yet different methods that can be used to delve into culture. These approaches penetrate the depths of people's lives and serve to generate insights that open opportunities for marketing and advertising.

Intermix: Listening to the Datastreams of Consumer Lifestreams

Robert V. Kozinets, Professor, York University, Schulich School of Business

There is little doubt that much of the momentum of contemporary social life can be found online. We book our travel, our dining, and our movies online. We check our friends and the weather. We find jobs, fellow hobbyists, and even dates (and, in some cases, spouses).

This is important for marketers—and, really, for everyone in business. If business is based on the understanding of people and their needs, then business also needs to understand what is going on online. The flow of electronic "conversation" of all kinds—words, texts, symbols, pictures, movies—provides us with an amazing opportunity to listen to consumers in action, as they interact and do, by sharing, recording, referencing, and evaluating what they and others do. Social media is not only a window into what consumers are saying, but also into what they are *doing*.

We are getting to the point where you cannot understand the course of someone's day—the way their time and plans, the shaping of their thoughts and goals are laid out before them [what I will call their "lifestream"]—without understanding the interactions and relationships that they are conducting online. We can make this ephemeral notion of the lifestream more applicable and concrete with some business-centered examples:

- A style-forward retail clothing brand building locations on the West Coast
- A manufacturer of children's cribs based in Europe
- A global financial services firm

These companies might seek to understand their consumers in traditional ways:

- Focus groups, where teens discuss their views of clothing
- Personal interviews with mothers
- A major global survey about how people use financial services

While all of these are valid and useful methods to inform listening, consider the knowledge that's left on the table. Think of the Seattle high schooler's all-important social life and the role of Facebook within it. Think of the brand-new mom in London and the role of online mommy forums in helping her deal with her anxiety and answer her many questions. And what about the way the Tokyo stock investor obsessively checks her online trading forums and financial advice blogs?

Could the keen business listener seek to understand the world of any of these individuals—and any of the groups to which they belong—and really, truly appreciate them without referencing the datastreams that feed into their lifestreams? It is likely that their online worlds will be mentioned, perhaps even detailed, in the focus groups, interviews, and (probably less likely) surveys. But it seems increasingly unforgivable that a marketer would miss investigating:

- The series of all-important Facebook updates
- That controversy on the mommy blogs about the risk of sudden infant death
- That amazing new stock prediction tool that everyone was talking about, which turned out to be a dud

To truly understand and empathize, you need to listen to the cultural conversations that take place through the Internet: on the Web, peer-to-peer, via video, and through services like Facebook. You would need to conduct *netnography*, a term that refers to online participant-observational research. Netnography inhabits the in-between spaces where large sample sizes coexist with rich, detailed, visual, textual, audiovisual, social, and naturalistic information. Netnography is electronic ethnography—cultural research that maintains and revels in the social qualities of social media. Netnography is not the automatic coding of data-mined material, or the semantic search engine by itself, although it can use such helpful tools. Rather, it is full-on human insight, the question-to-answer investigation that considers the gamut of human interaction and researcher intuition.

Exploring online cultural worlds is the very purpose for which netnography was designed, and is what it does well. But listening online exclusively, to the online worlds and interactions, may be insufficient by itself. In this age of social media, this time of digital connection and online advertising, of blind faith in buzzwords and the "next new thing," it is important for thinkers to also question these new methods. When is online enough? And when is it not enough?

Where is business, relating to the public and marketing, moving? It is moving to those places in between thought and action, imagination unbound and practice constrained. What is important, and where I see netnography and online listening developing, is in the interstices, the places between online avatars flying free and the physical world of gravity-entangled meat puppets.

The art and science of market understanding in the next three to five years should become increasingly obsessed with the relationship between what happens in the sphere of online social interaction and in people's physically embodied lives. That will require astute and rigorous application and integration of existing and new methods of listening. The astute listener would be wise to ask questions like the following:

- How do teenagers' Facebook conversations affect their sense of style? How do their online photo albums transmit their identity, and how does fashion play a role in this? How do they discuss them in school, face-to-face, over SMS?
- What questions does the new mom learn through her social media interactions on blogs and bulletin boards? How does she mention them in person, with her family, and her personal social circle? What new motivation does she find when online and in-person mix?

(continued)

(continued)

- How does the day trader learn about new techniques of valuation, new blogs, or new places to learn about undervalued companies? How does her real-world activity influence her online behavior, and vice versa?

In my recent book, *Netnography: Doing Ethnographic Research Online* (Sage Publications, 2009), I offer the integrative idea of the "intermix." I suggest that a good netnography will carefully investigate and take into account the interconnection of the various modes of social interaction—online and off—in culture members' daily lived experiences. It will do this through the incorporation of various methods.

We can follow the intermix by tracking the trail of consumers' own words and experiences. If we conduct profound and insightful research that asks the right questions and probes the right cues, then it leans in the direction of integration and of intermix. For example:

- Teens in a focus group may mention seeing clothing in a Facebook profile picture. The interviewer who listens would follow up by investigating which brands were mentioned, how they were mentioned, how the Facebook medium altered the marketing and lifestream message, and how the online medium translated into in-person conversations and action.
- The new mother might mention reading about a new crib controversy on "the blog I read" during an in-home interview. The interviewer would track this by carefully examining this blog, as well as other related online resources that the new mom uses. He or she would then explore the actual social application of this online information.
- Based on investigative qualitative research, a multidimensional understanding of the day trader's world would be formed. It would inform the kinds of questions asked on the global survey to include those about online resources, among them social media forums. Follow-up, open-ended questions would explore the interrelationships between online resources and in-person interactions and decisions.

In the final analysis, truly listening to consumers' communications—both online and off—becomes a voraciously credible, embedded understanding of consumers' lives as they take place, in multiple social and cultural worlds—both online and off. Cutting-edge netnography contributes increasingly to this understanding. When members of the business and research worlds attend to the intermix, the blending of social realities as communications take on myriad forms. Listening then blends into action, into an engagement with the many roles and worlds of the consumer, so that the deepest understanding—empathy—can emerge.

Following through the traces of the intermix, we lean into the social changes of today and tomorrow. We can listen through others' ears to the way their worlds combine.

Neo-Tribes: A New Listening Framework for Marketers

John Zogby, Chairman and Chief Insights Officer, IBOPE ZOGBY
International, and Joe Plummer, Columbia Business School

> We live in a world turned upside down. Old walls have crumbled and old patterns of doing business are vanishing. Consumers are different. Demographics are no longer destiny. Nationalism is no longer the predominant identity. Consumers are reorganizing themselves into tribes, and smart people are learning how to find those tribes.

As countless institutions that have offered Americans safety, security, and stability no longer generate public confidence, new technologies have enabled our country's citizens to reshuffle and reconstruct themselves into new versions of an institution as old as humans themselves: tribes. But our tribes are not due to birth or geography anymore. We are doing—albeit doing at the speed of light what used to take an epoch—what humans have always done best: organize ourselves into groups that reflect who we are, how we think, what we need, and what is most important in our lives. Based on ZOGBY International research, we identify the neo-tribes that exist today, as well as some smaller ones that are also firming, and suggest neo-tribes as a great framework for listening to consumers. Indeed, the notion of neo-tribes can become a robust structure for listening to consumer conversation on the Internet and elsewhere to better understand trends and countertrends, as well as patterns around brand preferences.

Marketers, political consultants, researchers, and people just looking for friends and lovers must understand that old-age cohorts and blue-collar/white-collar identities just don't fit any more. The public is actually creating new clusters of character and new sectors of interest for themselves. As we Americans abandon old individuality borders and lay waste to outmoded demographic models, we are coalescing around discrete common interests, forming ad hoc partnerships, and fitting ourselves (mostly unconsciously) into increasingly well-defined social clusters. Tribes today can come and go, but each one of us has at least one dominant tribe—two at the most. Virtually everyone can be found in the following examples from ZOGBY research:

Flash Drivers: These people distinguish themselves as "techies," and frequently have friends they know only online. They claim a greater-than-average reliance on the Internet, state-of-the-art PDAs, and other cutting-edge, high-tech gizmos. In keeping with their love of and reliance on technology, 39 percent of Flash Drivers would agree to have a computer chip implanted in their brain if doing so would provide them with a storehouse of knowledge.

Ecolytes: As far as Ecolytes are concerned, environmental problems comprise the largest danger facing the world today. Ecolytes spend significant time researching products they buy in hopes of living a greener, more environmentally friendly lifestyle. Far more liberal than the average, they voted overwhelmingly (96 percent) for Barack Obama in the 2008 presidential

(continued)

(continued)

election. Not surprisingly, most also identified Obama as their "hero," followed by the Dalai Lama. Demographically, Ecolytes are more likely than the general sample to be women (61 percent versus 51 percent), less likely to be married (49 percent versus 60 percent), and significantly less likely to consider themselves to be "born again."

Rule Breakers feel that they are justified in bending rules to get ahead, and that the ends justify the means if they personally benefit. We all know them: They are the ones who feel entitled to park in the handicapped zone because they will only be there for a few minutes. Look for areas where they hope to "break" new ground as you listen to this personally lenient group.

Nouveau Luddites find technology overwhelming, distracting, and/or too complicating. Megachains hold little charm for them. More so than almost any tribe, Nouveau Luddites say they work only to make money to live. It's not surprising, then, that this tribe also claims to most look forward to doing absolutely nothing in retirement. Listening to Luddites will often provide companies with hints on how to best simplify technology or complex products and services.

Mobiles are world travelers with a global perspective on life and work. Affluence and urbanity define them. If they could shop at only one store for the rest of their lives, Mobiles would pick Target. Forty percent of Mobiles would have a computer chip implanted in their brain if it would make them immune to disease.

God Squad: As their tribal name implies, the God Squad is staunch in their belief that the Bible is inerrant and Christianity the only correct faith. Eighty-three percent voted for John McCain in 2008, and are more likely to be married (74 percent versus 60 percent) and male (57 percent versus 49 percent). Half of God Squaders tithe, meaning that they give one-tenth of their income to organized religion. When asked who they would like to portray them in a movie, 17 percent of God Squad males name Mel Gibson, and another 13 percent Bruce Willis. No other tribe comes anywhere close to matching those numbers for either actor. If you listen to conversations among this tribe, you will discover the next moral backlash regarding specific brands, celebrities, and politics.

Mission Driven: Causes, not money, define this tribe's lifestyle. Like Ecolytes, the Mission Driven are politically liberal (70 percent versus 30 percent of the overall sample); the majority are female (61 percent versus 51 percent); and many are drawn to the Dalai Lama (13 percent call him their "hero," the most of any tribe). Mission-Driven individuals are the most likely of any tribe to believe that the American dream is about spiritual fulfillment.

Secular Idolaters: As strong nationalists, Secular Idolaters feel American culture is inherently superior to cultures elsewhere in the world. As such, they show little inclination to travel abroad or question the practices of their country. Secular Idolaters are big fans of fast-food chains, especially Subway and Wendy's, and of big-box stores such as Walmart. Listening to this tribe can help companies discover what Main Street finds attractive.

New Agers: New Agers are a 50-years-old-and-upward crowd that is far more focused on friends, family, or community than on owning things or making a living. This is a tribe that doesn't go bowling (21 percent versus 34 percent overall) but does love gardening. When it comes to cereal, New Agers prefer the tried and true: 36 percent choose Cheerios, and 37 percent Raisin Bran. No other tribe is so devoted to those morning classics. New Agers are also the neo-tribe most likely to call McDonald's McCafe coffee "as good as it gets."

Out-of-Boxers: Creativity and business entrepreneurship mark the lives of Out-of-Boxers. Along with New Agers, they are the most likely tribe to describe their work as "very fulfilling" to them as a person. They are also the most likely of any tribe to own a luxury car. Clearly, they are a leading indicator for affluent individuals and business viewpoints.

Left Behinds: Members of this group are wracked by fears that they will not be able to provide food, shelter, or other basic needs for themselves and their families. Not surprisingly, they are more likely to fall into the lower-income brackets, with nearly a quarter of them making less than $25,000 annually. But Left Behinds can also be found in the highest-income strata: One in nine of them reported an annual household income before taxes in excess of $100,000. Forty-eight percent of Left Behinds (versus 38 percent overall) fear losing their job. Half say their work is unfulfilling, a number matched only by Rule Breakers.

NEO-TRIBAL ANALYTICS

Multiple research techniques have been used over the years to connect people's characteristics to consumer decision making and leadership skills and potential. Though the most basic have been simple demographics, these usually don't tell us how people adjust to change. Psychographic profiling, on the other hand, takes polling a quantum leap forward. However, designing psychographics research surveys takes time, expertise, and money. And does it tell us anything about how we find structure and meaning in our lives while living in a world of chaos?

The fact is, we opinion researchers spend too much time within our own four walls, reducing our data to simplistic common denominators. To discover best how people are adjusting to and surviving the disorder in their lives, we simply do what we do best: listen to them to learn what they are asking about themselves and how they are dealing with change or new ideas. If we look for patterns in conversations, we can translate them into online questionnaires, or attempt to form tribes out of shared online content and conversation.

That's the great strength of Tribal Analytics. It doesn't rely on tricks; it gets beyond the surface texture of people's lives. It's built on self-identity—the fundamental questions that determine everything from consumption choices to media favorites to presidential ballots. In the end, it's not about yesterday's transactions or broad demographic indicators; it's about the kind of in-depth understanding that builds relationships. If you get the relationships right, transactions—and much more—will follow.

(continued)

(continued)

According to futurist Watts Wacker, one of the biggest trends to pay attention to in the short run is this: Although consumption is never going to go away, consuming as the defining criteria for individuals *is*. We are now using our media consumption, as opposed to our physical consumption, to explain who we are. You don't ask questions at a party such as, "Where'd you go to college?" "What kind of car do you drive?" "Where do you live?" anymore. Now you ask, "What do you blog?" "What Web sites do you surf?" "Have you read the article in *Vanity Fair* on terrorism in South America?" "Are you an Imus or a Stern person?" "Have you seen *The Departed*?" "Did you love or hate *Avatar*?" "Have you read *The Shack*?" These are the kind of questions that reveal so much about who we are.

This is what ZOGBY International has done to arrive at our tribe categories. After compiling and reviewing years of previous polling data, and listening to social media conversations, we developed the types of questions that would best help us assign people into tribes.

As important as the tribes themselves are, their borders matter, too, because that's where most people live. True, there's a hard core within every tribe—a group for whom the "greenness" of a product or its domestic content or a preacher's blessing is the absolute essential element. But the rest of us live with our right foot in one tribal zone and our left foot in another, and those border straddlings vary based on the product or service being offered. Clearly, this provides a rich opportunity for marketing products and services that fill the "crease" between tribes and that cross over into adjoining tribal territories. No matter how attractive, Macs are not suddenly going to outsell Dell PCs with God Squaders, just as Harleys won't suddenly make inroads with Flash Drivers.

However, the purpose of understanding and listening to neo-tribes is not to predict future purchase decisions with great precision. The value is to move beyond the simple stereotypes, such as affluent versus nonaffluent, young versus old, or urban versus suburban, which create division and limit markets. The idea is to listen to and interpret conversations at the deeper level of neo-tribes, whose shared values and connections expand opportunities for marketers and advertisers.

CHAPTER 21

CHANGE THE RESEARCH PARADIGM

Social media listening data furnishes companies with insights into what customers are doing, thinking, and feeling. Listening professionals we interviewed for this book reveled in sharing the data and working across departmental boundaries. For example, Jason Harty, then of vitaminwater, recounted the excitement of collaborating with various functions (marketing, sales, product development, legal, customer service, and the top brass) to create and launch a new customer-designed beverage in just a matter of months. His colleagues' enthusiasm for up-to-the-minute listening data became a type of social glue and fostered real camaraderie. And along the way, it changed Harty's researcher role from data historian to valued development partner (see Chapter 6 for case details).

As Harty's experience illustrates, listening brings changes in research approaches, the data generated, and the ways that data is analyzed, applied and acted upon, all of which raise fundamental issues about what the data is, its quality, and what researchers should become and do to drive their businesses foward. The essays within this chapter speak to challenging the established ways of working and changing the research paradigm.

Stan Sthanunathan, Coca-Cola's director of Insights and Strategy, argues that market researchers must unshackle themselves from their priestly past, and instead become more like prophets—in the spirit of those who are gifted with profound insight and exceptional powers of expression. Anicipatory and forward-looking, these research professionals should help their companies visualize and create more compelling and rewarding business futures. They need to predict, shape, and capitalize on change. Simply tweaking the research function won't cut it, he argues. Research needs to transform, and Sthanunathan provides a blueprint for getting there.

ESPN's research chief, Artie Bulgrin, stresses that decision making, and the research transformation Sthanunathan advocates, must use high-quality research processes, data with high levels of integrity, and trained professionals. Bulgrin strongly cautions that the river of free or cheap research and "insights," which companies utilize so easily, threatens a manager's ability to make decisions on quality data using guidance from an expert research counsel. Companies will wrestle with the challenge of making decisions based on data they can have confidence in versus data they can get, while evaluating the costs, staffing, and business risks of doing so.

The concern of Microsoft's Social Media Thought Leader R. Scott Evans speaks to improvements in social media analysis; progress that's needed in order to make rightful claims on management attention and research budgets, and, most importantly, contribute meaningfully to business decisions. Evans's piece is somewhat technical, but his central point is clear: Social media analysis must become more rigorous, empirical, predictive, and, for larger companies, global. These improvements make it possible for social media listening to achieve its promise of bringing the customer into the company. Businesses should aggregate and synthesize their insights and experiences to create their own playbooks. Doing so will allow them to operate from evidence and principles, and confidently respond to changes in marketplace signals. Although Evans's essay appears concerned with large companies, businesses of every size will benefit by finding ways to adapt its ideas.

Britta C. Ware, Meredith's head of Research Solutions, and Manila Austin, research director for Communispace, underscore the importance of communicating social media research findings, without which there will be no impact on planning or action, no research transformation, no esteemed role for researchers. They present a time-tested, five-step program for effective insights communication: (1) bring consumers to life through a killer insight; (2) tell stories to integrate ideas; (3) visualize data; (4) build relationships with stakeholders; and (5) inspire actions to take with them. The trick is to convey the stakeholders' perspective and language in order for the insights to impact the entire company.

Predict the Future; Don't Explain the Past

Stan Sthanunathan, Vice President, Marketing Strategy and Insights, Coca-Cola

When CEOs want to know how a product launch went awry, how purchase habits have changed, or where the company is gaining ground, they ask research for answers. But what if they ask about what is *going to happen* instead of what already did? Then researchers might be stumped. Yet if we want to increase the impact of market research, we need to focus far more on getting organizations to predict, shape, and capitalize on change than on carefully explaining their past.

Our role needs to shift to helping companies dream about and create a more compelling and rewarding future, and driving the transformational change that will get them there.

Instead of creating the newest, greatest research tool, which will quickly become irrelevant and outdated, both agency and client-side researchers must engage in a change of mind-set that puts the ultimate needs of the business front and center. A contemporary research approach should revolve around the four key elements described here.

1. ANTICIPATE NEW OPPORTUNITIES

- Inspire
- Transform
- Seek what we don't know and how to figure it out

If a researcher had gone to consumers in 1886 and asked them what they would most like to drink, not one of them would have asked for something loaded with bubbles and a strange, sweet, syrupy taste. But Dr. Pemberton didn't ask what people wanted then; he anticipated what they *could* want and carried a jug of his unique mixture down the street to Jacob's Pharmacy to be sold as Coca-Cola, for 5 cents a glass.

Similarly, if you asked people in the late 1850s how they would like to get from one place to another, there would not have been a statistically significant response for developing the automobile. Since one did not exist yet, no one knew they wanted one yet.

The pace of change in our society today and the diversity of its inhabitants make it ever more critical for market research professionals to act as anticipators, and even agents of change. We need to get closer to clients and consumers to find out what is keeping people up at night, and then tailor products and services to meet those needs. The goal is to shape change, not follow it. And we need to create the change people have not yet dreamed of.

2. USE INNOVATIVE APPROACHES

- Observe
- Listen
- Synthesize
- Deduce

Getting ahead of societal change rests on finely honed powers of observing and listening to people. It also relies on the ability to synthesize what we learn and to draw logical deductions about the kinds of products and service-delivery methods that might better meet their needs. We do this by tuning in to people with an open mind and waiting to see how they illuminate us. We start the process, as the ARF makes clear, by "listening for the unexpected," rather than quantifying the expected.

(*continued*)

(*continued*)

Thanks to techniques such as BlackBerry ethnographies and the practice of "netnography," there are many ways to "listen in" to people's hearts, minds, and lives today, which never existed before. We can develop ways to sweep the content of the Web and conduct advanced analysis on it to really learn about people's passions, dreams, and what is keeping them awake at night.

If you focus on the well-accepted adage of leveraging what you already know, you run the very real risk that everyone else in your industry already possesses that same knowledge—and is acting on it. There's more power in figuring out how to know what we don't know.

3. Turn Insights into Action—Now

- Capture info
- Organize insights
- Create impact

It is possible nowadays to calculate results immediately with real-time feedback from consumers. These responses drive an immediate reaction in terms of tailored marketing messages and even product development. We can use technology-enabled observation to stay ahead of the game.

Coke recently used social media to engage people in creating a new flavor of vitaminwater, right down to its packaging (see Chapter 6 for a case study discussion). A process that normally takes two years and millions of dollars of investment in formal market research and trials was turned on its head, and conducted in three months for a few thousand dollars, by harnessing the power of the crowd to co-create a new product.

Organizations are also now using responsive outdoor advertising, with messages that change based on the time of day. Even more sophisticated versions can quickly scan passers-by for key demographic data, such as age and gender, and then display an advertising message targeted to that demographic, or instantly transmit a coupon for the product to a mobile phone.

4. Focus on the Business Impact

- Connect results to business growth and health
- Demonstrate the connection to senior leaders
- Provide inputs for strategy

As research professionals, we are appropriately concerned with the quality of our methodologies and reliability of the insights we gather. That vigilance is critical in terms of our own professional ethics and in the trust others put into the new ideas we provoke. But we also need to understand that the "back room" machinations of good research are not what earns a seat at the decision-making table or the ability to influence corporate direction. In other words, a pristine research project is meaningless unless it shapes business and drives value for customers. We must always draw a straight line between what we're doing and learning and how it will impact our company's growth and health. We also need to be able to demonstrate that connection to senior leadership.

If we direct our focus on ROI and value creation, we'll be key players in help-ing the company figure out how to execute better in the marketplace and increase value in the business.

MAKING IT HAPPEN

Of course, there is a requisite skill set to conducting quality research, and there are new techniques to be learned almost daily. We also need to master new mind-sets (see Chapter 4) and be willing to experiment a little and get out of our com-fort zones.

Just a little open-mindedness can compel us to embrace new opportunities for learning what's important to consumers—even when they can't completely artic-ulate it yet themselves. And technology is making it possible for us to achieve the paradox of customizing our messages and products on a massive scale.

At the heart of doing market research right in today's marketplace lies a will-ingness to stretch out your neck and try to figure out where change is going to appear next. It lies in listening to people's thoughts and desires to learn what really moves them. Armed with that inspiration, you may be able to predict which products and services will help them meet those overwhelming needs.

The Future of Marketing Research and the Professional Researcher in a Digital World

Artie Bulgrin, Senior Vice President, Research and Analytics, ESPN

Irish philosopher and management specialist Charles Handy once said that "measuring more is easy; measuring better is hard." This has always been the case, but never more so than today. In fact, marketing or media research is often misunderstood and undervalued, due to its complexity, cost, and perceived limi-tations. Exacerbating that situation is the growing illusion that consumer mea-surement has become easier and even more robust, due to the instant gratification of data that flows constantly in a digital economy.

But while the quantity of data in today's world is apparent, the quality and clarity is not. Looking ahead, I strongly caution that this is most certainly an illu-sion. I believe that the near-instant availability of data—as a by-product of our digital transactions—will raise *more* challenges for marketers in the future, and will require us to rely increasingly on trained research practitioners to make sense of it all. My fear is that the ubiquity of transactional "analytics" will continue to lead some organizations to reduce any investment in or reliance on the tradi-tional marketing research process and classically trained research professionals—an approach that is both shortsighted and risky.

At ESPN, I am very fortunate to work in an organization that generally under-stands and appreciates the value of quality research. However, we didn't establish

(*continued*)

(*continued*)

this rapport overnight. Through collaboration, thoughtful communication, and strategic focus over time, my staff has been able to gain the trust and respect of our management team. But, as our business has evolved in recent years, especially in digital media, there has been an inclination toward democratization and decentralization of data throughout the organization. Though inevitable—and even practical—this trend inherently carries risks that the data's end users may not understand a dataset's limitations or operational definition, and what it represents, which could lead to misinformed decisions. Nevertheless, as these end users become more comfortable and independent using internal analytics—complemented at times with "free" research downloaded from the Web—there is the threat that the role of the traditional marketing research function may be compromised, moving us from data democratization to data anarchy. As a result, we increasingly find ourselves defending our own findings, while disputing conflicting claims from other sources or conclusions derived from our own internal analytics.

At times like these, it's important to revisit what the role of marketing research is to an organization. In 2004, the American Marketing Association revised its definition of "marketing research" to the following:

> Marketing research is the function that links the consumer, customer, and public to the marketer through information—information used to identify and define marketing opportunities and problems; generate, refine, and evaluate marketing actions; monitor marketing performance; and improve understanding of marketing as a process. Marketing research specifies the information required to address these issues, designs the method for collecting information, manages and implements the data collection process, analyzes the results, and communicates the findings and their implications.

The key word in this definition is "information," making it clear that the marketing research professional's essential role must continue to encompass managing the process that ultimately converts data into tangible and actionable information. This starts with ensuring the reliability and validity of the data that flows into the process. Whether it is internal analytics or a DIY online survey, there is no substitute for the traditional marketing research function to protect this integrity and manage the process. Though it certainly should not be replaced by self-serve knowledge solutions, that's my fear, as transactional, social, and behavioral data become even more inexpensive and accessible.

To me, research transformation means that analytics need to be considered part of the marketing research process to understand the consumer. While listening is also part of this transformation, it should not be limited to online or digital sources, either. In fact, this book makes it clear that, when not filtered properly or placed in proper context, there are concerns over the quality and representativeness of online sources. This affects the validity and reliability of the data. The author is also careful to point out that while the volume of branded conversations or buzz on the Web is well known, it actually represents a small percentage of *all* word of mouth. This is a great example of a digital knowledge gap which, in this case, is carefully filled today by research conducted by the Keller Fay Group.

Yet despite this available knowledge, so many organizations still rely solely on online sources. Why? Because it's easier and faster. Overcoming this challenge requires a professional who is able to communicate and demonstrate the value of the added cost and effort necessary to fill the knowledge gap. The benefit is broader vision and greater clarity.

At ESPN, we integrated the business analytics function with the marketing and media research functions two years ago. This allowed us to not only better understand the consumer, but also to improve and manage the quality of our internal data. The idea was to enhance the reliability of our internal analytic data and augment it with secondary and primary consumer data—including listening—to provide greater context, insight, and information. It has worked very well so far. But I know that maintaining this role in coming years will be a challenge, as it will be for all of us in this industry. Measuring better will continue to be hard work!

From Narrative to Insight: Trends in Social Media Intelligence Platforms

R. Scott Evans, PhD, Director, Social Media Thought Leader, Microsoft

Social media is only one of many sources for deriving business insight. But in order for it to become a primary contender for research budgets and business leader mindshare, it must advance on six fronts:

1. Master scalable technologies that allow researchers to build rich context-laden maps of the conversations taking place in social media.
2. Create reliable measures of sentiment and disposition so that prescriptive insights and evaluative benchmarks become central in the analysis.
3. Build an extensive framework for multiple languages so that social media analysis can be incorporated in truly global designs.
4. Measure influence in ways that cross all social media platforms and track the flow of information from agent to agent and platform to platform.
5. Demonstrate that social media can be a valid proxy of market trends, and that the issue of representativeness does not impact the extent to which patterns in social media can be generalized to any given market.
6. Integrate social media insights and data with the conventional sources for a more far-reaching and balanced approach to business decisions.

As social media analysis increasingly finds a place in corporate research centers, methodologists will challenge the validity of social-media-derived insights. Social media monitoring platforms suffer serious shortcomings when it comes to

(continued)

(*continued*)

thematic mapping, sentiment measurement, and language capabilities. In comparison to conventional survey research, there are serious concerns about the diversity of the sample. As for influence structures and data integration, these are far down the wish list of most platform developers. However, researchers will argue that these two capabilities will greatly contribute to both the prescriptive utility and overall validity of the analysis.

While my comments on the state of social media appear pessimistic, I am actually optimistic on this front, given some recent trends among platform developers and companies that seem to want to better understand the insight social media has to offer.

MAPPING CONVERSATIONS AND MEASURING SENTIMENT

The first important development impacting social media analysis is the rapid convergence of listening platforms with the more mature text analytics industry. Though accessing content is an ongoing dynamic enterprise, the fundamentals of the technological solution are in place.

Emerging text analytics hybrids, built on natural language processing (NLP), are offering researchers sophisticated tools for building detailed multitiered classifications. This makes prescriptive insights both intuitive and defensible, by being able to break down issues into their constituent parts and matching themes to changes in volume and sentiment.

NLP offers valuable advances for improving sentiment measurement. Capturing word relationships at the clause level lets emotive words be more readily associated with the appropriate subject. Comprehending sentiment at this level is a key building block for measuring disposition at the level of individual themes. Without an accurate gauge of emotion, it is difficult to translate themes and volumes into business insights.

THE LANGUAGE CONUNDRUM

While language is of lesser importance for regional businesses, it is critical for global companies. Understanding what social media can tell us about a message's impact in a global campaign can be a critical part of the evaluation process. Initiatives that focus on digital media must make social media insight a central part of planning and eventual evaluation. Without the requisite coverage, social media must take a back seat to more expensive conventional tracking surveys.

Fortunately, machine translation continues to improve. Both social media platforms and their text analytics platforms are continuing to experiment with automating the translation process. While success is mixed, there have been constant improvements, which suggest that a "good enough" solution may be on the horizon.

INFLUENCE AND OPTIMIZATION

Unfortunately, the multiflow nature of online influence means that considerable work still needs to be done to capture the way in which memes and meaning are generated and propagated throughout the Web. Memes are ideas and messages in the social media environment that encompass forms of expression that transcend written language. Videos, audio, images, and even certain types of online behavior are forms of memes that can spread rapidly across platforms. For example, simple Web analytics and mapping hyperlinks or followers do not address who should be targeted, and with what message. The road map may be in place, but the tools for understanding the actual traffic flow and the relevance of the goods being transported are currently inadequate.

From a tactical vantage, it is essential to know who is carrying what, and to whom. For example, the PR firm that needs to assess optimal communication solutions must combine the "who" with an understanding of *how* messages transform and cross platforms, as well as the role specific agents play in this process. It is absolutely necessary to have all the other elements in place. Exhaustive mapping and accurate sentiment are vital components for researchers to trace the permutations of memes across all social media channels. Aligning actual connections and content are crucial for building actionable influence analysis.

VALIDITY AND REPRESENTATIVENESS

The great advantage of social media is its historical record. The transition from telephone to online panels required extensive simultaneous surveys to calibrate the online medium with its conventional counterpart. This process can be replaced in part with time-series. Building benchmarks and trends for themes and sentiment enable researchers to compare results with both known events and already-validated datastreams from other sources. As these comparisons progress, we will begin to understand both the strengths and weaknesses inherent in social media as a means to generalize market trends.

Those who argue that social media analysis today focuses on unrepresentative voices and public expressions fail to recognize that such positions become irrelevant if social media proves to be a market bellwether. Critics who cite the requirement to cover private conversations—or the need to traverse the entire social media universe—fail to consider the implication of matching time-series events. Those who refer to the many gaps in the crawling profiles of most social media monitoring platforms do not recognize the inherent sampling limitations and weighting schemes of most inherent methodologies. Regardless of the nonrandom sampling of the social media universe, consistent matching of historic patterns does give credence to the potential validity of social media analysis.

INSIGHT INTEGRATION

The goal of social media analysis for business is simple: to improve our understanding of the market. This means that we must begin to integrate what social media offers with the numerous other sources of insight currently available to decision makers. Since social media represents a valid voice of customers and market influencers, you disregard its relevance at your peril. To the extent that social media analysis matures along the lines identified in this essay, it will increasingly become an important source of insight in decision-making circles.

Synthesize, Clarify, and Inspire Action: Keys to Effectively Communicating Listening Insights

Manila Austin, PhD, Director of Research, Communispace Corporation,
and Britta C. Ware, Vice President, Research Solutions, Meredith
Corporation

What is the future of listening? When we were asked to write an essay to explore this question, we put our heads together and wished we had a handy crystal ball—or even a geeky market research magic 8 ball—that could provide a ready answer. We don't have any such object, of course, but we do have a shared passion and point of view.

Along with countless others, we have first observed the remarkable shift in marketing and advertising from persuasion to engagement. We've witnessed the commensurate shift in market research from studying "respondents" to listening to consumers. Second, we have experimented with and embraced listening technologies as they have emerged, championing the voice of the consumer in our work. And, third, we have taken a step back to look at the state of listening today, and have found many examples of how brands are staying relevant, and leading, as a result of listening to real people in their own words.

But we also see room to grow. In our respective roles, we struggle day to day with a common problem, namely: how to manage the complexity that listening creates. We attend conferences and see a lot of data points; we read reports that faithfully describe findings . . . and more findings . . . and more findings; and we participate in the industry debate about how to transform market research, listen to and engage consumers, and maintain data quality.

Listening creates complexity on two fronts: It challenges many of the assumptions underlying traditional market understandings, and it generates a tremendous amount of information. If market research is going to evolve with the times, the future of listening will have to be about more than simply listening, in and of itself. While the act is necessary, and even critical, ultimately, it is not enough. Communicating what we hear in a way that synthesizes data points, clarifies insights, and inspires action is the second half of the equation. We need to do more than listen to the consumer's voice; we need to bring that consumer to life.

LISTENING CREATES COMPLEXITY

In the past decade, we have seen an explosion of online listening technologies. They are social, engaging real people in conversations and co-creation; they are nearly infinite in scale, incorporating a multitude of voices from nearly every walk of life; and they are evolving rapidly. Thus, the possibilities for every kind of listening—from passive eavesdropping to co-investigation and collaboration—can seem endless. While these developments create great opportunity for market research, the use of social-media-driven technology fuels the quality debate that's been raging for years. It fuels a sense of concern about declining response rates, questionable respondents, and sample representativeness. Listening, particularly to hundreds or thousands of people in a conversational way, blurs the boundary between quantitative and qualitative, quasi-experimental, and humanistic methods. This can be confusing, and can further complicate how we interpret what we learn, while undermining confidence in the insights we uncover.

Therefore, one factor that must certainly play a role in the future of listening is our ability to reconcile this conflict. We need new ways to understand and explain what quality looks like as we expand our repertoire to incorporate consumer-led versus researcher-led methods. It will fall to us as researchers to make informed trade-offs that allow us to continue to listen through technologies as they develop, and to educate colleagues and clients about what we are risking— and gaining—by shifting our focus and methods.

Rather than doggedly applying familiar standards to the rich, unstructured information generated through naturalistic online conversations, we find it is often more helpful to focus on what is actionable (as opposed to irrefutable). This means using a range of techniques to pragmatically generate and test hypotheses. Integrating elements of both humanistic and experimental approaches allows us to produce timely, "good enough" research targeted to specific business needs. It also requires that we generate a broader definition of quality and consider how online, social, consumer-led research can actually strengthen validity.

For example, we see quality enhanced by trading artificial for naturalistic settings. One of the great benefits of social media is that it brings research into the consumer's world and allows for comfortable, convenient participation. Creating an intimate, natural space for consumers to relate to each other and generate their own discussions yields authentic and detailed insights that are likely to be missing when we rely solely on quasi-experimental surveys. Our experience has also shown us that when we trade anonymity and distance for relationship, we do a better job of engaging and motivating consumers. Simply said, people are more forthcoming, and their input is more useful, when they know whom they're talking to. A common fear is that feedback from people will be inflated and biased when they engage in long-term, branded research. We have actually found that the opposite is true: Ongoing relationships result in higher-quality, more genuine feedback. When consumers care about a brand, they are more likely to provide useful insight—even when it's unfavorable—precisely because they feel more invested in the brand's success.

LISTENING REQUIRES SYNTHESIZING, SIMPLIFYING, AND CLARIFYING WHAT WE HEAR

The future of listening will entail evolving and clarifying the process of research; it will also require us to clarify the product of research. Listening to the customer's voice is potentially disruptive, in that it tends to provoke as many questions as answers. It is essentially generative in nature, which means it can produce a great wealth of rich information—more voices, more perspectives, and, ultimately, more specific and actionable insights.

But the volume and diversity of data generated through listening can be overwhelming. We live in an era of shrinking attention spans, where information must be transmitted and consumed in 140 character snippets. Therefore, the richness produced by listening cannot afford to be reported in all of its complexity

(continued)

(*continued*)

and detail. Somehow, we need to streamline the outputs of listening so that they are digestible and linked to business objectives.

This task is challenging precisely because—as Chip and Dan Heath explain in their bestselling book *Made to Stick: Why Some Ideas Survive and Others Die*—our awareness of all that detail and complexity can actually get in the way of our ability to effectively communicate what we know. Powerful ideas are both simple and creatively crafted; they reduce intricacy into pithy and compelling statements that allow others to absorb information and pass it along to others.

FIVE KEYS TO EFFECTIVELY COMMUNICATING INSIGHTS

While there are likely many ways we are all tackling this problem, here are a few tactics that have helped us synthesize, clarify, and communicate insights about the consumer:

Bring the consumer to life. One of the best ways we have found to communicate complex information is through powerful verbatim messages. Much like how the human face can convey a range of social and emotional information in a matter of seconds, literal quotes from consumers can—in one nugget—capture the essence of an insight, a segment, or a new direction or possibility. To that end, much of our work requires that we synthesize listening—all those myriad data points—into one profound statement that embodies the research and brings the consumer to life. We can frequently achieve this through a direct quote from the consumer; sometimes we need to create that statement ourselves, based on what we have heard. But it is on us to find the right words to communicate the message from the research in the most compelling way.

Be a storyteller. Reporting data points in an analytical way is not usually helpful to those who make decisions based on our work. Rather than rigorously describing each finding and the method behind the research, we need to focus on finding the big idea and telling a story. We have found it helpful to lead with the story—one slide, thesis statement, or headline—that seamlessly integrates findings from qualitative and quantitative efforts (details about method and analyses can be included as an appendix).

Visualize data. Not only do we need to learn to write more creatively; we also need to think more like designers, and communicate with pictures and visuals. We have found it useful to partner with our creative teams to produce booklets, presentations, and other deliverables that use design elements to tell a story. We've come to see how incorporating visual devices (such as word clouds or infographics) can be a concise way to convey rich information.

Build relationships. Insights—even ones that are succinctly and beautifully packaged—are not useful if companies do not connect them to business strategy or articulate their impact. In order to do this, we need to be tuned in to the key business issues our clients, both internal and external, are facing. This means that a large part of our job will hinge on our ability to build relationships, open lines of communication, and create common ground across functions and organizational silos.

Facilitate action. The voice of the consumer has transformative potential, but only when insights are translated into meaningful action. Listening entails that we combine the diverse perspectives it generates. To be effective, we must also involve decision makers across our organizations, to create a shared understanding, clarify business implications, and inspire action. Listening, then, depends on our ability to facilitate conversations and consult with our colleagues and clients. It also means that we must work across business units to bring relevant insights to bear on a range of problems.

The practice of listening will require all of us to elevate and evolve how we apply our expertise, how we communicate insight, and how we interact with business partners to help solve problems. It is true, of course, that many of us in market research are already doing these things. However, as the art and science of listening continues to gain traction and move into the mainstream, these qualities will shift from nice-to-haves to must-haves.

CHAPTER 22

RETHINK MARKETING, MEDIA, AND ADVERTISING

Social media conversations are transforming the very nature of media and marketing. In some quarters, conversations are becoming considered as a new form of media that blends content, community, and chatter. Social channels like Facebook and Twitter, blogs, forums, and review sites encourage people to talk with one another and with companies, express their views, amplify their voices, and provide the means to do so. As we saw in Part II, marketers as diverse as JetBlue, Comcast, Gatorade, Provo Craft, Fiat, and Naked Wines have committed to relating with customers—informing and entertaining, providing service, smoothing transactions, solving problems, consulting them and learning from them. That's a big change from the bygone era of "make and sell" companies of the mass media era who talked more than they listened. By bringing the voice of people into companies, listening to social media conversations has been central to these transformations, and will continue to be. This chapter's essays examine why they will.

Kantar Media's Richard Fielding and Networked Insight's Dan Neely engage in a virtual dialogue centered on the evolving role of conversation in marketing and advertising. The primary implication they set forth is no doubt both revolutionary and controversial: Marketer-controlled advertising will recede as companies engage in experience-driven and open-ended conversations, some of which—the ones that move through social networks with a momentum of their own—will be monetized by advertisers. As Neely claims, "Today we pay for media placements. Tomorrow's rewards will shift toward the actual users who carry the content and messages." Understanding, monetizing, and effectively manipulating "the ripple effect" of those conversations for the benefit of companies will alter media strategy and drive social media listening over the next few years.

Carat's Mike Hess and Michelle Lynn tackle several media-related issues that are critical to every business that advertises: evaluating "earned" media, understanding social networkers through their behavior, and learning how social networking influences the time people spent with other media, such as TV. They believe that listening sheds light on the question, "What did people do with our content that earned us a place in their media world?" The answers are not as simple as "they linked to us" or "they embedded our video." Social networkers are not all alike, and Hess and Lynn explain that segmenting networkers by their participation styles can quantify the impact of earned media and pave the way for planning social media strategy.

Hess and Lynn also dissuade those who think that social media is a never-ending trend of that notion. The "hockey stick" growth period appears to be ending, portending a shakeout in social media properties and vendors. When growth spurts end, the competitive game shifts, from growing in size to battling for market share. Changes in media behavior will exert additional pressure on the competitors, since time spent with media does not constantly expand. People appear to have daily media allowances that they adeptly manage. Although old and young people may have the same overall time allowance, they allocate it differently across their screens and different services. Consequently, media strategy is becoming more complex, requiring deeper insight into people's media behavior and the shifting social media landscape. Social media listening now, Hess and Lynn argue, plays a vital role that will be even more important in the coming years.

Leaving media and moving toward marketing, VivaKi's strategy and innovation chief, Rishad Tobaccowala, reveals the game-changing effects social media and listening are rousing, and that are challenging marketing thinking and practices. Tobaccowala sees the role of social media as creating a new marketing system he calls "the people's network." Emerging from interactions among people and between people and companies, this network becomes larger, more interconnected, increasingly global, and more mobile each day. The people's network generates, channels, and broadcasts word of mouth. Listening enables companies to place people at their centers, effectively turning their companies inside out. Tobaccowala helps professionals apply this to their own situations by sharing the eight rules he has established for effective marketing within the people's network.

Conversations, the Ripple Effect, and the Future of Media

Richard Fielding, Chief Client Officer, Kantar Media, and Dan Neely, CEO, Networked Insights

Note: Richard and Dan originally contributed individual futures pieces. After reading them, I realized how complementary their points were and thought that they should be combined—not by cutting and pasting—but by working their ideas into a dialogue to which they could then respond and advance with comments. Richard, a media agency executive, appreciated Dan's additional

(continued)

(continued)

perspective. Dan, an executive at a listening company, did some additional riffing on Richard's ideas from his. This essay results from that give-and-take.

RICHARD FIELDING, KANTAR MEDIA

Brand relationships have traditionally been framed by marketers, directing one-way communication from company to consumer based upon functional and emotional attributes. However, this relationship is now evolving into much more of a partnership based upon communities, with brands delivering experiences, not just marketing messages. In the future, brands will not only behave differently; they will communicate differently. The brand will become a facilitator, participating in conversations with its consumers that are experience-driven, open-ended, and nonlinear.

Media is constantly evolving to enable this new paradigm. It will continue to move from a system built upon a "push" mentality that's primarily focused on media investment efficiency measured by CPMs, reach, and frequency. It will gradually become a "participation" model focused on the optimization of brand value delivered via utility and content that are driven by experience and that involve consumer communities.

This new marketing is propelled by dialogue that starts well before purchase and ends long after the transaction—something that's already happening. If the late 2000s were the era of the social network, the future will see the rise of the "social graph"—that segment of a network focused on you, your friends, and the friends of your friends. New services will emerge that use social graph data more aggressively. We will stray further from the destination Web, and toward a social Web, whereby consumers get more and more information through their networks, rather than a specific Web site. Successful brands will tap into existing communities and create new ones. In this new world, success will not be measured by old-world metrics like reach and ratings, but by the breadth and depth of conversations.

DAN NEELY, NETWORKED INSIGHTS

Richard, I'm putting my money down on what I consider the single most important area of development for listening over the next few years: the understanding, monetization, and effective manipulation of "the ripple effect" of conversations that you discussed. Its simplest expressions are water-cooler talk and word of mouth. It wasn't invented by social media or listening; however, both trends accelerated the dynamic. In the coming years, marketers will willingly pay for messages that travel through social channels with a momentum of their own; and they'll demand proof, via measurement, that the ripple effect has been delivered.

Today we pay for media placements. Tomorrow's rewards will progress toward the actual users who carry the content and messages. Marketers and advertisers need to understand this, because Web sites and similar properties will cease becoming destinations in themselves. Instead, their value will be in the quality, nature, and kind of the conversations held among people connected to them. We see this already in Facebook: Some fan pages are getting millions of hits per day. Why? Because people are looking to converse with friends and the like-minded who are in their lives. They don't merely want to view ads, watch silly videos, learn new product facts, or get coupons.

Simply put, the ripple effect takes place when an event (e.g., a product launch, advertisement, TV show, etc.) registers in the consumer space. For a TV show, conventional ratings provide a static assessment: eyeballs on sets during the show, or merely the fact that the TV was on. But measuring the impact of the same show in social media gives you a more dimensional view. The best listening platforms can already measure this ripple effect. This metric is revaluing ad inventory and entertainment properties as I write. The coming years will bring great improvement in how we track the progress of messages and memes across sites and people so that we can predict the ripple. This will give marketers, advertisers, and agencies more powerful tools to plan communications and engagements, and to anticipate and adjust in ways that maximize their effectiveness.

The Triple Alliance of Social Media, Social Networks, and Social Listening

Mike Hess and Michelle Lynn, Carat USA

These days, it seems like anything with the word "social" in it is hotter than a New York sidewalk on an August afternoon. We have social networks, social media, and, more recently, social listening.

To determine the future of this phenomenon, we need to begin with the present. Social listening is a method of obtaining information and reading about what participants in social networks say about products, services, and people. We assume that what people say is authentic or objective when they participate in such groups. As such, we like to think that we "listeners" are like the proverbial fly on the wall that is hearing what participants "really think" about us, and our brands and services.

At present, social networks have 70 percent participation by those who are online. And since about 80 percent of the United States has online access, this means that over half of Americans are involved in them—definitely critical mass. No wonder marketers and advertisers are so interested in finding out what these people are saying.

AN INTEGRAL PART OF TODAY'S BOE MEDIA ENVIRONMENT

Certainly, a big part of the overall future for social listening lies in the role it is beginning to play as part of the bought/owned/earned (BOE) media paradigm that has emerged as we begin the new decade in 2010. To break it down:

- *Bought* media is what agencies have always provided: planning and buying television, radio, print, and, increasingly, digital, to address client media objectives.

(continued)

(*continued*)

- *Owned* properties have, of course, always been part of branding, in the form of the package, label, and store. However, they have become increasingly important as the firm's Web site has been added to the list of such owned vehicles to touch the consumer.
- *Earned* media is where social networks and listening play their own critical roles today.

Earned media is an example of good news and bad. The good news is that it's free, and you've therefore earned it from other activities that you've done. The bad news is that its content isn't really in the brand's control, but rather in that of the shopper and consumer. This dual nature as an "earned" entity will ensure that social listening will remain an important part of media and market research for years to come. In addition, we predict that one of the keystone attributes of the brand manager of the future will be how well he/she adapts to the ever-changing social feedback on the brand.

SEGMENTATION AND QUANTIFICATION

Social listening is anything but static. It allows us to monitor consumers' interests and passions as they find their self-expression through blogging, forums, online communities, and video. We have learned through CCS, Carat's proprietary Consumer Connection Study (an online study of 10,000 respondents fielded annually), that social networkers can themselves be segmented based on level of their digital participation and sociability.

This is especially true when we drill down to specific categories. A social networker who is passionate about skincare, for example, may choose not only to comment on a specific brand experience (good or bad), but also to build his/her own Web site, author his/her own blog, or create his/her own content/video to be uploaded on someone else's. This so-called amateur may end up garnering considerable influence.

On the flipside, when looking up consumer reviews for a new facial moisturizer, another consumer might be hesitant to trust a bad review from a faceless person who writes without punctuation. That consumer might also be reluctant to believe a glowing review that sounds more like an endorsement than an honest, unsolicited review from another consumer.

The point is that not all social networkers are created equal. We can address a need for increased granularity—to better understand and navigate through the social media landscape—by segmenting consumers. At Carat's, this means that we distinguish among four active groups, all of whom participate in social networks:

- Authors
- Commentators
- Connectors
- Spectators

Segmentation may be the first step in increasing our ability to quantify the value of contributors' feedback and what it ultimately means for a brand. Once we have done that, we can then more confidently begin to buy and sell social media programs. In addition, we will be able to truly activate these consumers to comment, raise their hands, or make an online purchase.

LIMITATIONS ON CONSUMER PROCESSING: INFORMATION OVERLOAD?

While there's no doubt that all things social—the triple alliance of networks, media, and listening—are here to stay, there is one truly critical aspect of these phenomena that almost no one has discussed: the ability, or lack thereof, of the average consumer to handle increasing amounts of information without making any trade-offs. Indeed, the way that social networks are regarded these days can make one think that there are almost no limits to them! Can a person really join 10 to 15 social networks, hold a day job, watch prime-time television after work, and have 500 friends on Facebook, all at the same time? At least two major pieces of research of which we were part suggest not.

The first of these is the "Video Consumer Mapping" study, published in 2009 by the Council for Research Excellence (CRE). Among its major findings was that all demographic age groups, except the 45–54 age cohort, average 8.5 hours of "screen time" every day, where screens are identified as television, computer, mobile, and all other (such as movie screens). The 45–54 age group engages in even more: 9.5 hours of daily screen time. And while the segments of 18–24-year-olds and 55–64-year-olds, for example, both use 8.5 hours of "screens" daily, they do so quite distinctly: The younger segment watches about 2 hours less television every day than the older segment, while using the computer and mobile screens more, to reach their own 8.5 hours.

This clearly outlines the limits on what "can" be done by the consumer, as well as reflecting limits on "how much" they actually want to do. After so many screen hours, perhaps it's time to play some touch football outside, or just go for a walk. Anything but more staring at screens!

The second study is Carat's own 2007 research, conducted in partnership with MySpace, and named "Never Ending Friending." In it, we clearly found evidence of what we termed "crowding out." Specifically, after controlling for age, we learned that social network users watched 2 hours less television every week than those in the same age group who did not belong to a social network.

These two important findings suggest that while the future is indeed promising for social listening, there is not unlimited growth potential in this space. We believe that what is likely to happen in the next few years is continued growth, followed by a shakeout and consolidation into a few core providers.

In the interim, we have already started to evaluate the decision to use a social listening provider, such as BuzzMetrics and Cymfony, based on a combination of the attributes of those services, as well as how well those fit the objectives of a given media plan. We know that some agencies have decided to go with just one social listening provider, but we feel that it's too early for that, as the market continues to grow and reshape itself.

To summarize, we believe that the future of social listening is very bright. As part of the BOE media environment, it will continue to play an essential role in evaluating and quantifying earned media. We believe that a big first step in this

(continued)

(continued)

direction lies in the area of enumerating the different segments, because authors, commentators, connectors, and spectators each have a different weight, depending on the category.

Beyond this, social listening can be of critical value in the generation of thematic material that enhances the understanding of a category and its brands. As such, we see listening as increasingly replacing some, but not all, focus groups (especially when timing is tight).

Finally, we expect that, due to information overload and the related problems caused by increasing consumer participation in social networks, there will be an eventual plateau in these groups' growth. This will be followed by a decline in both the networks themselves and those who glean, or "scrape," the information flow from those groups. In the long run, however, we fully expect social networks, social media, and social listening to occupy an important role in the media landscape for all marketers and advertisers. Understanding and capitalizing on that role will be an essential factor in their success.

The Rise of "The People's Network": Why Listening Will Grow More Important and Change the Way Marketers Think

Rishad Tobaccowala, Chief Strategy and Innovation Officer, VivaKi

Word of mouth has always been a potent form of marketing. Technology is now allowing word of mouth to be broadcast and to scale.

The broadcasting of word of mouth takes several forms. It can be liking or disliking an action or a post. It can be a comment that resonates against a social graph. It can be publishing a tweet, a blog, or a video. It can be passing along a positive or negative comment that one comes across. Importantly it is not necessarily initiated or contained in the digital world. It can start offline, move online, and then accelerate offline or vice versa.

This scalable broadcast word of mouth now creates a potent new marketing network, which we refer to as "The People's Network." Engaging with "The People's Network" is significantly different than most other activity marketers have become specialized at.

1. First engage, and then market: Most marketing efforts begin with a campaign, which is then modified as results filter in. Marketers must realize that today technology allows one to listen to what people are saying about your product and services independent of your marketing efforts and deciding how to react to these efforts is predicated on careful listening. How you decide to "engage" is more important than deciding how you "program" a response. Unlike other "networks" like broadcast or publisher networks, The People's Network rewards responsiveness, flexibility, and customization. It rewards conversation as communication. Conversational marketing is different than broadcast marketing.

2. It's what you do, not just what you say: Oddly, the most powerful form of conversational marketing is not what you say or how you say it, but what you do and deliver. Positive word of mouth is predicated on convincing folks that you are taking action, delivering a superior product or service, or fixing their problem (versus talking about fixing a problem). "Social media" is often less about media and advertising, and is more about customer service, product quality, and value creation. It is about giving a "gift" whether it is lessening a pain, providing a discount, or offering valuable content, among other things. Don't spend money on telling folks how cool your company is . . . invest in being cool.

3. It's voices—not just users—who are important: Most marketers focus on heavy and frequent users since this group drives a disproportionate share of profits. Often we confuse heavy influencers with heavy users when the opposite is often as true. There are two types of influencers: Advocates who speak positively about your product and detractors who complain about it. Our research has indicated that detractors are four to six times more likely to speak than an advocate. Thus, not only must marketers "arm the advocates" but also "defang the detractors." The detractor is likely to be a lapsed or non-user. Thus marketing today requires paying great attention to the non-user and light user as much as to the heavy user. Influential voices are not the same as heavy product and category users.

4. Engaging The People's Network is as much a bottom up as a top down effort: Every marketer is now preparing a central listening post and customer response unit somewhere central and at headquarters. While this is important, it is critical to note that a driving force of social is mobile. And mobility is really about place, location, and retail. It is about what happens at a restaurant, at a store, at an event. Marketers must train and empower their local and retail efforts to engage, and not just run things from some central command post far away from the action and often too slow in response.

5. It's about people and authenticity rather than technology platforms and buzz: Technology is especially important today. Technology allows for broadcast of word of mouth, and technology is allowing us to better understand and listen to what people are saying and sharing about our brands. It is understandable that many marketers are investing in technology platforms and creating "Facebook" and "Twitter" strategies. But it is like being in the water business and focusing on the plumbing and forgetting to pump in the water. Social media or conversational marketing is first and foremost about people and about being real. Machines are not real and will not be for some time. Marketers must invest significantly in people. Training people to respond. Training people to think and market differently in this age. Investing in additional people in customer service. Real people, real voices, and real conversations are the only way of being authentic.

6. Earned media is the most expensive form of media and needs to be integrated with paid media to be impactful: Earned media is not "free." The only way one gets positive word of mouth is by actually delivering value

(*continued*)

(continued)

through products, services, or experiences. This is expensive and limited in scale, but the positive word of mouth reflected in posts and comments, called "earned media," often has great impact. Those online and offline conversations can then be scaled via "paid media" to reach broad audiences. In fact a majority of times people hear about great "earned media" through "paid media."

7. It's not just about social media marketing, but all marketing: Often the insights you get from social media listening platforms will impact all your marketing efforts—not just your social media efforts. Make sure your social experts work closely with the rest of your marketing team. Avoid creating social media silos.

8. Not all social media experts are expert; separate signals from noise: Vet your experts and get sound advice: It's astounding that there are so many social media "experts" out there in an area only about five years old. LinkedIn's Social Media Marketing Group has nearly 94,000 members. Be careful when some "social expert" comes selling you snake oil for free.

CHAPTER 23

BECOME A LISTENING ORGANIZATION

Many companies want to know how they can become true listening organizations—this is one of the most frequently asked questions at listening forums and workshops put on by the ARF. At this early point in listening's adoption, few proven models are available to benchmark against, consider, and implement. For the most part it's been a matter of fit, feel, and finances (see the discussion in Chapter 1).

Companies that have embraced listening across their entire organizations, such as IBM and Lego, took different approaches that made sense for their individual companies. IBM created a center of excellence to support listening initiatives worldwide, whereas Lego completely streamlined and reorganized. A better idea than finding a model to abide by is to apply principles that lead to the right solution for your business. The following two essays reveal that principles combine ways of thinking with ways of acting.

Chris Boudreaux, head of management consulting at listening research and social media agency Converseon, outlines the various organizational obstacles that stand in the way of achieving meaningful business results from social media and listening. These include unclear, fragmented strategy; superficial, convenience measurement; staffing and training issues; and unaligned technologies. Boudreaux then delineates a five-step plan every company should consider, to maximize the contributions of social media and listening to the business.

Following Boudreaux, Wharton's Jerry Wind and I discuss the need to adopt a new "mental model" for listening. Mental models operate when we experience something and explain it to ourselves; they color our views of what is possible and achievable and what is not. Too often, they also act as barriers to progress instead of liberating energies to do remarkably great things. Sports history is rich with examples of athletes breaking restrictive mental models to set records that raise the bar for others to follow, like the four-minute mile. We contend that the current mental model for social media listening keeps companies from seizing its benefits, and so needs to be replaced by one that can. We propose a new model that aims to create companywide value through listening. For that to occur, we outline 10 shifts dealing with intention (why we listen), people (who we listen to), sources and content (what we listen to), and engagement (how we interact). Companies adopting this model will be able to deliver on the promise of listening, place customers squarely in the center of their businesses, and reap exceptional business benefits.

Organizing for Social Media Success

Chris Boudreaux, Senior Vice President of Management Consulting, Converseon

In 2010, social media reached a tipping point. It is no longer treated as an experiment or pet project. Leaders in very large enterprises are committing significant people and money to achieve business objectives through social media. CFOs are asking for real business cases, because managers are asking for real investments in resources. Vice presidents and directors are assigned social media goals in their personal performance plans. In short, corporate social media is finally "growing up."

As a result, we will soon begin to demand the same levels of reliability and accountability from social media that we demand from the companywide functions that social media support, such as IT, HR, marketing and finance. As the science of measuring social media matures, organizations will demand that this element deliver quantifiable business outcomes, and that performance measurement exist in full integration with existing measurement capabilities. Specifically, social media will not get its own dashboards; instead, metrics will appear within existing dashboards.

While the majority of leaders welcome the maturity of social media capabilities in the enterprise, most still wonder how to make it happen. In a lot of organizations today:

- *Ownership is unclear.* Everyone wonders, "Who owns social media?" For example, accountability for blogger relationship management and outreach remains vague, and is often contentious.
- *Strategy and planning are fragmented.* Even though every functional area can benefit from many of the same tools (e.g., Twitter, Facebook) and listening platforms, each functional area, business unit, and global region typically plans its social media efforts in isolation. As a result, there is a lot of redundant investment and activity across the enterprise.
- *Measurement is superficial.* Many social media teams simply report whatever metrics their tools provide, such as overall sentiment regarding selected keywords and keyword volumes. They are unable to tie social media activity to business outcomes, forecasting, or insight.

- *Execution falls short of expectations.* Too many organizations invest in social media without determining what they expect from their investments. As a result, they do not recognize when they are underperforming, and simply hope for better outcomes the next time around.
- *Staffing is reactionary.* Few companies have taken the time to define specific social media roles and responsibilities that allow the organization to proactively identify, hire, and develop proficient social media practitioners to lead and evolve their social media capabilities. As a result, any social media effort inevitably becomes someone's secondary responsibility.
- *Training focuses on individual tactics.* Most social media training that is sold to large enterprises still focuses on tactics and guidance that apply to individuals, but not to large organizations.
- *Tools do not align or integrate.* Most large enterprises have purchased multiple listening tools, all of which report different metrics, with little hope of reconciliation. In addition, social media measurement exists in isolation from Web analytics and customer analytics, leaving business leaders unable to determine where and how to invest.

Why is all of this occurring? Because most enterprises are still trying to figure out exactly how to achieve success in social media. The answers are available, fortunately; many of them rely on lessons from the past 20 years of business process reengineering, application rationalization, and functional shared services.

Most organizations' social media efforts look a lot like their e-businesses did in the late nineties: Each business unit had its own Web site, with its own Web infrastructure, its own shipping carts, and its own customer experience. Performance varied widely; the customer experience was very inconsistent; and redundant costs were everywhere. Eventually, most corporations determined to concentrate their e-business operations into a more centralized technical infrastructure, with IT operating as an insular shared service that optimized the performance of e-business capabilities across the enterprise.

At the same time, Michael Hammer, author and management expert, preached the benefits of business process reengineering and establishing internal "customer champions" to break down existing corporate silos. During that time, CEOs around the world selected influential senior executives to lead the charge across their organizations, with the goal of seamless and consistent performance for their customers. They mapped out business processes across various units, and consolidated many functional teams into shared services groups. The investments in these very large change initiatives were significantly fueled by fears of Y2K disasters, which led every large company in the world to rip out and replace many of their existing IT systems.

Throughout all of that change, the organizations that succeeded applied many of the same principles that led to enterprise-scale success in social media today, including:

- *Establish an internal champion.* Social media crosses every functional area of your business. You need a senior executive with strong internal

(continued)

(*continued*)

relationships to take the lead, invest his or her own dollars, and get everyone working toward common goals.

- *Begin with business objectives.* You must determine what social media investments to make, based on how you expect them to support your business objectives. The days of experimentation are over. If your managers still want to "test and learn," then you probably need to import some social media experience into your team.
- *Create a social media center of excellence.* Almost every organization benefits from sharing or coordinating certain social media resources and capabilities across the company. For example, someone should be accountable for defining a single social media measurement framework; and you'll want to deliver training consistently across the organization. Make sure employees are reporting performance regularly; and someone should ensure that all product marketing plans apply social media tactics reliably.
- *Focus investments on business processes.* Most social media efforts require significant coordination across functional teams. Think of that collaboration in terms of the business processes it is going impact. Examples include demand generation, lead management, customer analytics, customer service, recruiting, and staffing. Instead of investing in more Facebook fans, think about how that investment should drive awareness, gain leads, or lower costs per customer support interaction.
- *Remember culture and communications.* Consider the ways that your internal culture (or cultures) will impact your plans. Proactively communicate, and determine how you will manage cultural change where required. This is especially important for companies with lots of mergers or acquisitions in their history (or their future).

We've realized by now that social media imposes significant change on the way we do business—both inside and out. Successful companies begin internally, with careful examination of the people, processes, tools, and data required to achieve their business goals through social media. They then chart a reasonable course to continue social media performance at enterprise scale.

The End of Listening as We Know It: From Market Research Projects to Enterprise Value Creator

Yoram (Jerry) Wind, the Lauder Professor, the Wharton School, and Stephen D. Rappaport, the Advertising Research Foundation

Called "the world's largest focus group," "free mind-reading," and other superlatives, many researchers have grabbed onto social media listening as the latest way to harvest consumer "insights" from "rivers" of "authentic, unfiltered conversations" in the social Web. Listening is seen as a priority for companies of all sizes. However, we argue that listening's potential is severely limited by a widely held conventional mental model. The mental model is short term in focus and fails to lay the groundwork for a model of listening that will provide companies with insights, competitive advantages, and the ability to create value through time, and carry them through the disruptions we know will inevitably occur (though we're not sure when or how, quite yet.).

MENTAL MODELS

In both our business and personal lives, we have unique ways of seeing the world, mental models of how and why things work or fail, whether it's a business success, a new idea, or why Brad and Jen will not get back together again. Neuroscience teaches us that we actually discard most of what we take in through our senses. Instead, the world we experience evokes an internal model of reality—our mental model. When you stop to think about this, it makes sense: How else could we survive in the world if we didn't have a way for rapidly dealing with situations? Stereotypes perform a similar function. Without them, we would suffer from mental paralysis caused by the need to organize our understanding of the world each time out.

The fact that mental models are so helpful is what makes them so hard to break. That's not bad when they still explain things correctly in a stable environment. However, outdated mental models can be a detriment in today's complex, uncertain, and changing business world. What usually happens is this: We hold tight onto these models even after they've failed, and risk succumbing to insanity as Einstein defined it—doing the same thing over and over and expecting different results. What we need to do is replace those old, ineffective models with new ones. That's a considerable challenge, but it's one we can certainly meet.

Listening's mental model is no exception. In our view, it concentrates applications in two areas—consumer insights and customer service—the so-called sweet spots. Consequently the industry is only getting more of the same, as "smart" money bankrolls similar listening startups. And as the market takes shape around commodity offerings, researchers view listening as just another research method to be trotted out as a buzzworthy alternative to focus groups. "We're hip, we're listening," they claim. But they're not.

THE NEW MENTAL MODEL FOR LISTENING

The new mind-set must allow listening to become a continuous, sustainable activity that is embedded throughout the organization, and must become a resource for creating significant enterprise value. A new mental model must allow listening to achieve its promise.

We contend that the mental model has five aspects: *who* we listen to; *why* we listen; *how* we listen; *what* we listen to; and *engagement*. Each category has one or more rules. We use a straightforward method for presenting the current and emerging mental models through a series of statements beginning with "from" the old and "to" the new.

(continued)

(continued)

Who We Listen To

1. From a focus on consumers to a focus on all stakeholders (companies, regulators, interest groups, etc.).

Why We Listen

2. From market research and customer service priorities to incorporating listening into all other business functions, including, but not limited to, marketing, sales, R&D, legal, manufacturing, logistics, and investor relations.

How We Listen

3. From two-way company-customer listening to *n*-, or multiway, listening to the Web of conversations within and across communities of interest.
4. From subjective interpretation of conversations to more explicit, quantitative analysis, assisted and increasingly automated by technology.
5. From ad hoc listening projects to systematic, always-on listening.
6. From listening through the filters of our current mental models and stereotypes to one that's free of biases and enables people's voices to be heard as fully as possible.
7. From a single interpreter to bringing together multiple perspectives and viewpoints that enrich analysis and interpretation.

What We Listen To

8. From a focus on the written word to verbal and nonverbal information. Our view of verbal and nonverbal information is broad. It includes, but is not limited to: analysis of the way data are presented; videos and other enclosures; dynamics of the discussion captured; behavioral metadata; and biometric signals.
9. From shallow meanings derived from text to deeper meanings grasped through cues, such as vocal intonation or emotional correlations.

Engagement as *the* Priority

10. From listening passively to consumers, as one of the marketing research tools of the organization used tactically, to active "network listening" whereby companies are not just looking for feedback but fully taking into account all types of signals, engaging with and listening to all consumers and stakeholders across all touchpoints, and using listening to guide enterprise strategy and value creation.

PUTTING THE NEW MENTAL MODEL TO WORK

The first step in changing a mental model is, unsurprisingly, to change your own thinking. If you're a golfer or even follow golf casually, you've probably noticed that some pros are shooting lower scores than ever before. A short while ago, shooting 59 in a competitive round was an extraordinary, exceptional achievement; it's still rare today, yes, but it's happening more often. There are more scores in the low 60s than ever before. What's more is that these scores aren't achieved by the superstars, but rather by the capable and less-heralded tour players. And it's not due to the equipment; it's due to a change in golfers' mental models. Over the last several years, the golf school that has been rated most highly is run by two instructors Lynne Marriott and Pia Nillsson, *not* gurus like Butch Harmon, Hank Haney, or David Leadbetter. In Marriott and Nillsson's program, called Vision 54, they ask their pro golf clients the following question: "You've played this golf course umpteen times and birdied each hole at one time or another. Why not birdie every hole in one round?" Traditionally, golfers didn't think like this, but a group is beginning to do just that, and scores are dropping. Remember the four-minute mile? The common belief was that it couldn't be broken—that is, until Roger Bannister said: "Why not? I will." Over the following three years, 16 other runners broke the four-minute mile barrier, because it had been a mental barrier, not a physical one. The notion of physical limits to performance seems almost quaint, because our mental models have changed so much.

Adopting listening's new mental model requires a change agent, and it begins with you. But like scientific paradigms, new ideas don't simply win out on their merits. They require evidence, acceptance, a supportive culture and values, and business processes built on listening, sharing, and consultation, all to support enterprise value creation and increase accountability. Without those there's no reason why others should stick their necks out. They'll simply do what most workers do best: support the status quo ante.

BENEFITS OF ADOPTING LISTENING'S NEW MENTAL MODEL

We believe that listening's new mental model will help companies turn themselves inside out. This will enrich *all* management functions, by shifting their attention 180 degrees from their internal focus to an abiding external focus on all relevant stakeholders. Listening will be a force that drives the conversion of firms locked on managing customer relationships to management by customers. Instead of customers relating to a company in ways the company determines, the company will relate to its customers in ways customers want them to. That's a big flip; and although it will challenge management, it will help bond companies and customers more closely together, through better consultation and dialogue.

The day is coming when companies will furnish the right offering—whether a product, service, solution, or experience—to the right people at the right time; manufacture more effectively and efficiently; and greatly improve marketing, distribution, and service. Additionally, the mental model supporting enterprise listening is key to effective risk management and capturing new opportunities. These benefits can contribute to achieving the objectives relevant to all stakeholders, and becoming a source of sustained value creation.

You might be thinking, "Well, all that sounds great; we'll be set." Although we make the argument that effective listening, following our 10 rules, is a necessary condition to reap the benefits we list, it is not sufficient. You must implement your takeaways from "listening" to our words.

APPENDIX

VENDOR PROFILES
A RESOURCE GUIDE

Brands have an extraordinary array of solution types and vendors from which to choose for their listening research. In the following pages we organize solutions into the five categories described in Chapter 2, and provide capsule reviews of commercial products and services available today, organized by the marketplace so that you can become familiar with the types of solutions that may be best suited to your listening projects. The five groups are:

- Search engines
- Social media monitoring
- Text analysis
- Communities
- Full-service listening platform vendors

We chose vendors that have publicly available products for review. None were paid to be included; the companies we selected were based completely on our criteria. They run the gamut from established firms that were instrumental in launching the listening movement to newer startups whose innovative approaches are influencing the listening market. The space is constantly in motion and fermenting with investor interest. With so many new entrants, it's likely that the listening marketplace will consolidate over the next few years. For this reason, it is vital to carefully evaluate companies you may consider partnering with and make sure that their data is portable.

SEARCH ENGINES

We group solutions into two categories:

- General Search Engines
- Real-Time Search

General Search Engines

AOL Hot Searches   http://hot.aol.com

AOL Hot Searches provides a list of the top 10 search terms from the previous day and a blog that comments on searches or topics the blog editors find of
interest. Within the blog posts, the editors list a subset of searches related to
the topic, which offers some insight into searcher interests. One example is a
US Open story that was reported on September 11, 2009, for which the top
five searches were: Melanie Oudin, Serena Williams, Maria Sharapova, Rafael
Nadal, and Roger Federer. This tool also provides a helpful bit of context
by briefly annotating the top searches. Although AOL Hot Searches is not
searchable and does not report trend data, it does lend a social media twist
by allowing participants to comment on blog posts. Additionally, the service
solicits feedback by running occasional celebrity-oriented and topical polls,
such as awareness and use of Groupon.

ESPN Searches   http://search.espn.go.com

ESPN offers a handful of tools reflecting searches across ESPN.com: Recent
Searches (top 16), Top 10 Searches (last 24 hours), Top Mover, and Top Searches
of the Month (25), which also includes an editorial wrap on the most interesting
stories. Top Searches of the Month is archived and available from 2005 on.

Google Services   Google has three generally available products for analyzing
search trends: Google Alerts, Google Trends, and Google Insights for Search.
All draw upon a portion of Google's worldwide database of Web searches
performed across all its domains. Google only includes search terms that have
sufficient volumes for analysis, which must pass a minimum threshold. Search
terms can be any word or phrase or keywords purchased by search engine
marketers. Google positions Insights for Search as an advanced research, analysis, and display tool designed for researchers and advertisers.

Google Alerts   http://www.google.com/alerts

Google Alerts monitors Google properties Web Google News, Google Blog-
search, and Google Images for predefined keywords. Typically sent as a daily
e-mail roundup, alert frequency can range from "as it happens" to longer time
periods. News feeds are also available.

Google Insights for Search   http://www.google.com/insights/search

Google Insights for Search orders lists of the top searches and top-rising
searches. Users can enter one to five terms for analysis, and Google provides
filtering capabilities that tailor the information displayed: time period, Google
property (Web, image, news, or product), country, and category. The results
page shows graphs with search volume trends, news context, and geographic
distributions, and as a 12-month forecast of search volume for each term.
Google provides several features for downloading and integrating the Insights
data with other systems or displays through data feeds and embeddable widgets.

Google Trends   http://www.google.com/trends/hottrends

Google Trends positions itself as a resource for understanding popular or user-specified search trends. It furnishes the top 100 search queries on an hourly basis. Each term is hyperlinked to a page that presents a graph of the search volume index and related news stories, blog postings, and Web results. Google Trends also provides a search capability that allows users to compare multiple words over time, as well as by country, city, and language. Data mined here can be exported to other programs.

Yahoo! Buzz Index   http://buzzlog.buzz.yahoo.com/buzzlog

Yahoo! provides two listening services: Buzz Index and Y!buzz.

Buzz Index provides a ranking of searches organized into categories: Overall, Actors, Movies, Music, Sports, TV, Video Games, and Decliners. The service aims to present the terms of greatest general interest, which the service monitors editorially and then omits those that are irrelevant or ambiguous. Additionally, Buzz Index's associated blog features weekly reviews of the top 20 searches and daily commentaries on stories Yahoo! editors find postworthy. Buzz Index publishes different flavors—kids, Canada, United Kingdom, and France. Data is exportable via RSS.

Y!buzz reports terms in two groups: Leaders and Movers. Leaders rank Buzz Scores for each term, most popular first, by the percentage of searchers using that term. Movers charts and ranks the daily change in score from one day to the next. Leaders show the most popular searches; Movers show what's hot. Yahoo updates its data daily, and it reflects the traffic from two days earlier. Yahoo! explains in its FAQ that this lag is required because it takes 24 hours for data processing and verification.

Real-Time Search

Within real-time search we further organize solutions into these subcategories:

- Blog-centric services
- Twitter-centric
- "Real-time" Web
- Collaboration and workflow
- Analytic-oriented

Blog-Centric Services

BlogPulse   http://blogpulse.com

A service of Nielsen, BlogPulse combines blog search with analysis and reporting on various blogosphere events. This tool allows users to plot trends that compare one or more keywords and drill down into the supporting posts. The Conversation tracker aggregates posts related to search terms users enter, while BlogPulse Profiles provide metrics that help users understand the influence of the blogger. Like most services, BlogPulse reports on Featured Trends, and is a subset of Nielsen Online's MyBuzzMetrics, which covers virtually all consumer-generated media.

Google   www.google.com

Google presents real-time search results that are available in the left sidebar. When expanded, options are available for "recent results," "past hour," "past 24 hours," "past week," "past year," or alternate date ranges that the user can specify. It also includes Twitter updates, which appear as they happen.

Technorati and Twittorati   http://technorati.com

Technorati users search the blogosphere for topics using keywords or phrases, receiving results and automated trend graphs on daily blog post mentions. As one of the first services to measure online influence, Technorati's "authority" rating ranks blogs by the number of other blogs linking to them in the last six months.

Newer service Twittorati provides a Twitter-focused search by tracking tweets from the highest-authority bloggers, starting with the entire Technorati Top 100. The company claims it will include "many more of the Web's most influential voices."

Twitter-Centric

CoTweet   www.CoTweet.com

CoTweet couples Twitter management with a customer service platform that enables organizations to manage and respond to customer issues. CoTweet's capabilities include elements like keywords and trends monitoring; group collaboration features (letting teams control multiple accounts, set alerts, escalate and assign Tweets for action, schedule Tweets, and post to multiple accounts); and tracking and analysis tools.

CrowdEye   www.crowdeye.com

Dedicated solely to Twitter, CrowdEye graphs Tweet volume by time period, and organizes key terms into word clouds and drill-down capabilities, and surfaces the underlying Tweets. It also offers links to related searches.

DailyRT   www.dailyrt.com

DailyRT tracks the popularity of individual Twitter tweets by analyzing retweets. In addition to providing keyword search, it displays "hot tweets," those that receive the greatest number of retweets, and "profiles," which identify the authors of the most retweeted posts, as well as "resources."

hootsuite 2.0   www.hootsuite.com

Recent entrant hootsuite 2.0 offers similar features to CoTweet. Hootsuite provides integration with ping.fm, which allows users to update all their social networks with one push.

Topsy   www.topsy.com

Twitter-only measurement tool Topsy adds a social search component to searches. This service's ranking approach factors in a source's authority and how many times the content was shared. Source influence centers around what followers do with their tweets, such as respond or retweet.

Tweetmeme   www.tweetmeme.com

Tweetmeme's service collects and organizes popular links on Twitter into top-level categories—such as "entertainment," "science," or "sports"—and then divides these into subcategories. The sports category, for instance, is further broken down into "baseball," "extreme," "football," and "Olympics."

Twitter Search   http://search.twitter.com

Twitter's search displays results in real time, with the most recent first. Its results page shows what's buzzing around the Twittersphere in its lists of "trending topics" and "nifty queries."

"Real-Time" Web

Collecta   www.collecta.com

Collecta provides a constant stream of social media blogs, comments, status updates, photos, and videos relating to the search terms that users enter. The service puts forth "hot topics" and allows users to include all results or limit to one or a combination of sources. Collecta offers "chicklets," to share items, and an API for integration with third-party applications.

IceRocket   www.icerocket.com

By tracking blogs, the Web, Twitter, MySpace, news, and images including videos, IceRocket's real-time searches are ranked by timelines (most recent first) and organized by source. The interface and feature set concentrates on aggregating results, and presently offers little in the way of analysis, social media, collaboration, or reporting. However, IceRocket's integration features— RSS and a programmer's API—enable users to easily share results with colleagues or incorporate them into other systems for the heavy lifting. IceRocket also offers Ice Spy, a keyhole that reveals the terms and phrases being searched most frequently at that moment.

IceRocket's Trend Tool (http://trend.icerocket.com) lists out popular posts and sports, celebrity, and entertainment news. Its tracker allows users to search on one to five search terms and plot activity over 30- to 90-day periods. Graphs display the percent of all blog posts for which the search terms account over time, and furnish tables of posts per day, as well as average percentage of posts per day. For detail, hyperlinked search times fire off a query that returns results from IceRocket.

OneRiot   www.oneriot.com

OneRiot focuses on indexing the links people share on Twitter and social bookmark services, which they refer to as the "realtime Web." OneRiot shows the number of times that each result has been shared, who shared it, and the first person to share it. This capability, which several other services share, allows marketers to track down influencers and expose the viral path content takes. OneRiot allows searching within specific Web sites, and makes it possible to identify the content being discussed most frequently.

OneRiot presents results in two ways: "realtime" and "pulse." Realtime rankings list results by time, while Pulse Rank, with its proprietary scoring system, weighs posts by a number of factors, including freshness, Web site authority, personal authority, and acceleration (better thought of as "hotness").

Scoopler   www.scoopler.com

Scoopler collects, organizes, and indexes live updated content, such as breaking news, photos and videos from big events, and hot topics from real-time sources like Twitter, Flickr, Digg, and Delicious. Results are displayed in two columns: presented as a stream in one, and ranked by popularity in the other.

Social Mention   www.socialmention.com

Social Mention is a social media search platform that aggregates user-generated content. Categories such as sentiment, reach, time of mention, responses, actions, top keywords, top users, and number of unique authors are all used. Filters for managing result display include date, source, and post rank. Social Mention provides alert capabilities.

SOCIAL MEDIA MONITORING

Social media monitoring tools and capabilities allow end users to monitor, measure, analyze, and report on social media activity by querying their collection of social media sources. Monitoring tools help companies track mentions of themselves, competitors and industry, topics and issues, words or phrases of interest, the sentiment around them, and key influencers (which can be people, blogs, or sites). The primary purposes for monitoring, as mentioned in Chapter 2, are public relations, including reputation management; company and brand protection; and customer service, outreach, and engagement.

Alterian Techrigy SM2

http://socialmedia.alterian.com

Techrigy monitors mainstream media, blogs, and social media, and allows users to set alerts for selected conversations and topics. The program computes sentiments around each discussion and aggregates them to provide an overview of social media trends. Discussion clustering classifies and graphs all discussions around the brand. Charts offer drill-down capability, to see the buzz generating trends, and are customizable.

Brain Juicer

www.brainjuicer.com

Brain Juicer specializes in insights development and validation, concept testing, product evaluation, communications testing, sales forecasting, and brand personality tracking. The company uses listening research to support its services, such as predictive markets, hybrid qualitative/quantitative tools (MindReader), visual ethnography (FamCam), and, most recently, Digividuals, a "robot" avatar programmed to study trends in the Twitter environment.

Brandwatch

www.brandwatch.com

Brandwatch uses its own program, called Crawler, which visits microblogging sites like Twitter; blogs including Blogger and WordPress; video sites like YouTube and Vimeo; social networks like Facebook and MySpace; discussion forums; and news sites. Brandwatch also "cleans" the results by filtering out most irrelevant data, like ads and spam, which may match on key terms but are unrelated to the area of study. People use Crawler to collate information on topics called "queries," which are uploaded to a workspace where users can view all the Web activity trends on multiple topics simultaneously.

BurrellesLuce

www.burrellesluce.com

BurrellsLuce provides Media Contacts, Media Monitoring, and Media Measurement. Offering human-edited and automated services, they cover traditional and online sources, including social media and paid sources. Their automated metrics include: story volume, media type, audience segment, and DMA. Custom metrics add finer layers of analysis: tone, share of voice, key messages, prominence, and marketing power. Through the BurrelsLuce Portal 2.0, customers manage their results and can perform self guided searches with iMonitor.

ChatThreads

www.chatthreads.com

ChatThreads' Touchpoints service seeks to help brands quantify the reach, purchase, and trial impact of all their points of contact with consumers. Touchpoints evaluates many different media of consumer contact, including sampling; word of mouth; and online social, mobile, gaming, customer service, retail, and traditional media. All parts of the transaction funnel are considered to provide a picture of how consumers are receiving a brand's marketing efforts. Dashboards are used to show real-time results of brand buzz, where available, while monthly insight reports assess data in a more detailed way—looking at how each touchpoint is performing compared to others in terms of share of voice (SOV); how other related brands are performing, if and how touchpoints are leading to purchase; and more.

CyberAlert

www.cyberalert.com

CyberAlert 4.0 monitors domestic and international sources and has a family of products for "consumer discussion and tracking," which include message boards, forums, videos, blogs, and Twitter, for example. PR and media analysis included for each clip—such as a Web site ranking or news site it comes from—reach per million, national opportunities to see (an online data point similar to print circulation), and the print circulation of an Internet site (if a print version exists). Results are stored centrally in a digital "clip book," where users can manage, share, and import them into third-party tools. Account staff advises on user queries and handles any changes requested to terms or collection frequency.

General Sentiment

www.generalsentiment.com

General Sentiment is a technology company that produces comprehensive research products to help marketing, sales, and communications executives evaluate their brands' performance in the media and assess return on investment. Through natural language processing and sentiment analysis, the company analyzes social media content by listening to opinions expressed regarding companies, brands, products, and people in near real-time. General Sentiment considers its key differentiator to be its capability to translate the data into high-level insights for the marketing executive through dashboards and customized reports.

Giga Alert

www.gigaalert.com

Giga Alert's service searches the Web and news sources against keyword searches its customers specify. It offers various tiers of service, from Personal to Platinum, which differ in the numbers of searches performed, number of results returned, result frequency, technical support level, and the capability to share results with colleagues or workgroups. Giga Alert provides capabilities to refine searches by enabling end users to configure filters that eliminate unwanted or irrelevant results by example. Results can be organized, managed, and shared online, and results can be integrated through RSS or HTML.

Infegy Social Radar

www.infegy.com

Social Radar continually collects social content from across the Web and allows customers to search its database, which contains information that stretches back to January 2007. Infegy provides tools for mining and reporting. Customers specify search terms, set parameters or limitations, such as date ranges or level of influence, and generate charts covering topics, top influencers, tone (sentiment), and trends.

Itracks

www.itracks.com

Established online market research company Itracks recently launched a social media monitoring platform that, in partnership with social software application MutualMind, captures data from Facebook, Twitter, and YouTube, as well as data generated from other social media platforms. This information is then tailored for market researchers, who can develop their research design or monitor their clients' activity. The dashboard gives a quick view of what people are discussing online and includes a sentiment analysis graph of online activity. It also offers a very useful Respond function, whereby users can update multiple social network platforms simultaneously.

Meltwater Group

www.Meltwater.com

Meltwater offers media monitoring (Meltwater News), social media monitoring (Meltwater Buzz), and a collaboration platform (Meltwater Drive). Founded in Norway, Meltwater is strong in multilingual coverage. The company furnishes its services through a software-as-a-service platform.

Netbase

www.Netbase.com

NetBase's natural language processing engine (NLP) analyzes textual information at the sentence level. Patent-pending "lenses" provide context for search results and intelligently guide users to relevant results. NetBase products include ConsumerBase (social media analysis and brand tracking) and ScienceBase (insight discovery tool). Netbase provides its solutions as a software as a service, and provides consulting services.

OpinionLab

www.opinionlab.com

OpinionLab specializes in voice of the customer listening, specifically for Web sites, e-mails, and documents. OpinionLab solutions are, respectively,

OnlineOpinion (for enterprises), DialogCentral (for smaller companies), O-Mail (for e-mail), and DocRate (for documents). These programs collect opinions from individuals through online "comment cards" or special links that capture information anonymously at very granular levels, like individual Web or PDF pages. The company offers a variety of analytics, visualizations, and reports that include data drill-downs and trends in pages, opinions, and user experiences. Collaboration tools enable users to share and act on knowledge, as appropriate.

PR Newswire eWatch

http://ewatch.prnewswire.com/rs/login.jsp

EWatch is a self-service tool that monitors editorial sites on the Web, including print or electronic publications, customer-specified sites, and public discussion sites—newsgroups, online service forums, and investor message boards—which eWatch delivers after human monitors review them for relevance. The service provides the capability to manage and share results, and integrates with PR Newswire's MediaAtlas service.

Radian6

www.radian6.com

Radian6 searches the social Web in near-real time. Users can filter and segment results to narrow them down to specific areas of interest. Radian6 provides a suite of robust analytic and visualization tools. Workflow and engagement management features enable customer teams to route, track, engage, and report. Radian6 helps companies achieve holistic views of customers by integrating with Salesforce.com and WebTrends Web analytic data.

Scout Labs by Lithium Technologies

www.scoutlabs.com

Targeted to agencies, Scout Labs' platform provides social media monitoring, sentiment analysis, collaboration tools, alerts, filtering, and analytics. When desired, customers can add their own URLs, to ensure coverage of all critical sources. Scout Lab Workspaces allow agencies such as Razorfish to create "collaborative client dashboards" for "sharing the voice of the customer in real time, along with their own insights and recommendations."

Sentiment360

www.sentiment360.com

Sentiment360 evaluates social media activity concerning specific brands or topics across multiple mediums, including blogs, Twitter, YouTube, and Facebook. Analysts formulate qualitative and quantitative data and then organize it into customized market insight dashboards, enabling marketers to monitor the online discussion about a brand or topic in real time. Sentiment360 also offers clients strategic PR and advertising guidance, based on their market investigations.

Sysomos

www.sysomos.com

Sysomos specializes in social media monitoring for public relations, word-of-mouth marketers, advertisers, corporations, and API/data partners. This program uses a holistic "five Ws" framework for monitoring social media for clients: *What* are people talking about? *When* did the conversations occur? *Where* in the world did they happen? *Who* is doing the talking, and what kind of influence do they have? *Why* are the conversations happening; are they positive or negative? They claim this segmented approach to monitoring online sentiment, helps construct a detailed portrait of the state of a brand in the eyes of the online social public.

Trendrr

www.trendrr.com

Trendrr is a real-time social and digital media tracker of "trends," which the company defines as a search time or phrase tracked on a single news or social media service. Service categories include blogs, financial, news, jobs, music, sales, and search, for example. Trendrr shows its trend results as graphs, and offers the capability to combine one or more trends to show comparisons and contrasts. The community features allow users to search all active trends, to create mashups of one's own trends with any other, to embed charts, and to share trends on social networks. The PRO version provides more reporting options, alerts, and a developer's interface for incorporating company data and integrating with third-party applications.

Webclipping.com

www.Webclipping.com

Webclipping.com offers four major products—clipping service, competitive analysis, political campaign monitoring, and brand monitoring—through its Massive Internet Presence Profile. Reports include "key phrases, competing brand correlation, the mention of specific people or celebrities, and the geographical location of Web sites," for example.

TEXT ANALYSIS

Text analytics software companies furnish software that provides tools and capabilities for collecting conversations; processing, analyzing, and reporting them; providing workflow and collaboration tools for groups or teams; and data integration with CRM solutions, third-party, and in-house systems, to present a comprehensive view.

Offerings range from enterprise solutions to Web-based self-service tools that are installed on site or made available as a service. A number of vendors offer both deployments.

Adobe Online Marketing Suite: Powered by Omniture

www.omniture.com

Adobe's Online Marketing Suite, powered by Omniture, offers a wide range of social media monitoring services that can be used individually or collaboratively. The platform integrates data from multiple sources including the Web, mobile and social media interactions, as well as CRM, call center, and point-of-sale systems. Marketing channels reports can line up all of a marketer's promotional outlets for easy evaluation of which marketing investments are proving to be the most effective in influencing customers.

Attensity

www.attensity.com

Attensity claims to "empower better customer experiences" by emphasizing the integration of its text analysis with capabilities to respond to customers in self-service or through assisted customer service. Providing the features characteristic of enterprise vendors, Attensity's Response Management and E-Service suites appear to showcase its approach to linking text analysis to action.

Clarabridge

www.clarabridge.com

Clarabridge Content Mining Platform positions itself as providing a "customer experience management" platform that addresses several functional areas: product/service management, marketing, and service delivery that is applicable across industries. Clarabridge describes its process in three stages: Collect and Connect incorporates data from all relevant external and internal sources. Mine and Refine extracts meaning from text, through techniques like natural language processing and machine learning, classification, and sentiment analysis; stores it in a data warehouse; and combines it with structured data (databases and spreadsheets) to form a "360 view of customer experience." Analyze and Report uses analytical approaches like root cause, trends, and "advanced analytics," to gain understanding of brand dynamics, patterns, and trends. Reports are made available through online business intelligence portals, reports, or third-party tools.

For companies wanting alternatives to installed solutions, Clarabridge offers Content Mining Service, software as a service alternative. Social Media Analysis offers customers the ability to integrate the Alterian Techrigy SM2 social media collection.

Crimson Hexagon

www.crimsonhexagon.com

Crimson Hexagon's technology analyzes the social Web by statistically analyzing word patterns that express opinions on topics its customers identify. The company's platform, VoxTrot, provides two data views: VoxTrot Buzz reports mentions and sentiment trends on topics; and a proprietary metric, VoxScore, evaluates topic perceptions across media. VoxTrot Opinion is an analytics tool that enables users to understand drivers, patterns, and trends in opinions of interest. The company has a self-service offering in beta test.

Lexalytics

www.lexalytics.com

Sentiment and text analysis vendor Lexalytics concentrates on the OEM market, licensing its software and tools to third parties that integrate them into their product lines and services. Lexalytics customers include several reviewed here: BurrellesLuce, TNS Cymfony, and Scout Labs. Its core product, Salience 4, extracts entities (e.g., people, places, dates), entity relationships (e.g., people and their job titles), summarizes documents, and extracts sentiment or tone at the document and entity level. Lexalytics harvests content through Acquisition Engine and Classifier, which creates taxonomies. Lexalytics provides professional services and is considering expanding beyond the OEM market; the company is testing a self-service solution.

Networked Insights

www.networkedinsights.com

Networked Insights' platform SocialSense creates virtual communities drawn from preselected sites that focus on specific organizational or brand interests, and also tracks mentions across the Web, to explore the attitudes, behavior, and opinions of consumers. Networked Insights extracts themes, identifies trends and key verbatims, and integrates with comScore and WebTrends data for site statistics.

SAP Business Objects Text Analysis

www.sap.com

SAP's offering focuses on providing text analysis, reporting, and integration with its own or third-party tools to provide a rich view of customers. Multilingual capability is a particular strength, with analysis of more than 30 languages available.

SAS Institute, SAS Text Miner

www.sas.com

SAS Text Miner is a component available to licensees of SAS Enterprise Miner, the popular statistical and business intelligence software product. Text Miner stresses its integration with databases to provide a comprehensive customer view. Like SAP's offering, it is strongly multilingual. SAS Text Miner utilizes Teragram's natural language processing tools. Teragram is an SAS division that licenses its tools to the OEM market.

Temis Luxid

www.temis.com

The Temis Luxid product family tackles text analysis for scientific discovery, content enrichment, competitive analysis, and sentiment analysis. Temis works with online sources each customer configures, as well as with in-house databases. Its software identifies tonality, feelings, and perceptions around products, services, people, or companies, and offers analytics that enable drilldowns, cross-tabs, mapping, and clustering. The company's capabilities include voice-of-the-customer functionality, providing alerting and intelligent routing to subject matter experts or service representatives.

COMMUNITIES

Private branded communities allow the creation of invitation-only Web communities that combine brand interaction and social media. Communities run programs for brands that generate conversations among community members. Brand representatives may participate in the conversations, and feedback often is available using polls and surveys.

Private Online Community Vendors

Communispace   www.communispace.com

Communispace provides full-service community solutions that include project management, recruitment, facilitation, and insight generation. Facilitation helps make the community a familiar place and encourages regular participation through activities, discussions, polls, and surveys. Community managers report regularly to clients, highlighting actionable ideas, key insights, emerging trends, and important issues. Communispace research "has found that the smaller and more intimate the community, the more that people participate and provide value to clients' businesses." For this reason, Communispace limits community size to 300–500 participants.

Jive Software   www.jivesoftware.com

Jive Software's Social Business Software (SBS) platform provides a competitive feature set for creating and managing community. Its Market Engagement Solution combines listening within the Jive-powered community, with buzz monitoring from "outside" sources like Twitter, blogs, RSS feeds, or Google Alerts, or internal e-mails discussing issues, for example. Jive provides collaboration features that enable groups or teams to share knowledge and coordinate actions.

MarketTools   www.marketttools.com

MarketTools provides two different community solutions, branded Idea Networks and Insight Networks. Idea Networks brings together employees, customers, and consumers to "identify, refine, and prioritize ideas." Insight Networks enables marketers to listen to community conversations, and allows them to engage target customers directly, all to understand their "needs, perceptions, attitudes, and behaviors."

Passenger   www.thinkpassenger.com

Passenger's software platform provides a full range of community features and professional services. Passenger clients include B2C as well as B2B companies that create communities for their employees and partners. Whether "B" or "C," Passenger states its goals are similar: to improve products and services, customer insight, and evolving brands.

RightNow   www.rightnow.com

CRM vendor RightNow recently acquired pure-play community software company HiveLive and renamed it RightNow Community. The community is positioned for customer support, engagement, loyalty, and innovation.

Ripple6   www.ripple6.com

Gannett company Ripple6 offers a social media platform that helps companies implement their business strategy through social media. Its technology allows brands to create "cloud communities," which work across multiple social networks and sites. The content is the same but is integrated into each individual site, providing members with a seamless experience. The Ripple6 platform has multiple uses: a way for customers to create consumer engagements and relationships; to conduct research and generate consumer insights; and for social marketing. Ripple6 Social Insights is a package of capabilities and services designed for marketers. The company provides a variety of professional services.

SheSpeaks   www.shespeaks.com

SheSpeaks specializes in creating women-only private communities for brands, with features designed explicitly for research and creating brand experiences. After registering on the site, women members engage with each other through discussion boards, blogs, product reviews, and comments. Depending on their activities and profiles, members are selectively invited to participate in product tests. Once accepted, these participants are given products, which they then review, comment on, and discuss their feelings about and experiences with; participants also may interact directly with brand representatives. During an interview, SheSpeaks advised that its tests measure change by rigorously following a pretest, test, posttest methodology. Brand clients are provided with analyses of test activity and all postings related to the program.

Vision Critical   www.visioncritical.com

Vision Critical is a market research online community (MROC) company that blends interactive technology, strategic research, and panel expertise. Vision Critical's Sparq Platform offers a competitive set of community and social-networking features and capabilities that are fully integrated with the company's research service.

FULL-SERVICE LISTENING VENDORS

Listening-platform vendors provide technology, services, and consulting, and offer end-to-end solutions for analyzing both offline and online word of mouth. Some vendors extend their services beyond listening, to include agency services for planning, executing, and evaluating marketing, media, advertising, and public relations programs.

Attentio

www.attentio.com

Brussels-based Attentio provides Attentio Brand Dashboard, a hosted service that reports and visualizes social media activity and demographics for a company's own brands and competitors; it can filter by media source, topic, and country. Additionally, Attentio Buzz Report, written by analysts, furnishes deeper dives into brands. For context and planning, Attentio Industry Reports cover a variety of industries, their market leaders, and trends in areas like automotives, packaged goods, pharma, food, and media and entertainment.

BzzAgent

www.bzzagent.com

BzzAgent stimulates and measures word of mouth by enlisting "agents" to try products and introduce them to others as they see fit. BzzAgents are not a sales force; they are volunteers who share their knowledge and can provide samples and coupons. Bzz campaigns may involve thousands of agents, all of whom are expected to file reports describing context, such as people (e.g., with girlfriends), places (e.g., mountains), and activities (e.g., hiking); individuals' reactions, and those of the people they engaged with. BzzAgent collects, analyzes, and reports the data in a number of ways, in a real-time stream showing the number of conversations and favorability of the reports, tag clouds, and graphs listing popular words and phrases, geographic distribution of the reports, and demographics of the agents.

Collective Intellect

www.collectiveintellect.com

Collective Intellect uses Web-based, automated, real-time text mining and analytics software to focus on Social Customer Relationship Management. Its Social CRM Insight platform can provide both open- and closed-end analysis. The open-end analysis identifies popular themes, terms, and places "snippets" on the "hub" application, with links to viewing the discussions in their original context. This helps in forging a deeper understanding of the true breadth of views being presented online. Collective Intellect's closed-end analysis collates and quantifies customer considerations and preferences into more clear sentiment categories that the brand wishes to analyze and learn from.

Converseon

www.converseon.com

Social marketing agency Converseon provides listening, strategy, program execution, and creative services, and segments its services into four areas: Conversation Miner, Converseon's social media monitoring and analytics engine, discovers brand-related issues, opinions, ideas, and concerns; Brand Reputation Management manages and protects online reputations, and includes search engine reputation management; Blogs and Social Media focuses on increasing transactions and burnishing reputation; and Affiliate and Search Marketing concentrates on lead generation and sales.

Converseon positions its Conversation Miner as a core service whose results and insights drive the others. For maximum impact of listening and social strategy, Converseon believes that organizations need to "bake" these into their management and internal processes, and offers consulting services to help stimulate this process.

CRM Metrix

www.crmmetrix.com

Focusing on "brand backyard" sources, CRM Metrix combines and analyzes structured information through surveys with consumer-generated comments across marketing channels. Its family of tools, services, and reports aims to help marketers understand the drivers that prompt customer satisfaction, retention and loyalty, brand affinity, purchase intent, and revenue, and to help assess their marketing mix and marketing actions. SiteCRM measures Web sites and digital media impact on brands and business. Brand Scorecard measures and tracks brand health. BrandDelphi is used for developing and testing new-product concepts/advertising and improving message wording using an "adaptive conversation" algorithm developed and validated with MIT fellows. All reports are available through online digital dashboards, RSS feeds, and insight alerts (e-mail, SMS).

Cymfony

www.cymfony.com

Cymfony (a Kantar Media Company) offers its customizable Maestro Platform—a resource that combines information retrieval, natural language processing, and reporting—and provides the foundation for its array of services. Cymfony packages its solutions as Market Intelligence Studies and as Verismo, a Public Relations measurement model. Their Marketing Intelligence Studies are of three types: Competitive Landscape Study, Category Insights Study, and Holistic Market Research Engagement.

DigitalMR

www.digital-mr.com

DigitalMR is a market research and consulting agency that uses digital methods exclusively and specializes in listening via the Serendio platform. Company services include online qualitative and quantitative research for product design and development, brand and communications, customer experience, and tactical and crisis management.

evolve24

www.evolve24.com

Evolve24 is a "business analytics and research firm specializing in the measurement of perception, reputation, and risk." This program analyzes both traditional and social media to determine the marketer's overall "information landscape" and provide quantitative metrics that let clients measure and report the value of their marketing and communications efforts. Its showpiece program, the Mirror Dashboard and Analytics Suite, is a Web-based business intelligence application that integrates the real-time collection of traditional and social media with text-mining and analytics algorithms to allow the measurement of media conversations and programs, and, ultimately, evaluates the impact of online activity on business performance and corporate reputation.

Harris Interactive

www.HarrisInteractive.com

Market and opinion research company Harris Interactive offers its Text Analytics and Social Media Monitoring tools. Harris takes a business intelligence "data mining" approach to text analytics, by focusing on the combination of social media information and quantitative sources, such as surveys and databases, to gain a holistic brand insight. Harris uses Clarabridge Content Mining Platform (see the Clarabridge entry for a description). The company's Social Media Monitoring arm concentrates exclusively on social media, and features services such as collecting data through custom searching, analysis, and reporting results (e.g., daily volume, share of voice, demographics, sentiment, tone, conversation themes, and domains). Its report formats range from discussion to granular analysis, and are available through a portal or RSS feed.

InSites Consulting

www.insites.be

Belgian-based InSites Consulting structures its research practice into four areas: market insights, innovation, customer experience, and brand and communication. The company's research methods combine structured techniques, like surveys, with unstructured approaches by using text analytics and related techniques to understand buzz and extract themes from online discussions and social media. InSites aim to make its quantitative surveys more open-ended and expressive by providing a "shout box" for every question, wherein people can express their opinions. These "shouts" then go directly to a staffer, who responds and engages. Additionally, InSites provides "exit forums," where survey takers can discuss the survey with one another. This affords users with extra layers of conversation capable of generating insight beyond the questions asked.

J.D. Power and Associates Web Intelligence

http://businesscenter.jdpower.com/

J.D. Power and Associates Web Intelligence provides a competitive set of social media monitoring and analytic services, as the company claims to have the ability to segment the blogosphere by age, gender, and demographics. Its social media services include a combination of tracking, analysis, and consulting around areas such as competitive intelligence, marketing effectiveness, product development, and trend tracking. Web Connect allows marketers to identify bloggers based on age and gender criteria for targeting, influencer campaigns, seeding word-of-mouth campaigns, and creating communities. A new service called Tribes finds groups of people who share a common interest—for example, snacking on Doritos—and then collects and mines all of their posted content to find commonalities in their attitudes, attributes, and behaviors, and identify conversation topics.

Keller Fay Group

www.kellerfay.com

The Keller Fay Group provides word-of-mouth (WOM) research and consulting services. Through its syndicated product TalkTrack, the group continuously monitors "marketing-relevant conversations in America, in whatever form or context they occur, including face-to-face, telephone, and internet." The firm interviews a nationally representative sample each week, totaling 36,000 Americans ages 13–69 annually. TalkTrack measures more than 350,000 conversations about brands annually and covers all major consumer categories. The research uncovers what "talkers say" and what "listeners hear and then do."

Customers use TalkTrack for a variety of purposes, including situation assessment, targeting, channel selection, message development, and marketing effectiveness. Keller Fay consulting services help "clients plan and execute effective word-of-mouth programs, as well as monitor and evaluate their success."

MotiveQuest

www.motivequest.com

MotiveQuest specializes in understanding consumer motivations, discovering unmet needs, positioning brands, and finding new-product solutions. Using an "online anthropological" approach and toolset, the company mines brand-relevant online sources where consumers converse about client brands or product categories. Data reveals "peaks of passion," consumer language, and motivational drivers. MotiveQuest analysts supplement the data and add expertise for business analysis and strategic recommendations. The company gauges marketplace success through its proprietary Online Promoter Score (OPS), which correlates word of mouth to sales by measuring the number of people online who are promoting a brand to others. MotiveQuest offers services for direct clients and for agencies.

NM Incite

www.nmincite.com

NM Incite is a joint venture between Nielsen and management consultancy McKinsey & Company. Their solutions enable brands to extract value from social media as it relates to marketing, sales, product development, customer service, and business strategy development across industries. They include: Consumer Understanding; Defensive Branding and Threats; Brand Advocacy and Increasing Customer Value; Customer Service; and New Product Innovation. NM Incite provdes consulting services.

Onalytica

www.onalytica.com

U.K.-based Onalytica "offer[s] software, systems, and services that transform publicly available online information into actionable intelligence" through its online platform, reports, live briefings, and direct feeds into systems. Onalytica's solution focuses on advertising, campaign monitoring and evaluation, corporate communications, customer service, management information, marketing, and outcome prediction, like forecasting sales, market share, and customer satisfaction.

Visible Technologies

www.visibletechnologies.com

Visible Technologies' TruCast platform provides social media monitoring, analysis, and capabilities for participating in conversations. Visible Technologies organizes its solutions into four areas: Listen (conversation monitoring, perceptions, influencer identification), Learn (consumer insight, target audiences for word-of-mouth campaigns, and media buys), Engage (join conversations and manage them with collaboration and workflow tools), and Protect (executive and brand reputation management).

ADVERTISING RESEARCH FOUNDATION

Founded in 1936 by the Association of National Advertisers and the American Association of Advertising Agencies, the Advertising Research Foundation (ARF) is the preeminent professional organization providing fact-based thought leadership to the advertising, marketing, and media industries. The ARF's membership includes more than 400 companies in four major industries: advertisers, agencies (creative and media), media companies, and research companies. Additionally, the ARF's knowledge and thought leadership are leveraged by industry associations, educational institutions, and international organizations.

The ARF's core activities for advancing knowledge include multiday events such as the annual Re:think Convention + Expo and Audience Measurement conference; and daylong Industry Leader Forums. The ARF Council program addresses topics which are central to the industries we serve. Each council presents the latest cases, trends, practices, and insights from A-list brands, companies, and presenters. Additionally, the ARF publishes the *Journal of Advertising Research*, a peer review publication with contributions by leading academics and practitioners.

ARF members enjoy the many benefits of an engaged community: professional networking; opportunities to contribute to industry development; access to advertising, marketing, and media knowledge through state-of-the-art Web tools, such as ARF PowerSearch and ARF Morning Coffee; community forums; and personal assistance from the ARF Knowledge Center.

If you are interested in learning more about membership, send an e-mail to membership@thearf.org or visit the membership section of the ARF Web site: www.thearf.org/assets/member-benefits.

ACKNOWLEDGMENTS

In an emerging field like listening, there's no company, library, or database one can turn to, perform a search, and retrieve a ton of relevant results to review and write up. It takes detective work, finding people who know something, sniffing for clues, chasing leads, and, sometimes, nabbing one's quarry. This is an impossible task to do alone, and I was blessed to have the interest, support, and guidance of true leaders in listening.

Heartfelt thanks go to these individuals who sat for interviews, provided cases, contributed essays, set me off in the right direction, or reviewed drafts: Amanda Bird, David Berkowitz, and Sarah Hofstetter, 360i; Simon McDermott, Attentio; John Kearon, Brainjuicer; Jay Fischer, Calibre Consulting; Bob Woodard and Monica Corbett, Campbell Soup; Mike Hess and Michelle Lynn, Carat; Stan Sthanunathan, Coca-Cola; Don Springer and Marc Silberstrom, Collective Intellect; Joe Plummer, Columbia University; Manila Austin, Communispace; Rob Key and Chris Boudreaux, Converseon; Annie Pettit, Conversition; Bobby Thomas, Corner41; Dagny Scott, Crispin Porter + Bogusky; Laurent Florés, crmmetrix; Michalis Michael, DigitalMR; Steve Rubel, Edelman; Artie Bulgrin and Julie Propper, ESPN; David Geddes, Evolve24; Courtney Keating, GE Capital Credit; Eric Soloff and Greg Artzt, General Sentiment; Thomas Malkin, GeeYee; Michael Kassab and John Wittenbraker, GfK; Jenni Chapman and Michael Cooperman, Harris Interactive; Marcelo Padilla, Guy & Gallard; John Zogby, IBOPE Zogby; Carl Marci, Innerscope; Steven Van Belleghem and Annelies Verheage, InSites Consulting; Jennifer Zinn, J.D. Power and Associates; Richard Fielding, Kantar; Ed Keller, Keller Fay Group; Frank Cotignola and Paul Banas, Kraft; Jeff Catlin, Lexalytics; Britta Ware, Meredith Corporation; R. Scott Evans, Microsoft; Howard Moskowitz, MJI; David Rabjohns and Tom O'Brien, MotiveQuest; Linda Sonne-Harrison and Lisa Joy Rosner, Netbase; Brian Johnson and Daniel Neely, Networked Insights; Jonathan Carson and David Wiesenfeld, Nielsen; Pete Blackshaw and Dave Hudson, NM Incite; Katja Bressette, James Forr, Olson Zaltman Associates; Ethan Titelman, Penn Schoen & Berland; Jeff Rosenblum, Questus; Dannie Flanagan, Red Sky; Steve August, Revelation; Renee Murphy, Seek; Jason Harty, Snack Factory; Larry Friedman, TNS; Rishad Tobaccowala, VivaKi; Sarah Tunney, Westport Public Library; Yoram (Jerry) Wind, Wharton School; Geoffrey Precourt and Douglas West, World Advertising Research Center; Robert V. Kozinets, York University.

Special appreciation goes to Brendan Lawley and Antonia Miranda, ARF Knowledge Solutions interns, from the summer and fall of 2010, respectively. Both worked tirelessly on the project, tracking things down, finding and closing gaps, summarizing, and contributing their valuable perspectives, all the while staying on an even keel and maintaining their excellent senses of humor. Both of these able assistants built on the work completed by Chris Philp, intern from the summer of 2009.

Thanks also to my ARF colleagues: President Bob Barocci, Chief Research Officer Todd Powers, and Chief Financial Officer Felix Yang lent their executive support and made it possible for me to dedicate the time necessary. Jill Peled and Mi hui Pak of the ARF Knowledge Center provided valuable research and reference assistance. Catherine Gardner, Managing Editor of *Journal of Advertising Research*, offered many suggestions that improved the manuscript. Gwen LaFantasie and Leslie Hutchings of Member Services helped secure and schedule interviews. Kelly McSorley of the Events team, and Simone Moyle of Marketing, put on four important and successful Industry Leader Forums on listening. Bill Cook, Norman Cordova, Chris Ducharme, Michael Heitner, Kathryn Herrera, Heather James, Erin Jansen, David Marans, Ted McConnell, Erica Palmisano, Sheila Seles, Jeremiah Tucker, and Zena Pagan all offered suggestions, kind words, and encouragement, which were invaluable.

The team at John Wiley & Sons, Inc., that guided me throughout writing and production: Richard Narramore, Lydia Dimitriadis, Christine Moore, Peter Knox, Janice Borzendowski, and Susan Moran.

Lastly, I am grateful for the support of my family, Monica, Ethan, Renee, Laury, Wayne, Jodi, Michael and Sol, who were always there for me.

References

Part I: Introduction

Kozinets, Robert V. (2010). *Netnography: Doing Ethnographic Research Online*, London: Sage Publications, Inc.

Matson, John. (2008, November 17). "'Motrin Moms,' a-Twitter over Ad, Take on Big Pharma—And Win," ScientificAmerican.com news blog, www.scientificamerican.com/blog/post.cfm?id=motrin-moms-a-twitter-over-ad-take-2008-11-17 (accessed September 27, 2010).

O'Brien, Tom, and David Rabjohns. (2010). "Social Media Monitoring Is Not Research," essay prepared for the Advertising Research Foundation.

Pettit, Annie. (2010). "From Bit and Bytes to Brilliant Breakthroughs," essay prepared for the Advertising Research Foundation.

Verhaege, Annelies, Niels Schillewaert, and Emilie van den Berge. (2009). "Getting Answers without Asking Questions, www.insites.eu/02/documents/whitepapers/04_Getting_answers_without_asking_questions.pdf (accessed December 19, 2010).

Chapter 1

Austin, Manila, and Julie Wittes Schlack. (2010). "21st Century Market Research," www.communispace.com/uploadedFiles/ResearchInsights/Research_Patterns/MacroTrends_21CenturyMarketResearch.pdf (accessed October 31, 2010).

Grimes, Seth. (2009, December 9). "For Text Data Quality, Focus on Sources," BeyeNetwork, www.b-eye-network.com/view/12244 (accessed October 30, 2010).

Kanter, Beth. (2009, June 11). "Are You a Listening Organization?," Beth's blog, http://beth.typepad.com/beths_blog/2009/06/are-you-a-listening-organization-.html (accessed November 1, 2010).

Keller Fay Group. Offline WOM more prevalent, positive and credible than online buzz. www.marketingcharts.com/direct/offline-wom-more-prevalent-positive-and-credible-than-online-buzz-5144/ (accessed October 28, 2009).

Poynter, Ray. (2010). "A Taxonomy of New MR," London: Market Research Society.

Webster, Tom. (2010, October 28). "Six Steps to a Successful Social Media Survey," BrandSavant, http://brandsavant.com/6-steps-to-a-successful-social-media-survey/ (accessed October 29, 2010).

Chapter 2

Forrester. (2010, July 12). The Forrester Wave™: Listening, Platforms, Q3 2010, Forrester Research Inc., Cambridge, MA.

Grimes, Seth. (2008). "Text Analytics Basics," Parts 1 and 2, BeyeNetwork, www .b-eye-network.com/view/8032 and www.b-eye-network.com/view/833, respectively (accessed October 31, 2010).

LinkedIn. (2010, October 31). "Can anyone recommend a good social media monitoring tool?," thread of 294 responses in Social Media Marketing group (membership required) www.LinkedIn.com (accessed October 31, 2010).

O'Brien, Tom, and David Rabjohns. (2010). "Social Media Monitoring Is Not Research," essay prepared for the Advertising Research Foundation.

Stodder, David. (2010, January 30). "How Text Analytics Drive Customer Insight," Information Weeks, www.informationweek.com/news/business_intelligence/analytics/showArticle.jhtml?articleID=222600270 (accessed October 31, 2010).

Chapter 3

Berger, Jonah, Alan T. Sorenson, and Scott J. Rasmussen. (2009). "Positive Effects of Negative Publicity: When Negative Reviews Increase Sales," http://papers.ssrn .com/sol3/papers.cfm?abstract_id=1344363 (accessed December 14, 2010).

Forrester. (2010, July 12). "The Forrester Wave™: Listening Platforms, Q3 2010," Forrester Research, Inc., Cambridge, MA.

Grimes, Seth. (2008a). "Voice of the Customer Text Analytics for the Responsive Enterprise," BeyeNetwork, www.beyeresearch.com/study/794 (accessed November 1, 2010).

———. (2008b). "Sentiment Analysis: Opportunities and Challenges," BeyeNetwork, www.b-eye-network.com/print/6897 (accessed October 31, 2010).

J.D. Power and Associates Web Intelligence. (2009). "Marketing Campaign Effectiveness, www.jdpowerWebintelligence.com/case_studies/CS-quick-serve.php (accessed October 25, 2009).

Pettit, Annie. (2010). "6 Checkmarks Towards Quality Social Media Research," Social Media Today, www.socialmediatoday.com/anniepettit/168900/6-checkmarks-towards-quality-social-media-research (accessed October 31, 2010).

Chapter 4

Communispace. (2009). "CDW's Best Sales Strategy: Listen to your Customers," www .communispace.com/news/groundswell/default.aspx?groundswell=13 (accessed October 19, 2009).

———. (2010). "comScore Releases July 2010 U.S. Search Engine Rankings," www .comscore.com/Press_Events/Press_Releases/2010/8/comScore_Releases_July_2010_U.S._Search_Engine_Rankings (accessed August 28, 2010).

Engelbart, Christina, and Larissa Mats. (2010). "Pulse on the Economy: Using Social Media to Understand Today's Shopper Behavior," Cymfony.

Moskowitz, Howard R., and Alex Goffman. (2007). Selling Blue Elephants: How to Make Great Products That People Want Before They Know They Want Them, Philadelphia: Wharton School Press.

Springer, Don. (2009). Personal communication.

Wind, Yoram (Jerry), and Colin Crook. (2004). The Power of Impossible Thinking: Transform the Business of Your Life and the Life of Your Business, Philadelphia: Wharton School Press.

Chapter 5

J.D. Power and Associates. (2005). "Market Tracker." No longer on Web site (accessed October 25, 2009).

Knight, Kristina. (2009, April 7). "Reports: Female gaming habits accelerate," BizReport, www.bizreport.com/2009/04/report_females_are_now_gaming_more_than_males.html (accessed October 25, 2009).

Neely, Dan. (2010). Personal communication.

Networked Insights. (2010). "New Audience, New Product," www.networkedinsights.com/products/uses (accessed September 1, 2010).

Rosenblum, Jeff. (2010). Personal communication.

Ultimatemotorcyling.com. (2010, March 17). "Suzuki Hayabusa Busa Beats Goes Urban," www.ultimatemotorcycling.com/Suzuki_Hayabusa_Busa_Beats (accessed September 1, 2010).

Chapter 6

AgenciaClick. (2010). "Fiat Brazil Suggests the First Co-Created Car," http://clickaqui.agenciaclick.com.br/profiles/blog/show?id=924212:BlogPost:59912 (accessed September 2, 2010).

Banas, Paul. (2010). "Social Listening: From Observations to Insights," presentation to ARF Industry Leader Forum, January 28, 2010.

Dubroff, M. Dee. (2009). "BaconSalt: The Guys Behind the Dream," *Digital Journal*, www.digitaljournal.com/article/271459 (accessed October 17, 2009).

Harty, Jason. (2010a). "vitaminwater® connect(s) with Their Consumers: Flavorcreator case study," presented to ARF Social Media Boot Camp, March 29, 2010.

———. (2010b). Personal communication.

Janowski, Karen. (2008). "Top 10 Reasons New Products Fail," EcoStrategy Group, www.ecostrategygroup.com/top10reasons.pdf (accessed September 3, 2010).

Kincaid, Jason. (2010, January 7). "Facebook Just Got Its Own VitaminWater Flavor: 'Connect.' Seriously." http://techcrunch.com/2010/01/07/facebook-vitaminwater/ (accessed September 6, 2010).

Kuhn, Thomas. (1996). *The Structure of Scientific Revolutions*, 3rd ed. Chicago: University of Chicago Press.

Qualman, Erik. (2009). *Socialnomics: How Social Media Transforms the Way We Live and Do Business*, Hoboken, NJ: John Wiley & Sons, Inc.

Starbucks. (2009). Starbucks Web site, www.mystarbucksidea.com (accessed October 17, 2010).

Sthanunathan, Stan. (2010). "Don't Explain the Past, Predict the Future, *Admap Magazine*, July/August.

Ware, Britta C., and Manila S. Austin. (2008). "Meredith's Silver Bullet: Leading with Market Knowledge and Innovation," www.communispace.com/uploadedFiles/ResearchInsights/The_Customers_Perspective/BrandPerspective_MeredithsSilver Bullet.pdf (accessed December 19, 2010).

Wentz, Laurel. (2009, August 21). "At Fiat in Brazil, Vehicle Design is No Longer By Fiat: Automaker is Relying on Consumers and Social Media for a 2010 Concept Car." http://adage.com/globalnews/article?article_id=138594 (accessed December 19, 2010).

Chapter 7

Doublethink. (2009, November 25). "Listening Is Easy," http://thedoublethink.com/2009/11/listening-is-easy (accessed September 7, 2010).

Madsen, Flemming. (2006). "Who Are the Most Influential Authorities on Business Blogging?" Onalytica, www.onalytica.com/Who_influence_the_debate_on_Business_Blogging.pdf (accessed December 19, 2010).

———. (2008, January 27). "Predicting Sales from Online Buzz," message posted on www.onalytica.com/blog/2008/01/predicting-sales-from-online-buzz.html (accessed October 16, 2009).

Mica, Anca, and Joseph Plummer. (2010). "Measurable Emotions: How Television Ads Really Work. Patterns of Reactions to Commercials Can Demonstrate Advertising Effectiveness," *J. Advertising Research*, Vol. 50, No.2, 2010, pp. 137–153.

Neely, Daniel. (2010). Personal communication.

Onalytica. (2009). "An Introduction to Onalytica," www.onalytica.com/whatwedo.aspx (accessed September 18, 2009).

Ostrow, Adam. (2010, June 15). "Inside Gatorade's Social Media Command Center," Mashable, http://mashable.com/2010/06/15/gatorade-social-media-mission-control (accessed September 9, 2010).

Steel, Emily. (2009, November 23). "Marketers Find Web Chat Can Be Inspiring: Devising Campaigns, IBM, Harrah's Are Guided by What Consumers Are Saying—Or Not Saying—Online," *The Wall Street Journal*, p. B8.

WARC. (2009, November 24). "P&G Targets Leadership Level Marketing Spend." www.warc.com/News/TopNews.asp?ID=25980&Origin=WARCNewsEmail (accessed November 24, 2009).

Wentz, Laurel. (2009, August 21). "At Fiat in Brazil, Vehicle Design is No Longer by Fiat," http://adage.com/globalnews/article?article_id=138594 (accessed December 15, 2010).

Wiesenfeld, David, Kristin Bush, and Ronjan Sikdar. (2009, August). "Listening Up: Online Yields New Research Pathway." Nielsen Consumer Insight, http://en-us.nielsen.com/main/insights/consumer_insight/August2009/listen_up_online_yields (accessed October 30, 2009).

Wikipedia. (2010). "Linguistic Relativity," http://en.wikipedia.org/wiki/Linguistic_relativity, last modified September 3, 2010 (accessed September 8, 2010).

Chapter 8

Alterian. (2010). "Measuring the Social Web Increases Engagement with the Public for Leading Cancer Hospital," http://content.alterian.com/resources/casestudies/MD_Anderson_Cancer_Center_SM2_Case_Study.pdf (accessed August 19, 2010).

Carney, Heidi. (2010). Personal communication.

Kraft Foods. (2010). How to Submit Your Recipe, www.realwomenofphiladelphia.com/how-to-submit-phase-two (accessed September 15, 2010).

Miller, Claire Cain. Twitter Serves Up Ideas from Its Followers (2009, October 26). "Twitter Serves Up Ideas from Its Followers," *New York Times*, p. B1.

Morrissey, Brian. (2008, February 6). "Social Media to Weather Recession, *Adweek*, www.adweek.com/aw/content_display/news/agency/e3idcbc5d3b3d8cd7714b48c1ac99fb8b30 (accessed October 18, 2009).

Sigala, Sal Jr. (2010, August 27). "NASCAR Racing Series Goes Up for Sale—Buyer Beware Rules Are Included," Bleacher Report, http://bleacherreport.com/articles/441966-nascar-racing-series-goes-up-for-sale-buyer-beware-rules-are-included (accessed September 10, 2010).

Vision Critical. (2009, October 14). "Vision Critical: NASCAR Awarded Online Panel of the Year," www.marketwire.com/press-release/Vision-Critical-1059675.html (accessed October 24, 2009).

Chapter 9

Communispace. (2009). "CDW's Best Sales Strategy: Listen to your Customers," www.communispace.com/Clients/ForresterDetail.aspx?id=517&terms=CDW (accessed December 15, 2010).

Harty, Jason. (2010). Personal communication.

Innis, Harold. (1972). *Empire and Communications*, edited by Mary Quayle Innis and with an introduction by Marshall McLuhan, Toronto: University of Toronto Press.

Keller Fay Group. (2008). "Offline WOM More Prevalent, Positive and Credible Than Online Buzz," www.marketingcharts.com/direct/offline-wom-more-prevalent-positive-and-credible-than-online-buzz-5144 (accessed October 28, 2009).

MotiveQuest. (2007). "Radical Listening," Presented to the Word of Mouth Marketing Summit.

———. (2009a). "The Raging Debate Case Study." www2.motivequest.com/client/showpost.aspx?postid=33 (accessed October 21, 2009).

———. (2009b). "The Online Promoter Score," http://motivequest.com/main.taf?p=1,2,1,1 (accessed October 26, 2009).

Nielsen Wire. (2009, July 9). "Global Advertising: Consumers Trust Real Friends and Virtual Strangers the Most," http://blog.nielsen.com/nielsenwire/consumer/global-advertising-consumers-trust-real-friends-and-virtual-strangers-the-most (accessed September 12, 2010).

Pietruski, Fiona, and Kimberly Lang. (2009). "Heinz: Leveraging Women and WOM to Launch a New Product," presented at Word of Mouth Marketing University, May 13, 2009.

SheSpeaks. (2009). "Case Study: Ore-Ida Steam n' Mash," shespeaks.com/pages/img/client/OreIdaFinalCaseStudy.pdf (accessed October 7, 2009).

Titelman, Ethan. (2010). Personal communication.

Chapter 10

Bird, Amanda. (2010). Personal communication.

Crimson Hexagon. (2010). "Provo Craft Uncovers New Market Opportunities via the VoxTrot Listening Platform," case study.

Gibson, Riley. (2010). Interview with Brendan Lawley, ARF intern.

Johansen, Bob. (2007). *Get There Early: Sensing the Future to Compete in the Present*, San Francisco, CA: Berrett-Koehler Publishers.

Kraft Foods. (2010). "How to Submit Your Recipe," www.realwomenofphiladelphia.com/how-to-submit-phase-two (accessed September 15, 2010).

Lukovitz, Karlene. (2010, March 24). "'Real Women' Drive Philly Cream Cheese Digital," MediaPost, www.mediapost.com/publications/?fa=Articles.printFriendly&art_aid=124871 (accessed September 14, 2010).

Morrissey, Brian. (2010, August 4). "Old Spice's Agency Flexes Its Bulging Stats," *Adweek*, http://adweek.blogs.com/adfreak/2010/08/old-spices-agency-flexes-its-bulging-stats.html (accessed September 21, 2010).

Neff, Jack. (2010, July 26). "How Much Old Spice Body Wash Has the Old Spice Guy Sold?," *Advertising Age*, http://adage.com/print?article_id=145096 (accessed September 13, 2010).

Propper. 2009. Personal communication.

ProvoCraft. (2009, February 6). "Provo Craft Demonstrates New Cricut Cartridges at CHA Winter," press release, www.provocraft.com/news/press.releases.php?newsarticle=78&cat= (accessed September 16, 2010).

Rabinowitz, Ilana, and Paull Young. (2009). "Converseon Lion Brand Yarn Case Study: Internet Retailer 2009," www.slideshare.net/Converseon/converseon-lion-brand-yarn-case-study-internet-retailer-2009 (accessed October 24, 2009).

Richard, Laurie. (2010, August 5). "Tapping the Wisdom of the Crowd," *New York Times*, www.nytimes.com/2010/08/05/business/smallbusiness/05sbiz.html (accessed August 5, 2010).

Wikipedia. (2009). "ESPN," http://en.wikipedia.org/wiki/Espn (accessed October 24, 2009).

York, Emily Bryson. (2010, May 24). "How Philly Cream Cheese Gave Its Flat Sales a Kick," *Advertising Age*, http://adage.com/print?article_id=144036 (accessed September 15, 2010).

Young, Paull. (2009). "Converseon Case Study: Lion Brand Yarn Drives Measureable ROI with Social Media," message posted to http://blog.converseon.com/2009/09/01/converseon-case-study-lion-brand-yarn-drives-measurable-roi-with-social-media (accessed September 23, 2009).

Chapter 11

Communispace. (2010). Personal communication.

Dove. (2004, September). "The Real Truth about Beauty: A Global Report," www.campaignforrealbeauty.ae/uploadedfiles/dove_white_paper_final.pdf (accessed December 19, 2010).

———. (2006, February). "Beyond Stereotypes: Rebuilding the Foundation of Beauty Beliefs," www.campaignforrealbeauty.ie/DoveBeyondStereotypesWhitePaper.pdf (accessed December 19, 2010).

———. (2006, September). "Beauty Comes of Age," www.campaignforrealbeauty.com.au/proage/pdf/DoveBeautyWhitePaper.pdf (accessed December 19, 2010).

———. (2008). "Real Girls, Real Pressure: A National Report on the State of Self-Esteem," content.dove.us/makeadiff/pdf/SelfEsteem_Report.pdf (accessed December 19, 2010).

Elliott, Stuart. (2009, February 22). "Tropicana Discovers Some Buyers Are Passionate about Packaging," *New York Times*, p. B6.

J.D. Power and Associates Web Intelligence. (2010). Personal communication.

Tropicana Products Inc. (2009, January 9). "Tropicana Launches Campaign to Emphasize the All-Natural and Healthy Benefits of 100% Pure Premium Orange Juice," press release, www.bevnet.com/news/2009/1-9-2009-Tropicana_squeeze (accessed September 24, 2010).

Unilever. (2009). "Dove," www.unilever.com/brands/personalcarebrands/dove.aspx (accessed October 18, 2009).

Ware, Britta C., and Manila S. Austin. (2008). "Meredith's Silver Bullet: Leading with Market Knowledge and Innovation," www.communispace.com/uploadedFiles/ResearchInsights/The_Customers_Perspective/BrandPerspective_MeredithsSilver Bullet.pdf (accessed December 19, 2010).

Chapter 12

Cooper, Charles. (2010, July 19). "Are Steve Jobs' iPhone 4 Antenna Woes Over?", CBS News, www.cbsnews.com/8301-501465_162-20010955-501465.html (accessed September 27, 2010).

German, Kent, and Erica Ogg. (2010, July 15). "What We Know about iPhone 4's Antenna," (FAQ), CNET, http://reviews.cnet.com/8301-19512_7-20010714-233.html (accessed September 27, 2010).

Google Insights for Search. (2010, August 23). Searches on "apple" and "apple iphone," www.google.com/insights/search.

Greenpeace.org. Post by Laura K. (2010, August 9). "What happened after you left that comment on Nestlé's Facebook page?", www.greenpeace.org/international/en/news/Blogs/climate/what-happened-after-you-left-that-comment-on-/blog/26125 (accessed September 27, 2010).

Hickman, Martin. (2010, May 19). "Online Protest Drives Nestlé to Environmentally Friendly Palm Oil," *The Independent*, www.independent.co.uk/environment/green-living/online-protest-drives-nestl-to-environmentally-friendly-palm-oil-1976443.html (accessed September 27, 2010).

Infegy.com. Post by Gray. (2010, March 20). "Nestlé, Kit-Kat, Palm Oil, Facebook . . . What happened?", http://infegy.com/buzzstudy/tag/kit-kat (accessed September 27, 2010).

Kilar, Jason. (2009, January 13). "Consumer Trust Is Hard Won, Easily Lost," Hulu blog, http://blog.hulu.com/2009/01/13/customer-trust-is-hard-won-easily-lost (accessed September 27, 2010).

Qualman, Erik. (2009). *Socialnomics: How Social Media Transforms the Way We Live and Do Business*, Hoboken, NJ: John Wiley & Sons, Inc.

Rappaport, Stephen D. (2010, October 17). Analysis of Google search trends for Apple iPhone 4 antenna issue, performed for this book.

Rubel, Steve. (2010). "The Future for Listening," essay prepared for the Advertising Research Foundation.

Saleem, Muhammad. (2009). "HOW TO: Survive a Social Media Revolt," Mashable, http://mashable.com/2009/01/28/social-media-revolt (accessed September 27, 2010).

Shin, Annys. (2006, September 23). "2 Deaths Prompt Toy Recall," *Washington Post*, www.washingtonpost.com/wp-dyn/content/article/2006/09/22/AR2006092201370.html (accessed October 22, 2009).

Social Media Club of Sydney. (2010, video uploaded September 26). "Greenpeace Nestlé Social Media Campaign," www.vimeo.com/15312263 (accessed September 27, 2010).

TNS Cymfony. (2009). "Real-time Crisis in a Consumer-Controlled World: A TNS Cymfony Influence 2.0 Case Study." www.cymfony.com (requires registration).

WARC. (2010, September 29). "P&G Outlines Major Sustainability Drive," www.warc.com/News/TopNews.asp?ID=27298&Origin=WARCNewsEmail (accessed September 29, 2010).

Winterfeld, Sandy. (2010, July 19). "Rival's Reaction to Apple iPhone 4 Antenna Problems," World Correspondents, www.worldcorrespondents.com/rivals-reaction-to-apple-iphone-4-antenna-problems/887700 (accessed September 27, 2010).

YouTube. (2010, September 27). Stats from pages: "Levinator25, Tiger Woods PGA Tour 08 Jesus Shot," www.youtube.com/watch?v=h42UeR-f8ZA, and "EASports, Tiger Woods 09—Walk on Water," www.youtube.com/watch?v=FZ1st1Vw2kY (both accessed September 27, 2010).

Chapter 13

Agnello, Anthony. (2010, August 27). "Amazon (AMZN) e-reader Future Bright Thanks to Kindle 3," www.investorplace.com/NewsML/amazon-amzn-e-reader-future-bright-thanks-to-kindle-3.html (accessed October 3, 2010).

Allfacebook.com. (2010, September 30). Statistics for Scrabble, Scrabble Worldwide, and Wordscraper, http://statistics.allfacebook.com/applications (accessed September 30, 2010).

Boone, Louis E., and David L. Kurtz. (2006). *Contemporary Marketing*, Mason, OH: Thomson South-Western.

Cotignola, Frank. (2010, June 21). "Listening with a Mix of Free and Paid Tools," presentation to ARF University Social Media Boot Camp.

Crimson Hexagon. (2009, September 11). "Give Tylenol to the Kids, Take Advil for Pain," www.crimsonhexagon.com/2009/09/give-tylenol-to-the-kids-take-advil-for-pain (accessed October 2, 2010).

Eldon, Eric. (2009, January 6). "F-A-I-L: Official Scrabble Facebook Apps Still Smaller Than Scrabulous Was," VentureBeat, http://digital.venturebeat.com/2009/01/06/f-a-i-l-official-scrabble-facebook-apps-still-smaller-than-scrabulous-was (accessed October 22, 2009).

Hurst, Mark. (2010, August 5). "One Social Media Tip: First Build a Good Customer Experience," Good Experience blog, http://goodexperience.com/2010/08/one-social-media-tip.php (accessed October 3, 2010).

J.D. Power and Associates Web Intelligence. (undated). "Competitive Intelligence: When to Hold and When to Fold," www.umbriacommunications.com/case_studies/CS-CPG-competitive.php (accessed October 25, 2009).

Knowledge@Wharton. (2008, August 6). "War of the Words: Scrabulous Is Off Facebook, But Did Hasbro Win the Game?", http://knowledge.wharton.upenn.edu/article.cfm?articleid=2029 (accessed October 22, 2009).

Paddock, Catharine. (2009, July 2). "FDA Panel Votes to Restrict Acetaminophen," Medical News Today, www.medicalnewstoday.com/articles/156256.php (accessed October 4, 2010).

Ries, Al, and Jack Trout. (1981). *Positioning: The Battle for Your Mind*, New York: McGraw-Hill Inc.

Chapter 14

Barnes, Norah G. (2008). "Exploring the Link Between Customer Care and Brand Reputation in the Age of Social Media," Society for New Communications Research, http://sncr.org/wp-content/uploads/2008/10/customer-care-study.pdf (accessed October 5, 2010).

Boudreaux, Chris. (2009, December 16). "Analysis of Social Media Policies: Lessons and Best Practices," Socialmediagovernance.com, http://socialmediagovernance.com/downloads/Social-Media-Policy-Analysis.pdf (accessed December 19, 2010).

Charlton, Graham. (2009, April 21). "The Power of Social Media for Customer Service," eConsultancy, http://econsultancy.com/us/blog/3707-how-to-use-social-media-for-customer-service.

ForaTV. (2009, October 29). "Comcast CEO: Twitter Changed Our Company," www.youtube.com/watch?v=5q4n9iA2JG4 (accessed October 6, 2010).

Fresh Networks. (2008, November 22). "You're your Customers. Use Social Media." www.freshnetworks.com/blog/page/2/?s=zappos (accessed December 19, 2010).

Kawasaki, Guy. (2010, May 6). "How to Use Twitter to Support Customers," American Express Open Forum, www.openforum.com/idea-hub/topics/the-world/article/how-to-use-twitter-to-support-customers-guy-kawasaki (accessed October 6, 2010).

Klaassen, Abbey. (2009a, June 29). "Forget Twitter: The Best Customer Service Tool Is the Humble Product Review." http://adage.com/digital/article?article_id=137634 (accessed June 29, 2009).

———. (2009b, July 13). "What's Your Brand's Social Score?", *Advertising Age*.

Nordstrom. (2010, August 21). "Social Networking Guidelines," http://shop.nordstrom.com/c/social-networking-guidelines (accessed October 7, 2010).

Patel, Kunar. (June 21, 2010). "How AT&T Plans to Lift Its Image Via Social-Media Customer Care," *AdAge*, http://adage.com/digital/article?article_id=144561 (accessed August 14, 2010).

Pick, Tom. (2010, September 30). "How to Write a Social Media Policy," socialmediatoday, http://socialmediatoday.com/tompick/191412/how-write-social-media-policy (accessed October 7, 2010).

Postman, Joel. (2008, March 17). "JetBlue engages in real-time conversation on Twitter," www.socializedpr.com/jetblue-engages-in-real-conversation-on-twitter/ (accessed December 19, 2010).

Raffaele, Dave. (2009, January 28). "How JetBlue Used Twitter to Make Me Feel Like a Human," message posted to www.daveraffaele.com/2009/01/social-media-case-study-how-jetblue-used-twitter-to-treat-me-like-a-human (accessed September 10, 2009).

Solis, Brian. (2008, July 28). "Comcast Cares and Why Your Business Should Too: The Socialization of Service," @BrianSolis, www.briansolis.com/2008/07/comcast-cares-and-why-your-business (accessed October 6, 2010).

Twitter. (2009a). "@JetBlue: It's Fun, But Does It Scale?", http://business.twitter.com/twitter101/case_jetblue (accessed October 23, 2009).

———. (2009b). Stats on Joel Postman account page, http://twitter.com/#!/jpostman (accessed October 23, 2009).

———. (2010). Stats from JetBlue account page, http://twitter.com/JetBlue (accessed October 5, 2010).

Zanger, Doug. (2009, August 25). "Like It Or Not, You Have to Behave on Twitter." http://adage.com/smallagency/post?article_id=138637 (accessed August 25, 2009).

Chapter 15

Fulgoni, Gian. (2010, September 7). "The Lure of TV Advertising for Internet Businesses," comScore blog, http://blog.comscore.com/2010/09/lure_tv_advertising_for_internet_businesses.html (accessed October 17, 2010).

Key, Rob. (2009, September 15). "Social Media from the Inside Out," presented by Converseon at the iBrand Summit.

Networked Insights. (2010, May). "Social Sense TV: Network Ratings Report," www .networkedinsights.com (registration required).

Poniewozik, James. (2010, March 22). "Twitter and TV: How Social Media Is Helping Old Media," Time.com, www.time.com/time/magazine/article/0,9171,1971444, 00.html (accessed October 17, 2010).

Quenqua, Douglas. (2010, July 15). "Bringing It All Back Home," Mediapost, www.mediapost.com/publications/?fa=Articles.printFriendly&art_aid=131880 (accessed October 17, 2010).

Verhaege, Annelies, Niels Schillewaert, and Emilie van den Berge. (2009). "Getting Answers without Asking Questions: The Evaluation of a TV Programme Based on Social Media," www.insites.eu/02/documents/whitepapers/04_Getting_answers_ without_asking_questions.pdf (accessed December 19, 2010).

Yahoo! (2010, July 7). "New Study Reveals 75 Percent of Americans Use the Internet and TV Simultaneously," www.yadvertisingblog.com/blog/2010/07/07/new-study-reveals-75-percent-of-americans-use-the-internet-and-tv-simultaneously (accessed October 16, 2010).

Chapter 16

Butcher, Dan. (2009, September 29). "Lexus, Chevron Buy All Ad Inventory in CNN's New iPhone App," Mobile Marketer, www.mobilemarketer.com/cms/news/ advertising/4293.html (accessed October 19, 2010).

Florès, Laurent, and Mark Whiting. (2005, May). "What Can Research Learn from Biology?" http://www.crmmetrix.com/en/WhitePapers.asp (accessed December 18, 2010).

Johnson, Lynn, and Anita Lai. (2010). "Listening to Multicultural Consumers: Dispelling the Myths," presentation to ARF Re:think 2010, New York.

Keller, Ed. (2008). "Offline Word of Mouth," Word of Mouth Marketing Association, Summit 2008, www.slideshare.net/Frankwatching/offline-word-of-mouthindustrys-greatest-examples-presentation (accessed October 18, 2010).

Key, Rob. (2009, September 15). "Social Media from the Inside Out," presented by Converseon at the iBrand Summit.

Roth, Tom. (2010, September 29). Presentation to ARF People Council. For more information on the LGBT market, see Community Marketing, Inc.'s summary: "CMI's 4th Annual LGBT Community Survey Yields Historic 40,000 Respondents from Over 100 Countries; Provides Marketing and Communications Insights, While Tracking Motivations and Trends," www.communitymarketinginc.com/ gay-lesbian-media-room-press-releases/2010-lgbt-community-survey-yields-his-toric-response (accessed October 28, 2010).

Chapter 17

Bowman, Douglas et al. (2010). "Quantifying the Effects of Social Media Activity on Brand Sales and Market Share," paper presented to ART Forum.

Facebook. (2010). Official fan pages for Costco and BJ's Wholesale Clubs, Facebook .com, October 22, 2010.

Friedman, Larry. (2010). Interview.

IPA and Nielsen Analytic Consulting. (2009, July 29). "How Share of Voice Wins Market Share."

Keller, Ed, and Gregg Liebman. (2009). "The Marketing Value of Influencers," presented at ARF Audience Measurement 4.0.

Moore, John. (2010, November 9). "Talk Share and Market Share," http://kellerfay .com/2010/11/09/keller-fay-car-talk/ (accessed November 11, 2010).

Nail, Jim. (2008, November 12). "Effective PR and Word of Mouth Strategies to Maximize a Brand's Investment in a Super Bowl Ad," ARF Webinar presentation.

Nail, Jim, and Jeni Chapman. (2008, September 9). "Social Media Analysis for Consumer Insight: Validating and Enhancing Traditional Market Research Findings," TNS Cymfony ARF Webinar, available at: www.cymfony.com/modules/knowledge BaseRegister.aspx?dl=51.

Onalytica. (2008). "An Introduction to Onalytica," www.onalytica.com/whatwedo .aspx (accessed October 25, 2010).

Siefert, Caleb J., and Ravi Kothuri, Devra B. Jacobs, Brian Levine, Joseph Plummer, and Carl D. Marci. (2009, September). "Winning the Super 'Buzz' Bowl: How Biometrically-Based Emotional Engagement Correlates with Online Views and Comments for Super Bowl Advertisements," *Journal of Advertising Research*, 49(3), pp. 293–303.

Swedowsky, Maya. (2009, September). "A Social Media How-to for Retailers," Nielsen Consumer Insights, http://enus.nielsen.com/main/insights/consumer_ insight/september_2009/asocialmediahowtoforretailers (accessed October 26, 2009).

Chapter 18

Archak, Nikolay, Anindya Ghose, and Panagiotis G. Ipeirotis. (2010, February 10). "Deriving the Pricing Power of Product Features by Mining Consumer Reviews," NET Institute Working Paper No. 07-36, http://ssrn.com/abstract=1024903 (accessed October 25, 2010).

Asur, Sitaram, and Bernardo A. Huberman. (2010). "Predicting the Future with Social Media," HP Labs, www.hpl.hp.com/research/scl/papers/socialmedia/socialmedia .pdf (accessed October 25, 2010).

Berger, Jonah A., Alan T. Sorensen, and Scott Rasmussen. (2009, February 16). "Positive Effects of Negative Publicity: When Negative Reviews Increase Sales," *Marketing Science*, forthcoming, http://ssrn.com/abstract=1344363 (accessed October 25, 2010).

BuzzingUp. (2010, October 6). "Twitter Serves 1 Billion Queries a Day and 1000 Tweets Per Second," www.buzzingup.com/2010/10/twitter-serves-1-billion-queries-a-day-and-1000-tweets-per-second (accessed October 24, 2010).

Chen, Pei-Yu, Samita Dhanasobhon, and Michael D. Smith. (2008, May). "All Reviews Are Not Created Equal: The Disaggregate Impact of Reviews and Reviewers at Amazon.com," http://ssrn.com/abstract=918083 (accessed October 25, 2010).

Chevalier, Judith A., and Dina Mayzlin. (2006). "The Effect of Word of Mouth on Sales: On-Line Book Reviews," *Journal of Marketing Research*, 43(3): pp. 345–354.

Ghose, Anindya, and Panagiotis G. Ipeirotis. (2010, January 24). "Estimating the Helpfulness and Economic Impact of Product Reviews: Mining Text and Reviewer Characteristics," http://ssrn.com/abstract=1261751 (accessed October 25, 2010).

Gruhl, Daniel, Jasmine Novak, R. Guha, and Andrew Tomkins. (2005). "The Predictive Power of Online Chatter," Proceedings of the eleventh SIGKDD international conference on knowledge discovery in data mining.

Hu, Nan, Ling Liu, and Jie Zhang. (2008, January 7). "Do Online Reviews Affect Product Sales? The Role of Reviewer Characteristics and Temporal Effects," http://ssrn.com/abstract=1324190 (accessed October 25, 2010).

Johansen. (2007). "Get There Early: Sensing the Future to Compete in the Present," San Francisco, CA: Berrett-Koehler Publishers.

MotiveQuest. (2009). "The Online Promoter Score," www.motivequest.com/main.taf?p=1,2,1,1 (accessed October 26, 2009).

Nail, Jim. (2009, April 3). "Social Media Analysis: Finding the Path to New Insights," ARF Webinar presentation.

Neely, Dan. (2010). Interview with Stephen D. Rappaport.

Onalytica. (2009). "An Introduction to Onalytica," www.onalytica.com/whatwedo.aspx (accessed October 26, 2010).

Reicheld, Frederick F. (2006). *The Ultimate Question: Driving Good Profits and True Growth*, Cambridge, MA: Harvard Business Press.

Varian, Hal R., and Choi, Hyunyoung. (2009, April 2). "Predicting the Present with Google Trends," Google Research Blog http://googleresearch.blogspot.com/2009/04/predicting-present-with-google-trends.html (accessed December 2010).

GLOSSARY

Access Permission to read or view information online or in computer systems.

Advocate A brand enthusiast who posts messages and helps others understand features or aspects of brands and who may act to raise brand awareness or favorability.

Aggregating content Collecting information from multiple sources that may be Web-only or a combination of Web and in-house sources, like databases.

Aggregator A tool or program that collects content from the Web, including blogs, message boards, or forums.

Alert A notification system that advises when new content is added to a Web site, blog, or other online source.

API An acronym for Application Programming Interface. APIs allow different software programs to "talk" to one another and share information.

Archive An accessible history of Web site posts or other types of entries, usually organized by topic or data.

AstroTurfing A fake grassroots push to generate buzz or interest in a product, service, or idea. Often, an astroturfing movement is motivated by a fee or gift to the writer of a post or comment. (*source*: The Social Media Guide.)

Attitude A user's perspective, usually described in terms of positive or negative. Attitudes are commonly captured by thumbs-up/thumbs-down icons or buttons or links that indicate "liking."

Authentication The process of validating a person's identity, usually with a username and password.

Blog A Web page that serves as a personal journal that is accessible by others and often indexed by search engines. Major blogging platforms are Blogger, WordPress, and MoveableType.

Blogging Writing in one's blog.

Blogosphere The collection of all blogs.

Blog post A story of any type included in a blog. Blog posts may include text, pictures, video or sound files, or links to other blogs.

Blogroll A list of blogs that the blog owner finds interesting, and links to.

Boardreader An aggregator specifically tuned to collect message board posts and forum discussions.

Bookmarking Saving the address of a Web location, typically in a Web browser. *See also* social bookmark.

Brand backyard The compilation of sources controlled by brands, such as customer and private communities, blogs, discussion forums, e-mail, customer service logs, corporate Twitter accounts, and official presences on social networking sites like Facebook.

Brand page A page on social network specifically for brands to manage.

273

Bulletin board   A message system that allows an online community of people to post questions and submit answers. Bulletin boards typically offer "guests" read-only access and require registration for people who want to post and reply. Also called a *forum*.

Category   1. A term or phrase used to organize content on a Web site. 2. In text analysis, a heading used to group one or more topics. See *data structure*.

Chat   Usually, a text-based discussion held among two or more people using an online service. Video chats are becoming more common as Webcam penetration increases.

Classification   In text analytics, the organization of information into high-level groups, which are then divided further into topics, subtopics, and themes.

Cluster   A grouping of related concepts.

Collaboration   People, usually team members, working together for a common end. Software offerings may include collaboration features that support business activities, such as customer care.

Comment   A response that people reading blogs may make to a posting. Commenters may also remark on responses made by other commenters.

Communities (online communities)   Groups of individuals who share common interests and are linked by online tools such as e-mail or social networks. Private communities are organized and run by brands, often with third-party help, to focus on learning from key customers, prospects, or suppliers.

Community building   The process of recruiting and accepting community members against defined criteria, helping them feel comfortable, and encouraging participation.

Consumer backyard   A place where people interact that is not brand-controlled. Blogs, forums, ratings and review sites, Twitter, social networks, and media-sharing sites like YouTube and Flickr are all types of consumer backyards. Ethical listening harvests only publicly available information from the consumer backyard.

Content   A general term used to describe text, images, sounds, and video on the Web.

Conversation   In general, the variety of exchanges that occur online or offline among people.

Crowdsourcing   Utilizing a community or large group of people to help companies make product, marketing, or advertising decisions. This process usually includes presenting the "crowd" with a problem and then listening to and evaluating their solutions.

Dashboard   A display of key data and trends. Dashboards are usually configurable in some way to meet the needs of projects or analysts. Capabilities vary by vendor.

Data cleaning (or cleansing)   A quality control step undertaken to ensure that the data harvested for a listening project is relevant.

Data integration   The process of incorporating data from two or more sources for reporting and analysis purposes.

Data structure   Organizing listening data into meaningful units for analysis, and designing the relationships among them. Typically, data structures include entities, themes, subtopics, topics, and classification.

Delicious   A social bookmarking site owned by Yahoo! for storing, sharing, and discovering Web bookmarks.

Digg   A social news site that allows people to submit stories from anywhere on the Web. Digg users vote on stories, with the most popular making it to the front page. Digg provides tools for people to discuss topics.

Domain name   The name of an Internet site, such as thearf.org.

Engagement   Company interactions with customers and prospects in social media. Engagement can take many forms, including: answering questions through e-mail,

Twitter, or support forums; participating in conversations; providing content; or furnishing customer support.

Enterprise   The full scope of an organization.

Enterprise vendor   A supplier offering solutions designed to be used throughout an organization.

Entity   Generally, a person, place, organization, brand, date, or other named thing that is extracted through text analysis. Entities are discrete.

Entity analysis   The process of analyzing entities, which can include counts, like frequencies, trends, co-occurrences with other terms of interest, or sentiment toward the entity.

Entity extraction   The process of identifying entities, usually through software-based rules, and pulling them out of content.

Entry   An individual post or article published on a blog.

Event blog   A blog specifically launched as a companion to an event.

Facebook   A very popular social networking site, with more than 500 million active users, 70 percent of whom reside outside the United States.

Face-to-face   An offline meeting or encounter.

Fan page   A special type of Facebook page that may be either official—created by a brand or celebrity, for example—or unofficial—created by people for brands or celebrities. For the purposes of listening, fan pages are important because they are public and searchable, unlike groups, which are not.

Feed   Content that is "pushed" at regular intervals, or when updated. The most common type of feed is RSS (really simple syndication). People subscribe to feeds through feed readers.

Feed reader   A software program that enables users to subscribe to a feed, and automatically keeps track of updates. The reader provides functions that allow users to read individual items or manage numbers of items.

Filter   A tool that lets end users winnow results to manageable sizes by specifying the types of content (e.g., stories, comments, photos, etc.), categories of interest (e.g., lifestyle or entertainment), age of the content (minutes, hours, days, weeks, etc.), or people and brands.

Findability   The quality of content as locatable.

Flickr   An extremely popular photo-sharing site that allows users to describe their photographs with tags and content, which is searchable.

Forum   A discussion area where people can post and respond to messages.

Friend   (1. noun) A person with whom you agree to connect according to shared interests or relationships. Also called a *contact*. (2. verb) The act of adding a friend on a social network, such as "friend me on Facebook" or "add me as a contact on LinkedIn."

Friend list   A user's list of friends or contacts on a particular social network. People can have many friend lists.

Google   A very popular search engine. The company Google also provides valuable tools for analyzing search queries, such as Google Insights for Search and Google Trends.

Groundswell   A social trend whereby people use technologies to get the things they need from each other, rather than from traditional institutions like corporations.

Group   A collection of individuals who share common interests or values and form a community based on them. On social networks, groups usually have pages and require membership.

Hashtag   Short character-string tags, beginning with the number sign (#), used to identify Twitter posts so that they can be found easily by Twitter-capable search engines. For example, #ilfny09 was the hashtag used for the ARF Industry Leader Forum in November 2009.

Influencer   A person in a social network who is often recognized as an expert in one or more areas and capable of influencing others.

Instant messaging (IM)   The capability to chat online in real time with one or more persons using specialized software.

Lifestreaming   The process of aggregating a person's many digital communications in one place, such as photos, videos, Twitter posts, blog posts, and bookmarks.

Listening   The study of naturally occurring conversations, behaviors, and signals, which may or may not be guided, for the purpose of bringing the voice of consumers into a brand.

Listening level   Used to indicate a company's degree of sophistication in terms of social media listening. In this book, three levels have been identified: *fundamental*, companies that just launched a social media listening program and rely on free or low-cost tools; *intermediate*, companies that have some experience in social media listening and some internal expertise, a collection of listening tools, and vendor relationships, and that combine listening with traditional research; *advanced*, companies that have made a corporatewide commitment to social media listening, and make substantial investments in people, processes, and technologies.

Lurker   A person who visits a site to look around and read, but seldom contributes.

Media monitoring   The practice of regularly scanning traditional media and online sources for items of interest, such as brand mentions and people.

Media universe   The collection of media sources selected for a listening project.

Meme   An idea, behavior, style, or usage that spreads from person to person within a culture, and may mutate or evolve. A meme can be thought of as similar to a gene, but for a unit of culture.

Message board   An online discussion site where people discuss particular issues and post messages and replies.

Metadata   Information about information. In social media, metadata may include descriptors for posts, photos, video, or audio. Metadata makes nontextual information searchable.

Microblogging   Sending short messages to subscribers of a service. The best-known microblogging service is Twitter, where entries are limited to 140 characters. People often link to Web content in their posts by using URL shorteners, such as bit.ly or tinyurl.

Multimedia   Typically, video, audio, pictures, and graphic files that are uploaded to Web sites or services like YouTube and Flickr. Content owners usually tag their content so that it can be searched and retrieved.

MySpace   A popular online social network, originally populated by artists and bands.

Netnography   The use of online data to conduct cultural research. An electronic version of ethnography.

Network   On Facebook, used to describe a larger social grouping of which people can be part, such as a city, large company, or college.

News reader   A program that manages RSS subscriptions and provides features for reading and managing them. Also called a *feed reader*, *RSS reader*, or *news aggregator*.

Offline   Disconnected from the Internet or computer network.

Online   Connected to the Internet or other computer network.

Online community   Typically, a group of people sharing common interests who interact on the Web using social media tools.

Page   A Web page.

People's Network   A marketing system using a series of interactions between people and companies to generate and spread word of mouth. The People's Network is global, and increasingly mobile. (Term coined by Rishad Tobaccowala.)

Persistent search   A search run repeatedly on a schedule, usually for the purpose of collecting social media conversations on a regular basis.

Phrase   Usually, two or more search terms used in a query.

Podcast   A downloadable audio file meant to be listened to through a media player.

Privacy settings   Features provided by blogs, social networks, and other sites that allow users to limit access to their friends or content. Privacy settings can restrict the information that can be harvested for listening.

Private online community   A group made up of invitation-only members. For listening purposes, such communities are brand backyard sources, run by brands or by third parties for the benefit of brands.

Profile   Description of a person's interests, demographics, and other attributes. The display of profile information is often controlled by privacy settings.

Property   A generic term for a page, application, widget, or Web site.

Real-time search   An aggregation of social media content, such as blog postings, comments, tags, bookmarks, tweets, and status updates that are presented nearly as they occur.

Real-time search engine   A specialized tool that allows for the search and display of real-time search results. These engines may include social media details, like retweets, and capabilities for passing along content or links.

Registration   A process for creating a username, password, and, often, other details for opening an account on a Web site, social network, or other service. Registered users are given access to areas or features that are otherwise restricted.

RSS (Really Simple Syndication)   A standard method for delivering Web content, such as stories, blog posts, images, and video. Newsreaders enable users to subscribe to feeds and stay current on publications or producers without having to visit numbers of sites.

Self-service   Software and services designed for end users to use themselves.

Sentiment analysis   An evaluation that determines the tone of a blog post, article, or conversation, typically expressed as positive, negative, or neutral. Sentiment assessment can be made by humans or machines.

Share   The act of distributing an individual piece of content with friends. Some search engines now include sharing in their results to show the virality of content, or to trace the path content moves through.

Social action   An interaction on a social network that triggers a story to be posted to a user's profile.

Social bookmarking   A method for enabling people to locate, store, organize, share, and manage Web page bookmarks without being connected to a particular machine.

Social graph   The network of online relationships in which people are a part. Some form of permission, like friending, is required to be included in a social graph.

Social media   Generally, online technologies that allow people to publish, converse, and share content online.

Social media listening   The act of gathering data (relevant to a company, brand/product, or service) from social media outlets for research purposes.

Social media listening metrics   Measures derived to analyze social media data. Social media listening metrics include such statistics as brand mentions, sentiment, topics, and themes.

Social monitoring　The process of tracking online brand mentions on a daily basis for PR, brand protection, operations, and customer service outreach and engagement (MotiveQuest definition).

Social network　An online environment that allows individuals to interact with one another using a set of tools and features that typically include profiles, friending, communications, adding media, and groups.

Social networking　Socializing in an online community.

Social news (social sites)　Sites, like Digg, that encourage people to submit and vote on news stories or other links. The most popular are featured on the site's home page.

Social research　The process of analyzing naturally occurring online categories of conversation to better understand why people do what they do; the role brands play in their lives; and the product, branding, and communications implications for brand owners (MotiveQuest definition).

Software as a Service (SaaS)　Software solutions hosted by vendors and licensed for use; akin to a rental model. SaaS is an alternative to the traditional vendor software model that requires purchasing a license, and installing, configuring and maintaining it on company-controlled servers and networking infrastructure . . .

Standing search　See *persistent search*.

Status, or status update　Short descriptive comments, typically 140 characters or fewer, that describe what a person is doing at the moment. Popularized by Twitter, many social networks now offer their own status update capabilities.

Subscribing　The process of adding RSS feeds to an aggregator or newsreader. For many listening projects, subscribing is an important way to harvest content.

Subtopic　In text analysis, the grouping level under topic. A single topic usually has two or more subtopics. See *data structure*.

Tag　A keyword added to content to help users locate it through a search feature, classification scheme, or search engine.

Tag cloud　A visual representation of the popularity of the tags or descriptions used on a site. Tags are sized according to popularity.

Tagging　Writing and adding tags to content.

Technorati authority　A rating computed by Technorati that establishes the authority of a blog in the blogosphere by analyzing links. Technorati has recently added an authority rating for voices on Twitter, called Twitterati.

Term　A search term or phrase.

Text analytics　The process of analyzing unstructured text, extracting relevant information, and then transforming that information into structured information that can be leveraged for such purposes as creating topics and subtopics, or assigning sentiment.

Theme　In text analysis, an element of conversation. Themes are grouped into topics and subtopics. See *data structure*.

Threads　Strands of conversation that describe a discussion.

Topic　In text analysis, the category of interest. Topics are composed of subtopics. See *data structure*.

Trackback　A method, popular with bloggers, that lets one site "know" that a second site has made a reference to it. The collection of posts, comments, and trackbacks facilitates conversations.

Troll　A person posting controversial, inflammatory, irrelevant, or off-topic messages in an online community, and whose main intent is to disrupt on-topic discussions.

Tweet An entry on Twitter.

Twitter A popular social network where posts are limited to short messages, of 140 character messages or fewer. Considered a real-time social network, Twitter has spawned innovative ways for individuals and businesses to use the service.

Twitterverse The universe of people using Twitter, and their conversations.

Update A message sent to people who subscribe to being notified when new content is added to an online page.

Upload Transfer of a file or other content from one device, such as a computer or video camera, to an online site.

URL Uniform Resource Locator, the technical term for a Web address, such as www .thearf.org.

User-generated content (UGC) All forms of user-created online materials, including blog posts, reviews, podcasts, videos, tweets, comments, audio, ratings, and such. Also called *consumer-generated content*.

Videoblog (or vlog) A blog that contains video entries.

Wall A type of discussion board centered on an individual, and part of his/her profile. Wall postings are presented in reverse chronological order and are made by friends. Privacy settings govern wall behavior.

Web 2.0 A Web constructed in part from user-generated content and conversations. Also known as the *social Web*.

Web analytics The measurement, collection, analysis, and reporting of Internet data for the purpose of understanding Web site traffic and visitor behavior.

Wiki Technology that allows group authoring and editing by providing a trail of creations and edits that can be approved or undone. Wikipedia is the most familiar example.

Word of Mouth (WOM) Offline or online conversations that people engage in. For the purposes of listening, word of mouth related to brands is usually of greatest interest.

Workflow The logical steps and pathways of work, from starting a task or process to completing it.

XML (eXtensible Markup Language) A scripting language used to describe information so that it can be easily exchanged between different computer systems.

YouTube Video-sharing Web site, owned by Google, where people and brands can upload, view, share, and comment on clips.

INDEX

281